HOLOCAUST AND HOPE

Sara Guyer and Brian McGrath, series editors

Lit Z embraces models of criticism uncontained by conventional notions of history, periodicity, and culture, and committed to the work of reading. Books in the series may seem untimely, anachronistic, or out of touch with contemporary trends because they have arrived too early or too late. Lit Z creates a space for books that exceed and challenge the tendencies of our field and in doing so reflect on the concerns of literary studies here and abroad.

At least since Friedrich Schlegel, thinking that affirms literature's own untimeliness has been named romanticism. Recalling this history, Lit Z exemplifies the survival of romanticism as a mode of contemporary criticism, as well as forms of contemporary criticism that demonstrate the unfulfilled possibilities of romanticism. Whether or not they focus on the romantic period, books in this series epitomize romanticism as a way of thinking that compels another relation to the present. Lit Z is the first book series to take seriously this capacious sense of romanticism.

In 1977, Paul de Man and Geoffrey Hartman, two scholars of romanticism, team-taught a course called Literature Z that aimed to make an intervention into the fundamentals of literary study. Hartman and de Man invited students to read a series of increasingly difficult texts and through attention to language and rhetoric compelled them to encounter "the bewildering variety of ways such texts could be read." The series' conceptual resonances with that class register the importance of recollection, reinvention, and reading to contemporary criticism. Its books explore the creative potential of reading's untimeliness and history's enigmatic force.

HOLOCAUST AND HOPE

Literature, Testimony, Media

———|———

Geoffrey Hartman
Edited by Kevis Goodman and Brian McGrath

Fordham University Press
New York 2026

Copyright © 2026 Fordham University Press

All rights reserved. No part of this publication may be reproduced, stored in a retrieval system, or transmitted in any form or by any means—electronic, mechanical, photocopy, recording, or any other—except for brief quotations in printed reviews, without the prior permission of the publisher.

Fordham University Press has no responsibility for the persistence or accuracy of URLs for external or third-party Internet websites referred to in this publication and does not guarantee that any content on such websites is, or will remain, accurate or appropriate.

Fordham University Press also publishes its books in a variety of electronic formats. Some content that appears in print may not be available in electronic books.

Visit us online at www.fordhampress.com.

For EU safety / GPSR concerns: Mare Nostrum Group B.V., Mauritskade 21D, 1091 GC Amsterdam, The Netherlands, gpsr@mare-nostrum.co.uk

Library of Congress Cataloging-in-Publication Data available online at https://catalog.loc.gov.

Printed in the United States of America

28 27 26   5 4 3 2 1

First edition

In Memory of Renée Hartman
(1933–2025)

Contents

	Introduction: The Limits of Realism and the Future of Witness	1
1	Shoah and Intellectual Witness	20
2	Holocaust and Hope	33
3	Words Not from on High	47
4	Wounded Time: The Holocaust, Jedwabne, and Disaster Writing	52
5	Elie Wiesel and the Morality of Fiction	59
6	Afterword to *Lodz Ghetto*	66
7	Unbearable Truths	71
8	Breaking with Every Star: On Literary Knowledge	79
9	Learning from Survivors	94
10	Public Memory and Its Discontents	107
11	Shoah Literature: The Universal Aspect	120
12	Defining a Living Genre: The Survivor Testimony	131
13	The Ethics of Witness: An Interview with Ian Balfour and Rebecca Comay	140
14	Terror and Art: A Meditation	160
15	Future Memory: Reflections on Holocaust Testimony and Yale's Fortunoff Video Archive	172
Acknowledgments		183
Notes		185
Index		221

HOLOCAUST AND HOPE

Introduction: The Limits of Realism and the Future of Witness

Kevis Goodman and Brian McGrath

The preface to the last full book of literary criticism and essays that Geoffrey Hartman published before his death, *The Third Pillar: Essays in Judaic Studies* (2011), ends on a promissory note: "Moreover, I have not included my writings on the subject of the Holocaust. These must be left for a further publication."[1] Hartman died in 2016, after a period of illness, before he could get that further publication to a press. In 2008, however, he had drafted a proposed list of contents for a large two-volume set of his writings, which he revised in 2010. Volume 1 of the set, which he had been calling *Essays on Jewish Studies*, was soon to be published as *The Third Pillar*. Volume 2, as yet unnamed, included most of the essays in this book, which he later also handed in hard copy to a colleague at the Yale Archive for Video Testimonies, Joanne Rudof, along with the instruction that two other pieces—which had appeared in his 1996 collection of essays on the Holocaust, *The Longest Shadow: In the Aftermath of the Holocaust*—be included in the volume that he realized he would not be able to see into production.[2] We have followed Hartman's most recent wishes in including them as well, recognizing that he may have hoped thereby to signal that the essays in this volume were to extend the explorations begun in *The Longest Shadow*. Similarly, when we subsequently found, among the many electronic files conveyed to Hartman's literary executors after his death, revised versions of several of the essays handed to Joanne Rudof (Hartman was an inveterate and tireless reviser to the last), we have used the latest versions we could identify. Finally, we decided to add one late essay that Hartman had not written when preparing the table of contents ("Terror and Art"), because we find it relevant to the concerns of the rest.

Holocaust and Hope, then, seeks to realize Geoffrey Hartman's wish for that next and final volume of essays on the Holocaust promised in the preface to *The Third Pillar* and frequently mentioned to colleagues after that. As such, this volume concludes over thirty-five years of Hartman's work on the literary, cultural, political, and historiographical implications of the Holocaust and its aftermath in Europe and America. In addition to *The Longest Shadow*, this large subset of his life's work included two collections of scholarship that he edited and contributed to—*Holocaust Remembrance: The Shapes of Memory* (1993) and *Bitburg in Moral and Political Perspective* (1986)—and dozens of his own uncollected essays, written both for scholarly and for more popular audiences.[3] While each essay in *Holocaust and Hope* is distinctive, they all take most seriously the difference between our being "after" Auschwitz and our being "past" it. They explore, with Hartman's characteristic intensity and humanity, the full complexity of how to transmit knowledge of the Holocaust to the future in ways that avoid simplification, the illusion of synthesis, and the aspiration to final closure, on the one hand, or compulsive repetition, on the other. A significant part of the answer, for Hartman, requires special attention to the role of literary and audiovisual forms in promoting an active relationship to extreme suffering and, in particular, a response to them that does not run into either of two opposed yet fully complementary extremes: on the one hand, indifference, amnesia, or denial; on the other, the repetition, prolongation, or transmission of the original state of trauma.

The essays that follow do not just rehearse the problems or the situation of *The Longest Shadow*. In part because some of them were written later, they address a different, emerging reality: the passing away of the survivors capable of bearing immediate witness to the atrocities of the Holocaust and, not too long from now, their children and grandchildren. In another twenty to forty years, as Hartman writes in the first essay of this collection, "Shoah and Intellectual Witness," "a community sensitive to matters touching on the Shoah will be more of a public," and public memory is "increasingly affected by new events and contexts—by the continuance of history." Does the passing of the survivors and, soon enough, those who knew them first-hand, mean the passing of witnessing? If the answer is no, as Hartman himself hopes, then there will have to be a new kind of witness, whose position will be more ambiguous, beyond the survivors and their immediate family and beyond what Marianne Hirsch has called the "postgeneration."[4] And with these, there will have to come new ways of witnessing from a distance of time and space, quite different from the situated eyewitness who can, as in a courtroom, attest to a plaintiff's testimony. The question is all the more pressing because, as a number of the essays in this volume argue, the future of witness is intertwined with the possibility of hope, and, conversely, "witnessing cannot take place without some hope for the future, in generational transmission."

Hartman did not choose "Holocaust and Hope" as the title of this volume; it is the title of one of its essays, published in 2003, which he intended—and we preserved—as the second chapter, right after "Shoah and Intellectual Witness." In other words, we have decided to follow Hartman's own frequent practice of taking the title of an essay as the title of the book in which it appears.[5] We have selected "Holocaust and Hope" for this role because we feel that the essay raises to a particular pitch the challenge of the whole. As Hartman notes, placing the words "Holocaust" and "Hope" together can invite serious misunderstanding. Hope after Auschwitz—and after Cambodia, Rwanda, Bosnia, Darfur, Gaza, and so many more—and hope still? After all, Hartman himself refuses, repeatedly and firmly, anything like a story of redemption or its corollaries, including epistemological or affective closure or didactic satisfaction. Even history, he states, is not "a source of definitive meaning whose influence could integrate a catastrophic past." What he admires in Maurice Blanchot equally describes his own position: Hartman, too, "rejects Hegel's 'imposture of completed meaning' and Christian triumphalism." There cannot be and must not be any final solution to *the* "Final Solution." And yet—and this is the difficult but necessary balance Hartman's essays sustain—there is a very different but similarly dangerous kind of foreclosure. The last chapter in this volume describes this other foreclosure: that of denying to "those living *in* the present as well as *at* present, those who do not evade the past ... the energizing hope that is their very birthright" (emphases added). Hartman's essays work to energize hope even as they deny hope's fulfillment. Hope remains (and must remain) necessarily inseparable from the despair that accompanies it: It is, Hartman writes, "something impermanent, a simple repetitive moment of hope, a shimmer unattached to fulfillment."[6]

In the later sections of this introduction, we discuss these issues and the related strands of argument central to the whole collection: Hartman's commitment to a "nonescapist thoughtfulness," his scruples about the desire for immediacy, the delicate relationship between knowledge and the means of representation, imaginative literature and Holocaust truth, video testimony and the testimonial alliance. But first, because the study of the Holocaust is not a single study but expansive, co-evolving, and interdisciplinary fields of research—composed of historians, philosophers, psychologists, political scientists, and other scholars—we start by offering a brief account of Hartman's own path to the subject from the other areas for which he is famous: the study of European Romanticism, widely construed, and literary theory. For he brought to the study of the Holocaust a distinctive set of gifts and concerns that were long in the making, developed over a sixty-plus-year career as one of the greatest literary critics and critical theorists of the second half of the twentieth century.

1

Over the course of six decades, Geoffrey Hartman took up an astounding range of critical issues and authors. In 1954, he published his first book, *The Unmediated Vision: An Interpretation of Wordsworth, Hopkins, Rilke, and Valéry*, describing a modern, poetic drive to immediacy that was doomed to fail.[7] It might be only a slight overstatement to describe much of his career after that as a meditation on the inevitability of different kinds of mediation, in the original sense of "mediation," which described the difficult process of interceding between incommensurable entities or levels that cannot otherwise communicate.[8] Hartman returned to William Wordsworth in *Wordsworth's Poetry: 1787–1814*, first published in 1964, a watershed study that helped transform not only the prevailing discussions of Wordsworth's poetry but also the field of Romantic Studies more generally, both at the moment of its appearance and for decades after.[9] Among its other accomplishments, it focused critical attention on the precarious, never-triumphal dialectic between consciousness and the natural world, or what Hartman, in a separate essay on I.A. Richards, called the delicate "ecology or interanimation of mind and world."[10] Hartman never stopped writing about Wordsworth, publishing, for instance, *The Unremarkable Wordsworth* in 1987 and numerous other articles on his favorite poet, but in the meantime his commitment to a wider range of authors emerged in collections of his essays, starting with *Beyond Formalism: Literary Essays, 1958–1970* (1970) and *The Fate of Reading and Other Essays* (1975). These collections presented transformative, prescient, and, for many readers, unforgettable articles on other poets and genres: "Milton's Counterplot," "Poem and Ideology: A Study of Keats's 'To Autumn,'" "Christopher Smart's *Magnificat*," "Romantic Poetry and the Genius Loci," among many others. Other influential books of literary and cultural criticism followed in the 1980s, 1990s, and early 2000s, positioning Hartman as a major literary theorist with a brilliance impossible to categorize in any single school of criticism, including the deconstruction associated with his colleagues in the Comparative Literature and English Departments at Yale. Prominent among such later books were *Saving the Text: Literature/Derrida/Philosophy* (1981), which ended with a significant counterstatement to Derrida; *Criticism in the Wilderness: The Study of Literature Today* (1980); *Easy Pieces* (1985); *Minor Prophecies: The Literary Essay in the Culture Wars* (1991); *The*

Fateful Question of Culture (1997); and *Scars of the Spirit: The Struggle Against Inauthenticity* (2002).[11] This list is incomplete, but taken individually and collectively, these and Hartman's other books on literary criticism, history, and theory marked a stunning achievement, and they solidified his prominence and a widespread recognition, by scholars of varying commitments and temperament, including his critics, of his deep originality, as well as his calm open-mindedness. Hartman, Adam Phillips observed in 2008, "has never been a critic with animus": His strong preferences "are not sponsored by complementary hatreds, and he has written some of the most distinguished literary criticism of his time without sounding embattled, or outraged, or even territorial." He has been mindful of competing ideologies, as Phillips added, but—uncharacteristically for an often-contentious field—"he has not been tempted to unmask the unmaskers."[12]

In 1979, Geoffrey Hartman co-founded Yale University's Fortunoff Video Archive for Holocaust Testimonies, the leading and largest video testimony archive at the time.[13] Although his criticism and various commitments to literature never wavered, a new, parallel chapter of his career emerged in the 1980s, as he began writing more explicitly about questions of witness and testimony and the heightened demand for each in the context and aftermath of the Holocaust. In a short memoir that opened his 1999 collection, *A Critic's Journey*, Hartman explained that after the 1980s three issues preoccupied him. First, he took an interest in supporting Jewish studies in the curriculum and worked to expand available interpretive methods through an understanding of "the exegetical imagination."[14] Second, he worked to develop the notion of the aesthetic and especially aesthetic education. Though the aesthetic risks becoming "a dirty word rather than one describing the system of the arts generally," Hartman understands the spirit of the literary, or the linguistic in the literary, as "counter-propaganda," a force that exposes "every dubious movement toward unification or consent."[15] Broadening the exegetical imagination develops a critical scrutiny capable of denouncing various political and ideological attempts to stifle the creative spirit and monopolize the public as well as the private imagination. The third issue, and one that most preoccupied him, concerned extreme experiences and the response to genocidal violence—specifically, "the limits of realism, the effect of the Holocaust on culture, the relation of words and wounds (the psychological complexity of communication), and the possibility of a specifically literary knowledge related to trauma."[16] Not only in the founding of Yale's Fortunoff video archive but also, as time went on, in the books and articles of the later 1990s and early 2000s, Hartman pursued his abiding interests in the relationship between literature and the audiovisual genre of testimony, which when combined raise complicated questions about memory, pedagogy, and cultural transmission.

As several of Hartman's phrases just quoted ("the relation of words and wounds," "the complexity of communication," and especially "the possibility of a specifically literary knowledge related to trauma") indicate, in approaching the study of the Holocaust from his earlier work, he brought a special sensitivity to the impact of trauma and extreme violence on the way we consider language, and especially literary language, as something different from or more than the delivery of information or news. "Words and Wounds" was the title of an essay published in 1979, but even earlier, from the early 1970s, Hartman had been interested in how literature, no matter the genre, searches for a way to put wounds into words. In other words, since the Greek word "trauma" (τραῦμα) means "wound," we should recognize that he had been theorizing trauma, or, more precisely, the specifically literary and linguistic expression of trauma, long before his work on the Holocaust.[17] At the same time, he had been very wary of attributing to literature a simply curative function. His attention gravitates just as much, and usually more, to literature's silences, stutters, aberrations, ellipses, periphrases, or more broadly its turns to metaphor and figuration. These are not aporias, sites of unrepresentability, but marks that, like a scar, point to the presence of a wound that has not yet found other expression. In addition, Hartman has always pointed out that "where there is a word-cure" there is also a "word-wound," for "words are always armed and capable of wounding."[18] Sometimes, he argued as early as a 1973 discussion of the poet Christopher Smart, that wound comes from an awareness of language's deficiency: "Words commonly present us," he wrote, but what if "we feel that words are defective" in this crucial respect and fail to do so?[19]

The study of the Holocaust and its aftermath intensifies this last question and others that are inseparable from it. In the totalitarian and dehumanizing world of Nazi Germany and, above all, in *l'univers concentrationnaire* of the camps, such "self-presentation" was systematically denied to inmates. As Dori Laub, a medical doctor as well as both a survivor and scholar of the Holocaust, explains, in the camps "there was no longer an other to which one could say 'Thou' in the hope of being heard, of being recognized as a subject, of being answered."[20] Then, in the aftermath of the Holocaust, when survivors were not actively prohibited from speaking, they often did not do so, whether because they did not have sufficient terms to signify their experience, or because they worried that they lacked an audience that could hear and understand those terms, or for another reason.[21] In several essays in this volume, including "Holocaust and Hope," Hartman agrees with Maurice Blanchot that one of the victims of the Final Solution was language itself. The fact "that the breach of civilized speech had occurred, even among intellectuals and professionals"—and "the Final Solution," of course, would be just one example of abused speech—suggests that coming to terms with this casualty "should lead to a new consciousness of words as the most responsible of human gifts." Yet, as the wishful subjunctive in "should" makes clear, both word-consciousness and responsiveness to a past that has not passed remain an ongoing project—that "shimmer unattached to fulfillment"—now and in the future.

2

Much scholarship in recent years has focused on the next generation after Holocaust survivors and witnesses, especially within their families or among those who had some direct contact with them. Marianne Hirsch offers a list of phrases Holocaust scholars have used in attempting to name the difference between the first- and second-generation witness, as they work to formulate transgenerational acts of traumatic transfer: "absent memory," "vicarious witnessing," "received history," "haunting legacy," and Hirsch's own "postmemory." "Postmemory," writes Hirsch, "describes the relationship that the 'generation after' bears to the personal, collective, and cultural trauma of those who came before—to experiences they 'remember' only by means of the stories, images, and behaviors among which they grew up."[22] In "Holocaust and Hope," Hartman recalls that at first he, too, referred to the "'second generation witness,' a concept that made sense because the pressure of the event on the sons and daughters of the survivors was such that 'witness' [i.e., a term usually limited to eyewitness testimony] seemed justified."

But then what? Not too long from now, witnessing will increasingly occur from greater distances of time and across space. Bearing witness—if it can even be called that—will increasingly be the responsibility of the large and abstract group that Hartman, as we noted earlier, calls "the public." Public memory, for Hartman, will be increasingly separate not only from personal and familial memory but also from what Hartman, following Maurice Halbwachs, calls "collective memory"—the collected plurality of different but converging individual memories within a community—a plurality but not a unity.[23] Public memory is therefore virtual, stretching across space, and, for Hartman, more "anonymous and occupied by impersonal networks of information," lacking the "'living deposit'" that, for Halbwachs, characterized collective memory. It is also vulnerable to "official memory," which tends to be more monolithic and is usually promoted by the apparatus of the state to a specific end. Yet even if it is not co-opted in that particular way, public recall of the Holocaust will be thoroughly shaped by later events and contexts, a "subsumption of the past in the present."

Some degree of such a subsumption is of course inevitable, a function of the passage of time and history, and Hartman does not resist it. But there is, he argues, a greater if less obvious challenge to public memory's ability to remain sensitive to the Holocaust and other atrocities of the past. This challenge, which need not be inevitable, derives from the current public's susceptibility to the numbing and abstracting psychoaesthetic effects of contemporary media, even apart from their explicit content. Many of the essays in this book argue that the news networks, and especially their uninterrupted, streaming flow of extreme and troubling images, makes active response *to the present itself*, not just to the past, more difficult. And how can we remain sensitive to the receding past when responsiveness to the present *in the present* is challenged by ongoing atrocities? As Hartman writes in "Public Memory and Its Discontents":

> Perhaps until news from Bosnia reached the screen, we clutched at the hope that had the indifferent masses in Germany or America known what was going on in the concentration camps, known with the same graphic detail communicated today by TV, surely the atrocities could not have continued. There would have been an outcry of popular conscience and so much protest that the Holocaust would have had to stop. Yet right now we are learning a new truth about human indifference. As the media makes us bystanders of every act of violence and violation, we realize that this indifference or lack of focus was not so incomprehensible after all. For we glimpse a terrible inertia in ourselves and even find reasons for it.

This inertia, for Hartman, is not, or at least not necessarily, evidence of widespread or inherent human callousness. It is rather a function of what he once called "the sympathy paradox."[24] Human sympathies are not unlimited, and the extension of consciousness and sensibility made possible by increasingly powerful and global telecommunications and related technologies makes us spectators to more and more distant sufferings—Hartman later dubbed this long-distance sensibility "telesuffering"—as well as those nearer to home. These place "an intolerable burden on feeling," hard to sustain, and as a result, "emotional defenses and self-protective doctrines come into play" to limit the demand.[25] Instead of feeling pain more often or more intensely, we respond with something like what John Keats called "the feel of not to feel it."[26] Hence the paradox of the sympathetic imagination: In Hartman's words, the more successful an "expanding sensibility becomes, the more evidence we find of actual insensibility."[27] "Bearing witness" to suffering (acknowledging and affirming its truth) depends on *bearing* (enduring) that suffering, and both depend on how—the particular means by which—we come to know it, as well as on how we act and respond once we do. This is part of what Hartman has in mind when he writes, more than once and across several essays, "today the relation of knowledge to the means of representation has changed."[28]

Hartman's references to news media and media technologies can often seem too sweeping and abstract, a point that he tacitly acknowledges, especially in the essays on videotaped oral testimony, which, he knows, would not be possible without the modern technology that he warns against when he comes to discuss news reportage. His essays make clear that his objections are primarily to those media and uses of media that blunt our capacity to respond to violence, suffering, and other extreme sights. These are the "glossy and accelerated displays of the human condition that allow less and less time for reflection," which he identifies most often in the round-the-clock stream of broadcast news and, less frequently but with no less wariness, certain blockbuster and spectacular Hollywood film productions, like *Schindler's List*.[29] These media, he argues, call forth our indifference not—as one might expect—because of their failures and limitations but rather because of their very efficiency and success. Their immense speed and scope, as well as their simulation of immediacy, introduce the possibility that Hartman has called "secondary trauma," and their 24/7 operation may end in something that looks very different from shock but that is often its other face: the "routinization, the constant viewing of extreme pictures ... and the coldness with which we eventually stare at such pictures."[30] Seeing traumatizing and traumatized subjects becomes a habit, and as with any habit, the threshold for evoking a response keeps increasing, such that we need more and more before we respond at all. The public's indifference, in this sense, simultaneously expresses and protects itself from secondary trauma.

For these reasons, Hartman's wariness is not a simple or Luddite resistance to technology; nor is it backward looking or unrealistic. In fact, when discussing technology, his concern is at every point for the future, and his worry is precisely about engaging reality. We need the news and need to be informed by it, Hartman makes clear; he knows that without it there can be no witnessing at all, and the capacity to witness now and in future (and the two are linked) is Hartman's own greatest hope—that hope that lies at the horizon of the explorations in this book. The chapter that closes *The Longest Shadow*, "Holocaust Testimony, Art, and Trauma," strives for the difficult but necessary balance. "To deal honestly with extremity may require extreme representational means and an acceptance of a degree of desensitization that is the by-product of realistic media," Hartman acknowledges, but he continues:

> One consequence of secondary trauma is indefensible. A massive realism which has no regard for representational restraint, in which depth of illusion is not balanced by depth of reflection, not only desensitizes but produces the opposite of what is intended: *an unreality* effect that fatally undermines realism's claim to depict reality. Yet precisely an effect like that is usually blamed on the aesthetic element in art which is mistakenly targeted for not being close enough to realities.[31]

Crucially, then, Hartman's critique is not about the technological means; it is a scruple about the end. Where others of Hartman's generation worried about how and where we can find means strong enough to depict extreme events in all their detail, Hartman's concern was quite different: What happens when we *do*? Do there need to be careful limits to the matter and modes of representation *in the interest of representation itself* and its reception? The late essay "Terror and Art," included in this volume, summarizes his point most forcefully: "Realism, in any case, does not always reinforce reality." It will not reinforce reality, Hartman suggests, unless we ask, at the same time, what "allows what we call reality to enter consciousness and word-presentation."[32]

The essays in this volume thus articulate and confront contradictions that pose a challenge for our present and near future. The passing of the survivors and their immediate families makes continued acts of witnessing more necessary even as distance in time makes the identities and acts of future witnesses more complicated. In addition, the particular kinds of amplification that we may expect or be accustomed to from our contemporary media environment can call forth not an intensity of response but rather an inertia, an "unreality effect" that can come unexpectedly from the heightening of the real, or the hyperreality of too much, too fast, too strong. Whereas in 1975 Hartman could write that "responsibility begins with the ability to respond," in the new millennium, some thirty to forty years later, he worried just as much about the ability to respond with responsibility. The chapters that make up *Holocaust and Hope* therefore ask what kinds of representation can encourage "an active reception that is relevant both for our time and the encroaching future, that could address with similar force a community and a public." That active reception will depend on what one of the essays published here for the first time, "Shoah Literature: The Universal Aspect," calls a "nonescapist thoughtfulness." It will also require a witness in the future who can at once retain some reflective distance yet "look at the Shoah not as something enclosed in the past but as a contemporary issue, a crisis that has not safely passed."[33]

3

Hartman does not pretend to offer an exclusive or final answer to the question of what makes possible this kind of active but thoughtful response. But the essays in *Holocaust and Hope* tend to explore two areas, sometimes together and sometimes separately, although in neither case as forms that guarantee historical knowledge. The first is the role of imaginative literature or "fiction," although that term will need some attention and explanation in this introduction. The second is the function of a deliberately low-tech form of survivor video-testimony, whose representational restraint resists the "glossy and accelerated displays of the human condition" and related shock effects that Hartman finds in many instances of contemporary news media and in some blockbuster Hollywood films. One central aim of *Holocaust and Hope* is to understand these two forms of representation together and to discuss the ways in which they complement each other as they engage the Holocaust.

Why, one might ask, not just rely on historical narrative and the massive amount of historical documentation provided by many sources, from the bravery of the prisoners to the obsessive punctiliousness of the Nazi record-keeping? For Hartman, the histories and factual records that we have and will continue to assemble are essential, but they are not sufficient. "To transmit the 'dreadful experience,'" he wrote in *The Longest Shadow*, "we need all our memory institutions: 'history-writing as well as testimony, testimony as well as art.'"[34] Yet if "realism does not always reinforce reality," more history writing does not by itself ensure the reception of history. In the earliest text published in this volume, Hartman's "Afterword" to *Lodz Ghetto: Inside a Community Under Siege* (1989), a collection of 128 primary texts from those imprisoned in the ghetto, he describes the cumulative experience of reading the documents as "haunting," adding that "one becomes ashamed of one's own voice, and wishes to do exactly what the compilers of this book have done: to quote, and avoid commentary." But that worries him because he feels that, decades after the end of World War II, "the burden is shifting from historian to reader": "We are at the point where the historical and memorial activity, while it must continue (for there is still much to be done), may not neglect the issue of interpretation: of how to say more, after reading this, than *never forget*" ("Shoah Literature," emphasis in the original). A similar concern for supplementing documentation with interpretation or reflection emerges in "Unbearable Truths," a review essay of Gitta Sereny's *Albert Speer: His Battle with the Truth.* Speer was Hitler's favorite architect, appointed Reichsminister in 1942, who denied awareness of the concentration camps to the Nuremberg tribunals. Sereny's own interest is forensic; her book collects a mass of data to prove just how much Speer knew and when he knew it. While Hartman acknowledges that her search for knowledge "may be useful to strengthen foresight and post warning signs about future behavior," his interest is not forensic. Instead, Hartman uses the example of Speer, who found the truth of what he knew so unbearable that he remained an accomplice to a lie, to think about how flimsy the relationship between knowledge and ethical response can be and about how, because that relationship is flimsy, more and more factual knowledge, more and more detailed accounts of history, by no means guarantees an ethical or just response. It may not "say more … than *never forget*," and it can leave unresolved how to act on that warning.

Moreover, as Hartman and others have remarked, even all the historical documentation imaginable does not necessarily prevent forgetting, especially when forgetting takes on many forms that do not look like literal forgetting. In "Wounded Time," engaging the work of Maurice Blanchot, Hartman finds that Blanchot's "subtlest point … is that responding with a vehement temporal demarcation is part of the disaster." To pretend that one can mark the end of a catastrophe—that one might set it off and file it as past (and passed)—can be a form of forgetting insofar as it assumes or suggests that the disaster is not still ongoing or, if it concludes, that considering and responding to its effects in the present do not have to continue now and extend into the future. Assuming that facts can supply intelligibility can also be a kind of misrepresentation, as well, when it involves forgetting the Holocaust's core of unintelligibility: "If I remained true to fact," the survivor Aaron Appelfeld remarked, "no one would believe me" (quoted by Hartman, "Shoah Literature").[35] Epistemological closure can thus paradoxically become a way of not knowing. Thinking of Blanchot's eloquent imperative, "to keep watch over absent meaning," Hartman argues that the goal of commentary "should be to guard the space of absence created by that sudden incursion of the unintelligible."[36] To do so is *not* to give up on intelligibility as a goal; it is rather to acknowledge that we do not yet have it and therefore must guard what we still do not understand "from explanations and consolations seeking to fill a void, from anything that pretends the factors contributing to that moment are over, like a freak storm."[37]

Therefore, Hartman concludes his review of Sereny's book by suggesting that "it may be that fiction—though less referential, factual, and probative than historical research—can guide us toward a limited form of understanding in this sensitive area of knowing and not-knowing." This statement surprises and may seem counterintuitive at least. "Fiction" would seem a most implausible guide to the unbelievability of Holocaust reality. It has going against it as well the "art-shame" (as Hartman calls it) that was captured dramatically and influentially in Theodor Adorno's dictum that "poetry after Auschwitz is barbaric."[38] Thinking about Appelfeld's statement ("no one would have believed me"), Hartman goes a step further in "Shoah Literature: The Universal Aspect," suggesting that "Aristotle's criterion of probability has been injured by the Shoah" and that "this, moreover, may have caused collateral damage to fiction more generally." As a result, "it is harder than ever to define fiction's type of truthfulness."

What Hartman means by "fiction" is far from self-evident here. He does not mean it in the everyday sense, and in this volume, it is never the designation of a particular genre (whether novel, short story, or poetry). Across a number of the essays in *Holocaust and Hope*, it often functions as something of a shorthand for uses of language and narrative that crucially insert time to respond to a reality whose force might otherwise be coercive, or for formal and figural qualities that leave open and flexible a range of responses to it, including that "nonescapist thoughtfulness." This process may involve, as it does in "Terror and Art," the possibility of an "imaginative or cognitive modification of a haunting site, its resetting in a tolerable frame narrative."[39] Elsewhere he thinks about fiction as a relationship to language that does not insist on single or determinate meanings. Writing about Blanchot in "Words Not from on High," Hartman comments:

> Improgressive sentences, close to aphorisms, intensify rather than diminish the distance between words and their direct signification. The vessel of understanding keeps breaking into fragments, as if the parts were more signifying than the whole. These essay books are less containers than empty rooms amplifying a silence in the words spoken. Everything resonates without moving toward a central focus or defined reference point. "The writer no longer belongs to the magisterial domain where to express oneself signifies to express the precision and certainty of things and values...." There is no triumphal *ergo* binding the "I think" or "I speak" to the "I am."

Elsewhere, too, Hartman discovers in metaphor, ellipses, reticence, resistance to closure, and other techniques *neither* the hope to explain the unexplainable nor (as Adorno worried) the aestheticization of reality but instead the chance to approach a catastrophic reality more gradually, in a manner that does not overwhelm, that does not, like a repeated or relentless newscast, leave us indifferent or frozen mute.

While Hartman often foregrounds writers like Blanchot and Paul Celan, whose language is confrontationally improgressive, he is not only interested in this literary style. The conclusion of "Holocaust and Hope" acknowledges that writers like Jean Améry, Primo Levi, and Elie Wiesel do not problematize the recession of signification or deploy the same disorienting style, but Hartman emphasizes the ways in which they, too, unsettle the triumphal *ergo*, so that Blanchot's radical direction is sustained by them. "Elie Wiesel and the Morality of Fiction" explores related features in Wiesel's fiction: "No one reads Wiesel without admiring his versatile storytelling in all the genres," Hartman comments, "yet the specter of the impotence of words, even of the divine word, is always present." We respond to Wiesel, he continues, precisely "because we continue to sense a precariousness within his eloquence." In Wiesel, Hartman finds a fine balance: No one may speak for the dead, no one may interpret their mutilated dreams and vision, yet speaking for the dead is precisely (and unavoidably) what Wiesel does—but, and to some extent because, he does so in fiction.

4

At first glance, literature and survivor testimony may seem altogether opposed—after all, literature may be fictional while survivor testimony is most decidedly not. Literary (in the original sense of *litterae*, i.e., written, lettered) texts are a very old medium, whereas filmed oral testimony "is partly a creation of modern technology and so has a chance of influencing that environment"—or so Hartman hopes in "Defining a Living Genre." Yet, while they are obviously different, they are not opposed, and Hartman is drawn to some of their common properties and possible collaboration in shaping tomorrow's witnesses. First, both challenge modes of history and Holocaust representation that assume the self-evident power of understanding. Second, neither takes for granted the assured relation between epistemology and morality—between what or how much one knows and how one responds to or interprets that knowledge. Third, the case that Hartman makes for art during times of terror—namely, that its "engagement with realities ... is not realized by constantly trying to shock, or transmit an actual moment of terror"—is also crucial to his understanding of testimony. Yet (and fourth), while they resist shock, survivor video testimonies, much like the literary texts that interest Hartman the most, can foreground the intellectual and emotional difficulty of engaging extreme or genocidal violence and traumatic experiences—a challenge that Hartman considers elided or downplayed in those news media and other kinds of spectacles aspiring to (the appearance of) transparency and immediacy. Tellingly, one of the aphoristic refrains of Hartman's later career was the insistence that "media are not mediations" because, or at least when, media seek to ease the cognitive difficulties of engagement: "The discontinuities they remove, and the apparently transparent or faultless pathways they create, cannot resolve existential human problems, persistent social conflicts. Mediation involves a risky engagement."[40]

Video testimony, for Hartman, brings that "risky engagement" to center stage, but it does so—and this is the crucial, perhaps paradoxical, balance—in a way that minimizes the "secondary trauma" in the viewer and therefore the disconnect and apathy he worries about from less restrained media. For that to happen, much depends on the various choices that shape how testimony is elicited, delivered, archived, and filtered. Indeed, the interpretive or hermeneutic strategies called for by survivor video testimony follow from the formal situation of the interview that the viewer—the new witness in the making—encounters. Similarly prioritizing questions of infrastructure and institutions, Noah Shenker's *Reframing the Holocaust* details the differences between the Fortunoff Archive at Yale, the United States Holocaust Museum, and Steven Spielberg's Shoah Foundation at USC, quoting Hartman's account of an important feature of the Fortunoff strategy: "'While the video testimonies have an unusually direct emotional impact, they are mediated by frame conditions.'"[41] In the interview with Ian Balfour and Rebecca Comay in this volume, for instance, Hartman emphasizes that when considering the frame conditions for the Fortunoff Archive it was important for survivors or witnesses offering testimony to appear in the present. They are dressed in their present clothes. They are well-fed. They are not represented as victims; they are *survivors*. Discussing his sense of the best practices in taking testimony of this painful intensity, he argues that video is important because without seeing the survivor's face, the voice remains ghostly: "We feel it essential to add a face to voice, to reduce the ghostliness, even to re-embody the voice." At the same time, Hartman explains, they decided to restrict the visual aspect to "talking heads" against a plain background, and he contrasts the filmic techniques used by other video testimony projects, like the Visual History Archive of the USC Shoah Foundation, which tapes in the survivor's home and at the conclusion of the interview surrounds the survivor with family, which not only increases the visual interest but also combines it with a sentimental one. (Spielberg's training in the entertainment business is an influence, of course.) At Yale, explains Hartman, "we are resolutely ascetic." "We found, almost by accident," he continues, "that this bareness helps the survivors to go into themselves."[42] Against this bare background, attention shifts to the survivors. The interviewer lets the survivor speak, for the survivor's own voice is of paramount importance. But that speech is deliberately *not* edited for coherence or for production. These video testimonies preserve the halting speech, the silence, the hesitations of the survivor. The testimony puts the focus neither on the horrors of suffering nor on the success story of survival but on something very different from both: the slow, challenged action of memory. It may be in those hesitations, haltings, and falterings—a version of the "improgressive" prose of a Blanchot—that we see most clearly the ways in which, for Hartman, video testimony can counter other audiovisual media, even as it partakes of some of the same technology.

In the past, Hartman remarks in "Defining a Living Genre," survivor testimonies were "treated mainly as death stories and mined for perpetrator data," and their use as data placed the value on fact. While the correction of error and proof of veracity are both necessary and intrinsic to history as a discipline, nonetheless, Hartman argues, "when that hygiene becomes predominant in the analysis of witness accounts, as if their sole value were historical veracity, other dimensions are lost." For that reason, in testimonies recorded at Yale, errors of historical fact are not corrected during the filming itself:

> Objectivity is not an exclusive aim. There is a performative as well as informative dimension to the testimonies. Despite well-known types of error, such as the conflation of incidents or the retroactive blending-in of what was revealed in print or movie afterward, each witness account places us in the presence of an individual, communicates something of the original impact of what was experienced.

The decision not to correct is neither an indifference to fact or information nor a devaluation of necessary documentary and historiographical knowledge, which testimonies supplement but do not supplant. It is a recognition that a carefully guided survivor video testimony can contribute something that other kinds of historical documentation cannot when they prize factuality exclusively: a truth that Hartman here identifies with "original impact" and elsewhere calls "*Wirklichkeit.*" *Wirklichkeit*, he explains, is "better translated as 'actuality' or 'worldly actualization' than as reality" (in the limited sense of reality as factual reality).[43] Hannah Pollin-Galay has recently explored the tension between reality as fact and reality as lived actuality in her discussion of the USC Shoah Foundation Visual History Archive, where in the current apparatus the human face of the survivor appears beside a digital map to help viewers orient themselves geographically in and through the testimony. But while these maps may be useful, they also inspire in viewers what Pollin-Galay calls a "geo-curiosity" that is sometimes at odds with the survivor testimony, especially when the testimony appears at times to contradict the narrative told by the map. As Pollin-Galay writes, "The survivor's loss of physical, indexical orientation is one severe consequence of Nazi persecution and is thus a meaningful, historical truth about the Holocaust."[44] To correct the testimony so that it matches the narrative told by the map would be to ignore how the "errors" or "metaphors" or "black holes" are also real elements of the violence endured.

Strikingly, Hartman suggests that at moments testimonies take on formal attributes that approach the literary: "Especially in the context of the Holocaust, witnesses go beyond reportage and transmit not only factual but also intensely burdened autobiographical stories, whose natural metaphors or imaginative condensations capture our attention." Talking to Balfour and Comay, he calls attention to the proximity of metaphor and error. They are different, of course—and Hartman would be the last to excuse an error on the grounds of its metaphorical punch. Yet there are metaphors that, while wrong as matters of fact, find out truths that are hard to describe empirically. He gives the example of one woman who says, in a very emotional testimonial interview, that when the sun rose it was not the sun, because it was black. "Sure," Hartman explains, "rhetoric can just be artificial, just rhetoric, but when you meet it in this situation, there is something incredibly spontaneous about it and you do seem to touch something elemental," a historical truth that may not be the same as a factual truth. If one reacts to the spontaneous image of a black sun by discounting the survivor's veracity, then one has diminished one's own responsiveness to the real force of trauma and even one's openness to the actuality of the Holocaust.[45]

With the emphasis on the performative as well as the informative function of testimony, we return to Hartman's question about the future of witnessing and the witnesses of the future. We return to his concern for an approaching time not only after the passing of the survivors, the primary witnesses, the "postgeneration," and those who knew them but also (and especially) as the Holocaust moves into that virtual, anonymous, and unstable sphere of "public" memory. At the same time that they contribute to the collective memory and form a lasting archive, the filmed testimonies also model the possibility of "social sharing." To the primary witness, delivering testimony, the interview may return some faith in communicability, for if, as Laub suggests, those caught inside the Holocaust were deprived of the ability to present themselves to others as human, as a subject to whom someone else might say "you," the interview can restore the promise of being listened to and perhaps help recover the internal "you" lost in the Holocaust. In other words, the interviewer becomes a secondary witness not only to the Holocaust past but also a "witness for the witness."[46] But there is a further performative dimension: The interviewer becomes the delegate of a larger audience willing and able to listen. This aspect is what Paul Frosh and Amit Pinchevski, discussing the practices of the Yale archives, call "audiencing." As they write in their introduction to a 2009 collection of essays, *Media Witnessing in the Age of Mass Communication*, "the function of media technology in this project was more than the establishment of an audiovisual archive: video cameras effectively constituted a technological surrogate for an audience of the witnessing process underway."[47] Hartman is well aware of the irony of a "technological surrogate," given his critique of other uses of technology—indeed, he courts it—but he is hopeful about the ways in which the filmed testimony, located as it is on the cusp of private and public memory, with its Janus-faced view of the past and toward the future, might build a community of many out of the community of two. But it is a *different* community from the ones he describes as vicariously "telesuffering." "Audiencing," in this case, avoids the effects that trouble him about mass media events that use extreme representational means: the overextension of sensibility that calls forth some degree of insensibility as a defense, the unreality effect that results when there is no regard for representational restraint.

5

It has been nearly a decade since the last of these essays was written. The streaming broadcast news and cinematic displays that worried Hartman for their dangerous immediacy and for their failure to create space or time for reflection have new competitors in the changing media environment—TikTok, Facebook, Instagram, and X (Twitter), and more undoubtedly are on the way. However, with respect to the particular traits and effects that Hartman focuses on—traits such as immense scope, lack of representational restraint, or hyper-reality; corollary effects like desensitization, numbness, and skepticism about reality—one may find in these newer platforms some distinction but arguably not much difference. Other things have not changed at all. Take, for example, just these three sentences from "Shoah Literature: The Universal Aspect," published now for the first time but drafted as early as 2004:

For the Holocaust has not turned out to be the genocide to end all genocides. In fact, at this point in time insistence on its uniqueness produces bitter awareness of a repetition. The historical circumstances or motives of each genocidal occurrence are different, the scope and duration are different, but the extreme brutality and suffering are overwhelmingly the same.

So it was in 2004. We write a year after the Holocaust Remembrance Day of May 2024, when the prime minister of Israel, Benjamin Netanyahu, marked the date at Yad Vashem, the Holocaust Memorial in Jerusalem, with a speech that declared—or rather repeated—"Never Again Is Now."[48] The ongoing war and genocidal violence not many miles away in Palestine and elsewhere in the world at present could not make it clearer that, no, "Never Again" is not yet and not, it seems, near at hand. In this context, it is hard not to be struck anew by Hartman's question in the "Afterword" to *Lodz Ghetto: Inside a Community Under Siege*: "How to say more, after reading this, than *never forget*?" Or by this recognition from "Shoah and Intellectual Witness": "We are obliged to think of the problems that surround the transmission of the Holocaust as a living memory. What if such a legacy—as it is now called—has a despairing or traumatizing effect and the "Never Forget" becomes an impossibility?" In other words, once intended to warn against the possibility of a recurrence, has the phrase "Never Forget" come to describe instead the reality of traumatic repetition and therefore to undermine, rather than secure, the possibility of "Never Again" by redirecting the aggression elsewhere in the name of self-defense? Hartman's awareness of that irony and his behest here, the reminder of a continuing obligation to think about the problems that surround the transmission of the Holocaust into the future, remain urgent. It is among the strengths of the essays in this volume to pose these questions, alongside the others we have described, and to model the kinds of reflection that must happen—more often, more widely, and more assiduously—if we are to hope for a "never again" that lasts.

1. Shoah and Intellectual Witness

The culture of remembrance is at high tide, but we cannot foresee how far it will reach or how much will remain valuable. At present, three generations are preoccupied with Holocaust memory. They are the eyewitnesses; their children, the second generation, who have subdued some of their ambivalence and are eager to know their parents better; and the third generation, grandchildren who treasure the personal stories of relatives now slipping away. Bonds of love reinforce the golden chain of oral tradition, which had been in danger of breaking, because of terrible and burdensome experiences that could not be integrated into family life. Among the first generation there are also child survivors, the last direct witnesses, whose significance increases when we focus on adolescence and pedagogy.

As the tide recedes and eyewitnesses pass from the scene, public memory of the Shoah, so crucial to contemporary thought, is increasingly affected by new events and contexts—by the continuance of history. According to an old saying, truth is the daughter of time; we might also say that whatever leads to disclosure, there is always a difference in the reception of that disclosure between a community that feels close to the event and the public at large.

In another twenty or forty years a community sensitive to matters touching on the Shoah will be more of a public; that is, it will respond in a more complex or self-reflective way. I wish to call *intellectual witness* an active reception that is relevant both for our time and the encroaching future, that could address with similar force a community and the public. I will be looking at the possibility of intellectual witness in those who did not directly experience the Nazi era as well as in survivors whose writings are extant and exemplary.

The idea of intellectual witness is overdetermined. "Witness," unless employed in a specifically legal or religious sense, is usually limited to eyewitness testimony. But then we would not ordinarily qualify it by "intellectual," since it is the immediacy, the sheer, wounding weight of experience that counts. In *The Longest Shadow* I used the expression "second generation witness," a concept that made sense because the pressure of the event on the sons and daughters of the survivors was such that "witness" seemed justified. Almost imperceptibly, however, the phrase broadened to embrace what Terrence Des Pres and Lawrence Langer name "secondary witness"—a concept without generational limit. It includes all who could be called witnesses because they are still in touch with the first generation or who look at the Shoah not as something enclosed in the past but as a contemporary issue requiring an intensity of representation close to eyewitness report. But should the term "witness" still apply, three generations and over fifty years from the event? And why substitute "intellectual" for "secondary" to characterize those who portray the Shoah with a special sense of obligation?

The first question is somewhat easier to answer than the second. The Holocaust refuses to disappear into time's "dark backward and abysm."[1] It has created a magnetic field stronger than that of the First World War. ("The Great War is a magnet," Wyndham Lewis wrote in the 1930s, "the 'postwar' its magnetic field.")[2] In 1985, on the fortieth anniversary of the end of the war and the liberation of the camps, Jürgen Habermas declared: "The presence of the past remains uncannily real and preoccupies discussion more forcefully today than in the 1950s and early '60s." Nazi history, Amos Elon wrote in 1997, "seems more 'alive' now than it did 30 or 40 years ago. Few people then would have foreseen that it would still weigh so heavily in the public life and culture of Germany.... It is a shadow that not only lengthens but also darkens as time goes by."[3]

There is nothing mysterious about this. The Germans were unable to mourn, according to the Mitscherlichs, who published a famous book on that subject.[4] A reluctance to confront what happened, both in public life (where many Nazis remained in the government) and in the intimacy of the family, not only postponed the reckoning but made it more painful when public memory refocused on the perpetrators in the '60s and '70s. The delayed impact made Helmut Kohl's remark about a later generation's "luck" (*die Gnade der späten Geburt*) particularly inept. In France, the role of the police as enforcers in the roundup and deportation of Jews was occulted into the '80s, and in Poland, where the Shoah had been an open and daily reality, full acknowledgment has still not come. A battle over the conscience of that nation continues to this day because many Poles were both victims and onlookers. For them the historical trauma is the war itself, the double aggression of Hitler and Stalin. Sometimes collaborators in the Holocaust, more often powerless or unwilling to intervene, they did not face the moral issue until Lanzmann's *Shoah* appeared and in the wake of a courageous article by Jan Blonski.

Eventually the "memory-wave" surged everywhere, and individual testimonies gained new life. The survivors began to speak and write once more, especially after the Eichmann trial, and the claim of the second generation to family memories of which they had been deprived by the murder of relatives and the destruction of their culture produced an explosive return to the event. Memories that do not exist have to be replaced; with Georges Perec and others new fictional modes are created, not so much to fill a void as to make it visible, to "present memory *as* empty."[5]

Despite attempts to forget, then, and dire warnings about the obsessive effect of Holocaust consciousness, interest has reached a new high. The passing of the survivor does not mean the passing of witness. Many have become witnesses by adoption and investigate what happened with religious fervor. What should be called the reception or resonance, rather than understanding, of the Shoah is, when measured against the lapse of time, a disruptive series of revelations following upon a latency period lasting from shortly after the war to the Eichmann trial in 1961. In this democidal century, each further genocide does not weaken the memory of the Shoah but revives it as an event that founded the exemplarity of testimonial acts.

Let me turn, then, to the second question: How appropriate is the slippery term "intellectual" to this intense and continued interest in the Holocaust? I have indicated that if anything threatens remembrance today it is not, so far, our increasing distance from the catastrophe. A more constitutive distance, however, intrinsic to intellectual inquiry, does matter profoundly, and we have some difficulty with it when it comes to radically shocking events. Yet without a struggle for or against that distance, our reception of what happened is impoverished.

The intellectual, a descendent of the Enlightenment's "impartial spectator" (important to Adam Smith's *Theory of Moral Sentiments*), plays a role similar to that of a bystander after the event who observes it from an ambiguous position. On the one hand, detached or belated, he has no obligation to take account of the Shoah. On the other, once he learns what happened and does nothing—treats it as of little or no concern—he is not unlike an observer of the event who failed to react.

The position of those implicated in this way can also be compared to that of a spectator in the theater. This analogy, though it may seem offensive, is challenging and suggests how intrinsic art is to moral perception. Spectators go to see a tragedy, and their judgment remains active despite the sympathetic imagination provoked by what unfolds on stage. The distance between spectator and tragic action is bridged, if at all, without psychological transvestism (permitted and even necessary for the actors), yet most viewers, while they might not feel pain, would not admit taking pleasure from a suffering that is known to have been actual rather than imaginary. In fact, we find it so difficult to value the feeling of pleasure, or seeming mastery, that comes from the ability to face painful events through thought or mimesis, that we justify this voluntary witnessing as a kind of labor. Dominick LaCapra, for example, describes it as a "labor of listening and attending that exposes the self to empathetic understanding and hence to at least muted trauma."[6]

In such statements, the labor metaphor not only removes the suspicion of illegitimate enjoyment but modifies the spectator theory of knowledge by evoking a more participatory state of mind. As LaCapra suggests, it seems impossible to experience something so traumatic as the Shoah, even at a distance, without suffering a secondary form of trauma. In the political sphere, we often talk of a person being "radicalized." A parallel radicalization among the survivors as well as those coming later is evidenced by their consuming effort to "see," to find a way of telling others—and even themselves—what happened.

The artistic intellect, combining with the testimonial imperative, plays an especially effective role in capturing and communicating a traumatic ordeal. In *Literature or Life* (its original title was *Writing or Death*), Jorge Semprún confronts "deadly riches" of memory that surge when he happens on a film about the camps a few months after his liberation from Buchenwald. "Seeing on the screen, under an April sun so near and yet so far away, the *Appellplatz* of Buchenwald, where cohorts of survivors were milling about in the disarray of their recovered freedom, I saw myself brought back to the reality of it, installed once more in the truth of an incontrovertible experience. Everything, then, had been real, and continued to be so: nothing had been a dream."[7] To counter the phantomization or dissociation endemic to trauma and the ensuing fragility of transmission, a medium more permanent than the individual mind is necessary. Art and the communal memory interact to achieve this end.

Yet a postwar hunt to deaestheticize art blocked the question as to whether the pleasure derived from it could have ethical value when its subject is the Shoah's enormous, state-sponsored atrocities. The issue was displaced by

Adorno's famous strictures. His emphasis fell exclusively on the moral difficulty of representing—or admitting into thought—a catastrophe of such magnitude. Adorno does not doubt our technical powers of mimesis but our moral and intellectual stamina. The horror of the Shoah must never be stylized or become fodder (*Frass*) to satisfy a craving for entertainment.

Indeed, what pleasure could result from art that depicts the Shoah? Perhaps there is no single, unified feeling and therefore no single word like "pleasure" that adequately describes it. But whatever we name that response, it cannot be related to a delight in imitation and only with many qualifications to emotional catharsis. In part it involves a distinction between memory and imagination. Those who cannot remember because of massive trauma or because they have lost places and people whose names and photos still haunt them must recover some of that lost density of life (or specificity of death) through an imaginative recreation. They work from "post-memory," as Marianne Hirsch calls it, to lessen its emptiness, and that very effort, impossible or grotesque, is often part of the subject.[8]

Some comfort, then, however tenuous, may come from this imaginative effort. Yet those who can remember also need relief—from a tormenting sense of discontinuity, which, as I have mentioned, phantomizes the survivor. So one of Charlotte Delbo's characters declares, "I am not among the living. I died in Auschwitz, and no one notices it." Semprún too, brooding on Primo Levi's suicide, feels compelled to ask: "Have we really survived?"[9]

The rhythm of Semprún's entire book enacts a tension between deathly (*mortifères*) recollections and his activist postwar life. No incident he recounts is merely punctual or described without being returned to, elaborated, mixed with associations, reprised. Semprún uses these liberties of fiction to integrate threatening anniversary symptoms of his Buchenwald trauma. He objects to the film about the camps by evoking the difference between documentary realism and lived reality. "The film," he writes, "should have been worked through, in its filmic substance, by arresting the march of images, by fixing an image to enlarge certain details: sometimes the projection should have been slowed, and, at other times, speeded up. Above all, the scenes should have been provided with a commentary, to make them less cryptic, to place them not only in historical context but in a continuum of thoughts and emotions.... In short, documentary reality should have been handled like fictional material."[10]

Semprún may be taking his cue from Alain Resnais's *Night and Fog*, which appeared a full decade after the war. Resnais filters Holocaust reality through the self-conscious use of cinematic techniques and a poetic voiceover commentary. Semprún too, as novelist or memoirist, is influenced by the cinema.

Yet he does not share Adorno's anxiety about mass media or the aesthetic exploitation of the Holocaust.

I believe that the problematic nature of Holocaust representation does not arise primarily from a temptation to aestheticize that reality (though Semprún's self-conscious devices serve to buffer as well as acknowledge shock). It comes, rather, from the damaged condition of modern life—damaged severely enough to affect its communicable core. On this issue Adorno was clear-sighted. Modern experience, he declared in *Minima Moralia*, is becoming less communicable, perhaps even unthinkable. A comment by Jürgen Habermas, the best-known philosopher of contemporary Germany, suggests both this damage and the hope of undoing it. The Holocaust has touched "the deep stratum of solidarity between all who bear a human countenance."[11] Restoring that solidarity, that *entente*, is what motivates public remembrance as a collection of testimonial voices and a collective of hearers. It also motivates our greatest writers after the war.

Their effort is shadowed, however, by a temptation that has not been talked about very much and that stems from intimacy rather than aesthetic or intellectual distancing. Writers often transgress a boundary. Imaginative power can push them across a threshold into overidentifying with victims or a victimized generation, to the point of seeking a mystical correspondence with the dead. (One thinks of Nelly Sachs but also of Walter Benjamin's suggestion that "a secret date" exists between past generations and the present one.) Documentary or reified detail, in any case, does not satisfy the bereaved imagination, which demands a greater, more fully imagined solidarity.

This desire for solidarity is reinforced by a fraternal ideal inspired by the French Revolution and the international camaraderie of the Spanish Civil War; it makes Semprún choose for one of his epigraphs to *Literature or Life* Malraux's "I seek the crucial region of the soul where absolute evil stands in opposition to fraternity." As an *imaginative* need, however, the solidarity-drive is equally present in Ida Fink's stories. Having escaped death by passing as a Christian, she looks back from the position of bystander as well as victim and expresses in various ways a temptation to join those who disappeared, to envision their end by merging with them. Yet the compassionate thinker should not try to identify with the victims any more than the teller of a story with its characters. "I should not have written 'we,'" one of Fink's narrators confesses, "for I was not standing in the ranks [of those rounded up for deportation and death]."[12]

Every identification approaches overidentification and leads to a personifying and then appropriation of the identity of others. The distance between self and other is violated and the possibility of intellectual witness aborted. So, too, Lanzmann's identification with the witnesses in his film *Shoah* is bound to be anti-intellectual. His angry, quasi-religious comments about the "obscenity" of seeking to understand the Holocaust betray this. He remains, at the same time, very present in the film as an ironic and often domineering questioner. He relentlessly pressures the victims as if uninterested in their human needs or their life beyond the traumatic event and subordinates all other considerations to a revelation of the event in its full horror.

Artists like these reveal that the intellectual part of consciousness always keeps us in the position of spectator or bystander. It is a deeply uncomfortable place to be in, because we are exposed, at one and the same time, to trauma *and* the anxiety of not empathizing enough. In this crucial area little can guide us. We say, for instance, that, on the part of historian as well as artist, there must be partial identification or some kind of emotional relation: a rational or therapeutic empathy that does not result in compulsive bonding or ecstatic loss of self. Like LaCapra we are tempted to use Freud's "Mourning and Melancholia" to distinguish between "working through" and "acting out."

Yet everything we know about empathy suggests how destabilizing it is. The memory of atrocity is often haunted by images of the human body violated by torture, as in the case of Jean Améry, or by random and savage acts of mutilation. What can empathy mean here? It is at best an escape from disremembering dismemberment and somehow piecing together the afflicted body through a narrative courage that evokes the once *integral* person. Empathy can also surprise and go out to the ex-perpetrators, the very people who betrayed the principle of human solidarity. Drawing a lesson from his own imprisonment in Dachau and Buchenwald, Robert Antelme insists that the perpetrators remain persons, subjects with rights, members of humanity. "From now on a man who is imprisoned is a man we have to 'think' about; we are able to identify with him" (*nous sommes dans son intimité*).

Fraternity, however, extended from immediate blood relations to nation or mankind has proved to be a corruptible ideal. Instead of reinforcing the concept of humanity, of Antelme's *espèce humaine*, it turned coercive and underwrote the political religions of fascism and Stalinism. Even in its Christian form it is not as universal as it claims to be, and it often subordinates humanitarian perspectives to fervid national demands. An exploited ideal, then, helped promote the German *Volksgemeinschaft* and its crimes against humanity, yet it could not be discarded after the Holocaust.

The quality of postwar intellectualism, however, is influenced by that fact.

Hoping to discover less corruptible forms of solidarity, contemporary writers have subjected the language of social and ethical thought to a painfully complex scrutiny. As a consequence, public discourse is sometimes jeopardized by the very means adopted to save it, the deconstruction of commonplaces and the outwitting of words emotionally abused by totalitarian regimes. I will instance only Derrida's *The Politics of Friendship*, which explores, among other texts, Maurice Blanchot's *Friendship* and *The Writing of the Disaster*. Blanchot belongs to the generation that matured before the war, but he survived an earlier self marked by right-wing journalistic agitation. Central to Blanchot's and Derrida's efforts is the attempt to reexamine and radicalize an older ideal: that of friendship. By the time they have analyzed it and removed solace and sentimentality, it poses a significant challenge to the intoxicating mass appeal of fraternity, community, humanity. Yet the anxiety of being seduced by words also creates a less communicative style, one that saves friendship by becoming less reader-friendly. The style may have a realism of its own, however: In the words of Yves Bonnefoy, it "aggravates instead of resolving, points to what remains obscure, takes clarities to be clouds that can always be dissipated...."[13]

Having described some aspects of intellectual witnessing, I want to turn to the intellectual as witness. Without seeking a firm definition of the intellectual, I can say that the Holocaust made his status even more problematic. The obvious reason for this is related to the behavior of many well-educated Europeans, especially those Max Weinreich called "Hitler's professors." After Hitler and Stalin, Irving Howe once wrote, "intellectuals must never, no matter what the occasion or pretext, allow themselves to provide ideological rationales for the suppression of liberty."[14] But there is also a less obvious reason for doubt about the professional thinker: While writers, journalists, and academics in Nazi-occupied Europe were often active accomplices, there was also a large group who waited it out as bystanders. The very concept, therefore, of bystander seems tainted. Given the passivity of so many who knew or could have known, is it possible *now* to "stand and wait"?

A clear sign of our impatience with the bystander mentality is the controversy over America's and also the Yishuv's (relative) inaction during the War Against the Jews. The dubious claim, moreover, that most Germans were ignorant onlookers, shielded from or accidentally happening upon the murderous events, has often been challenged and may not recover from Daniel Goldhagen's book *Hitler's Willing Executioners*.[15] Also important is a renewed and exacting interest in rethinking agency and culpability.

The intellectual's situation is paradoxical. If, yielding to the call for action, he engages himself on one side or the other and that side loses, he finds himself compromised. If, avoiding action, he becomes a bystander who takes his time, anti-intellectualism increases. Intellectuals tend to be among the most pressured groups in society. But the most significant factor affecting *all* bystanders since 1945 is that the technology of real-time reporting now brings every disaster and evil in the world to our attention and so takes away all excuse. Through the media we become onlookers exposed to daily violence and global misery in the same quasi-involuntary way that Germans after 1933 were directly exposed to overt incidents and vicious propaganda. These bystanders saw yet did not see what was before their eyes.

Media exposure, then, may lead to more tension than ever between knowing and not-knowing, between a guilty conscience and deliberate palliation or forgetting. The constant spectacle of misery is already causing a low-grade, perpetual anxiety. The very absence of feeling pains us instead of the pain we think we should be feeling. We suffer a split, so that one part of us cannot accept an insensibility for which the other quietly decrees forgiveness. And, after Bitburg, the issue of premature closure, or what Adorno called *erpreßte Versöhnung* (coerced reconciliation), comes to the fore. Instead of the passage of time setting a limit to liability, the delay—as often in fictional narratives—may now be deemed necessary to a full disclosure of trauma or guilt. In sum, the innocence of the bystanders has become less clear with the passage of time.

It is natural to focus on the bystander, for in the last fifty years, while scholarly and critical interest shifted from perpetrator to survivor (or rescuer) and back, the bystander was often neglected. The category is somewhat vague and confronts us with the ambiguities of Primo Levi's "gray zone" (*The Drowned and the Saved*) in which the demarcation between victim and collaborator, or bystander and collaborator, remains unclear. Bystanders after the event, however, such as the belated thinker and artist, struggle with a different dilemma. As in epitaphic inscriptions admonishing the traveler, a voice comes from the past, and each must decide whether to heed it or pass by.

This moment of brooding is essential. We know that during a catastrophe there is not enough time; thought is needed for coping, for meeting the emergency. After the crisis, however, an awareness that it had, if not an end, then a datable structure leads to a repeated act of recall that tries to become a reflection. We experience, as after a nightmare or serious illness, a feeling of relief, even of gratitude, that the immediate danger is over. The intolerable, though we did not know it directly, gives way to perplexity: How could it happen, how could they let it happen? And, since daily pressures, not only catastrophic ones, short-circuit this kind of reflective time, it has to be maintained and refurbished—despite the taint of spectatorship or the bitterness of the victim. So Tadeusz Borowski writes in *This Way for the Gas, Ladies and Gentlemen*: "We were filthy and died real deaths. They were 'aesthetic' and carried on subtle debates."[16]

Catastrophe, then, reduces time. As the threat advances, we rapidly lose the reflective space needed for decision making. Any kind of playing for time becomes impossible. Fink describes how haste and hesitation prove equally fatal during the Nazi roundups. In such moments, however, moral actions do occur, whether or not they succeed. The father in "A Spring Morning" fails to save his child: She runs at his urging toward the safety of some bystanders and is shot down. If we see his decision, nevertheless, as a brave act, it is because of the closeness of the family previously portrayed by Ida Fink. We infer the father's moral courage in separating from the child.

Eventually an indefinite respite allows us to make time for time, and this recapture is humanizing. Those murdered in the Shoah, Habermas writes, "have a claim to the weak anamnestic power of a solidarity which those born later [he is thinking mainly of young Germans] can now only practice through the medium of memory."[17] Habermas's "weak anamnestic power" and Benjamin's "weak messianic power," to which it alludes, suggest something potentially redemptive, insofar as historical knowledge is converted into remembrance or the risk—through art—of an anabasis, a descent to the dead, is undertaken.[18]

But is there an aesthetic truth—is art a form of intelligence as trustworthy as historical or scientific inquiry? This long-standing debate revives again. Before "aesthetic" became a dirty word, the rubric of "aesthetic distance" had a place in the analysis and judgment of works of art. Though often superficially understood, the concept made us aware of the artist's responsibility vis-à-vis subject-matter and audience. The Greeks fined playwrights who merely quickened their pain or fear, and Primo Levi, in "The Memory of the Offense," shows how difficult it is to be a messenger of bad news—also to oneself. I suspect that aesthetic distance struggles with a dissociation that results from trauma and seeks to achieve a balance between over- and underidentification. The key factor here is art's decorum of disclosure, its sense of *timing*.

We receive a strong impression of such timing from a text that represents the opposite of Holocaust annihilation: the ritual creation sequence that opens Genesis. God takes time out to recognize or bless what He has made. An image of sheer power is modified by this predialogic acknowledgment of creature by creator. But periods of decreation—when we are devastated or returned to nothing—are something else. Time as the steadfast ground of being has disappeared; how do we talk *then* with the traumatized part of ourselves or others? What kind of dialogue or recognition is possible?

"Entmündigte Lippe," writes Paul Celan, "melde / daß etwas geschieht, noch immer, / unweit von dir." I can only paraphrase, not translate, "Mouthless, disenfranchised lips: announce that something is still happening, not far from you."[19] Those who are lost, though far away, never disappear completely. Active in memory or activated by fantasy, their internalized presence may be so haunting that our own voice is jeopardized and becomes mute. Written words, silent but not mute, represent a compromise, and the tradition of written art, or rhythmic and ritual forms, will try to reintegrate something of the lost world, despite pain or trauma. The combination of form and feeling in art or some other, more discursive recovery of hermeneutic patience is especially effective in creating a mode of disclosure. The very difficulty, however, of "seeing" an event of such human ferocity, or of presenting it *untraumatically*, should make us more cautious about an axiom of our culture: that, to quote Justice Brandeis, "Sunlight is . . . the best of disinfectants."[20]

What are the chances, then, of encouraging an intergenerational conversation, through art or essays, to forestall silence and solipsism? Though "conversation," in this context, is a misnomer, I have yet to find a better word. To introduce facts about the Shoah into casual talk—or even into the less casual space of the classroom—produces an embarrassed silence. Silence of this kind can be propaedeutic, however, a step toward mature conversation, toward that very *Mündigkeit* by which Kant defined the enlightened person or humanity's collective exodus from a self-incurred *Unmündigkeit* (immaturity).

The conversation I consider essential to intellectual witness includes such questions as: Was suffering meant to end in a book or a movie? Must every good story presuppose a fascination with crime and disaster, with the heart of darkness? Can we look at the calamity of the Holocaust without taking some comfort from representation, discursive or artistic? Has the culture in which it happened changed? Does emphasis on the Shoah raise the suspicion that the Jewish community is monopolizing suffering, or is there a way of bringing this disaster into the framework of comparative genocide? Are there moral lessons to be drawn from the Holocaust, more compelling than a vague appeal to humanitarian or democratic values?

As time passes and the terror that threatened to blank the screen is lessened by the very stories and pictures that accumulate as partial defenses against that blankness, we are obliged to think of the problems that surround the transmission of the Holocaust as a living memory. What if such a legacy—as it is now called—has a despairing or traumatizing effect and the "Never Forget" becomes an impossibility? Finally, is there a limit to the bitter logic of accusation, or does that always depend on the triage of particular ideologies?

When the topic is the Holocaust, moreover, the cautions that weigh on intellectual essays are sometimes distinct from those that burden artistic or fictional projects. In art, scruples about representability often take over: Can or should the Shoah be depicted in graphic and realistic ways? But in intellectual witness the constraint comes more from an equivalent to the third than the second commandment: "Thou shalt not refer to the Holocaust in vain."

We are always under the injunction not to multiply words needlessly. In the matter of the Shoah, however, "silence" takes on a particular value, and speaking and writing are more at risk than in fictional modes, which often experiment with shock or create, through the magic of art, what Boileau called "agreeable monsters."[21] Silence as a value does not mean keeping quiet but evokes an internal monitor or threshold demon. The way we write about the Shoah has a bearing on the viability of culture after the Shoah.

In conclusion, "intellectual witness" is partial to itself: It brings forward those aspects of rationality that contribute to humanity, those writers who refuse to sacrifice their intellect despite the inhumanity of modern experience. Although I will not enter into arguments about Gadamer's ideal of "conversation" or Habermas's "communicative action," these relate rationality to democracy and continue to challenge a skeptical or *realpolitik* doctrine of social survival. In such debates the intellect becomes a witness to its own survival rather than being seduced into guilt, self-flagellation, or abdication.

Witnessing, moreover, cannot take place without some hope in the future, in generational transmission. Perhaps all writing presupposes this hope—the manuscript in a bottle as well as the buried milk canisters of Ringelblum's "Oneg Shabbat." Yet the scorched intelligibility Nazism left behind and modern efforts to rebuild and recover from it in a time of accelerating change have produced an uncertainty about who will transmit, or who can identify long enough with a self to become a subject, to establish a consistent sense of place, emplacement, belonging.

Because the identity of the survivors is so thoroughly shaped by their experience, this may not seem to be an important consideration. But the literature puts us on our guard. The Nazi Holocaust systematically denied the victim any identity except of the most shameful and dehumanized kind. An unbridgeable gulf appeared between being human and being a Jew. "If This

Be a Man" is Primo Levi's title for his Auschwitz experience. "A different creator made me," Dan Pagis writes, comparing the shade (*tsel*) he has become to the booted, uniformed guards usurping the *tselem elohim*, the image of God. The victim's identity became a nonidentity. It is far too easy to claim that 1945 brought reversal and restoration. Who is speaking, who is testifying, if Paul Celan speaks truly when he says: "Speaks true who speaks shadow"?[22]

Here the necessary function of intellectual, or secondary, witnessing is disclosed once more. It provides a witness for the witness; it actively receives words that reflect the darkness of the event. For "blackbird" Celan, for Ancel/Amsel, intelligibility is not the aim of witnessing. His poetry does not shine in the darkness to abolish it. Rather, the poetic word is as "darkness to a dying flame."[23] Celan's skeletalized "I" testifies to the missing other as well as the missing self, the "you" or "we," what Maurice Halbwachs called the "affective community" (basis of all memory) and Michael Pollak called the need for social identity.[24] Intellectual witness stands in for that "you" or "we" by a commitment to the survivors' or eyewitnesses' words. Like literature itself it moves within the damaged space of speech, specifically conscious of past betrayals and caught between the distancing and the discovery value of time.

2. Holocaust and Hope

> Thinking and the death camps are opposed ... thought entails as much a moral hope (that it may be triumphant, mastering its object, dissolving the difficulties, containing and elucidating the conundrum) as it is the investment of skill and dispassion in a methodic procedure. The death camps are a reality which, by their very nature, obliterate thought and the humane program of thinking.
> —Arthur A. Cohen

> One cannot write the history of Jewish hope without a parallel history of Jewish despair.
> —Yosef Yerushalmi

What are we to think when Jorge Semprún changes the title of his book on the aftereffects of his experience in Buchenwald from *Writing or Death* to *Writing or Life?*[1] Was it hope that fluttered up from the depth of Pandora's box, or was it the knowledge that writing is a form of life after death for survivors of the Shoah? I would like to say something of hope about hope, which I might do more effectively if hope could be separated from its opposites: not only from despair but also from muteness and suicidal grief, and above all from the fear of coldness, of becoming insensible to new life—its sorrow or joy. "Sometimes," Semprún tells us, and many survivors say the same, "I felt certain that there hadn't really been any return, that I hadn't really come back.... I was nothing other than a conscious residue of all that death."[2]

It could be considered hopeful that, despite the pain, so many are dealing with the Holocaust antiworld. Beyond the eyewitnesses themselves and the exemplary writings of, among others, Primo Levi, Elie Wiesel, Imre Kertesz, Charlotte Delbo, Ida Fink, Robert Antelme, Dan Pagis, Yitzhak Katznelson, and Paul Celan, there is a second-generation witness, there is a third-generation witness, there are what may be called witnesses by adoption; above all, and in spite of taboos and cautions, there exists a growing attempt via literature, history, film, video testimony, monuments, and art to focus on the madness of genocide.

Moreover, there does exist a tradition of comfort, if not exactly of hope. God and the Shechinah weep, they mourn, they go into exile with Israel. But those who quote such texts do so hesitantly, to show that they persist from the time of the destruction of the First and Second Temples, not that they would reconcile us to the Holocaust. And Christian theologians, insofar as they have broken their silence and acknowledged the role of religious antisemitism, realize that the plea for reconciliation remains precarious.[3] So Wilhelm Marquardt concedes, in one of those many waves of self-confrontation Germany has gone through, this time after the mediocre and yet—in Germany—effective TV serial *Holocaust*: "How could anyone of us be at peace with himself, who must be shunned like a fearful abnormality [*Abscheu*] by the victims. It would be an important Christian task to learn how one can keep living as a human being, when one is shunned by other humans."[4]

I limit myself to a literature that rarely suggests a redemptive value in what it continues to value: writing and language as such. This literature respects a reversal in the status of the victim but honors no myths. As an early article by Robert Antelme discloses, the concentration camp inmate, immediately following liberation, was asked to be the same person as before this experience, or to get on with life as if nothing had happened.[5] (In some cases the deportees were even greeted with suspicion, as tainted personalities who may have survived because of their collaboration.) The reversal of status that came about was attributable partly to the Eichmann trial and partly to the persistent writings and activities of Elie Wiesel, who viewed survivors as embodying the duty of remembrance and compelling the world to see Auschwitz as a rupture in history amounting to a second origin, as defining in its way as Sinai.[6]

Early postwar witness accounts from East Germany that glorify communist and worker resistance are not always, moreover, without justification. Even as the Nazi terror turned against the Jews, it also targeted whoever might have become a base for political resistance, in particular German social democrats and communists. Yet the only general myth or "grand narrative" we find in addition to a "chaos narrative"—fragmented, wounded, plural memories that need stitching up—is that of *Überleben*, of surviving in order to tell the story and becoming by sheer act of will an Ahasver, or, as in the Book of Job, the "I alone have escaped to tell thee."[7]

I do not feel confident enough to speculate on what may have nourished hope during the Holocaust itself, or whether such hope contributed to survival. Certainly for some like David Weiss Halivni, the Jewish learning tradition was so powerful that the recovery of a single page of Talmud, rescued from a guard who had wrapped his meal in it, seemed a miraculous event.[8] And Roberto Benigni's controversial movie, *Life Is Beautiful*, carries to the point of absurdity an insight already expressed in Jurek Becker's *Jacob the Liar*, where the hero, claiming to have access to a clandestine radio, lifts the morale of the ghetto by inventing broadcasts that keep hope in liberation alive. The logic of *Life Is Beautiful* pits the desperate make-believe of a father against the unbelievable inhumanity of the events he reinterprets. The very absurdity of the father's wager, that the death camp is simply a challenge, a game he and his son must win, even as it offends us in this context, even as it flouts historical possibility and artistic probability, not only prolongs a lifesaving vision of innocence but recalls the precarious habit of euphemism, without which ordinary life, too, is not bearable.[9]

Yet when the full extent of the disaster became known, what diminished hope was, in addition to the fact that such a genocide had been systematically carried out, the realization that the German public had been thoroughly brainwashed, how everyday speech and the media had been debased by a massive, state-sponsored propaganda. Heinrich Mann would diagnose the literary situation as early as 1934. "Everything is prefabricated, paid for, distorted" [*Alles gestellt, alles bestellt, alles verstellt*].[10] The interpretive spin that produces the humor and pathos of *Life Is Beautiful* was totally reversed, during the Nazi era, into a boundless malignity. Victor Klemperer, in notebooks that scrupulously record, like the philologist he was, what he calls LTI, the Language of the Third Reich, shows how thoroughly both public and private discourses were contaminated during the thousand-year empire's twelve years.[11] Leo Spitzer, the émigré scholar, wrote as follows after the war to a former associate: "The pain that a continuous self-purification should have brought with it, would have been so severe that you must have gone mad."[12]

State control of the media was total in Nazi Germany: Thought was besieged, day in, day out, by a mixture of exalted and criminal ideas. After the war, therefore, liberation meant more than restoring freedom of speech. The subjection of the populace had been too great: Its belief in Hitler, but also in the Nordic myth, seemed in retrospect a kind of trance or intoxication (*Rausch* is the word often used by commentators who lived through this period),[13] and, when it was over, when the war was lost, there seemed to be no basis for discussing what had happened.[14] For language itself had fallen under a spell and would have to be liberated.

Not only the material and psychic powers of Germany were exhausted but also its cultural heritage—squandered by a shameless appropriation. This heritage with its honorable words had shrunk so much through Nazi misuse that, according to Elisabeth Langgässer, the writer could no longer live in the German language as a natural home. It became "a remnant, a last primal rock formation identical with the writer, who suffered this fearful contraction as a trial of its indestructibility."[15]

I do not want my emphasis to be misunderstood. The corruption of language is a topic central to modernism and is often alleged against modernism itself—before postmodernism made it seem like an archaic scruple. Even Heidegger's revision of philosophical language is involved. Premonitions during the rise of totalitarianism (both of the right and the left) revealed their full ethical implications only after the war. We should recognize, George Orwell wrote in "Politics and the English Language," his well-known essay of 1964, "that the present political chaos is connected with the decay of language, and that one can probably bring about some improvement by starting at the verbal end.... Political language ... is designed to make lies sound truthful and murder respectable."[16]

—+—

I wish to go a step beyond this modernist concern to focus on the generic impact of the Holocaust on the way we consider language, especially literary language. The writer I will mainly take up is Maurice Blanchot, influenced by Emmanuel Levinas yet an original thinker and one of those responsible for a distinctive mode of writing that has remained enigmatic to many. Blanchot came to realize that language had to be reoriented, that the breach of civilized speech that occurred, even among intellectuals and professionals, whose behavior can only be called a culpable self-disenfranchisement (the German *Entmündung* captures that meaning), should lead to a new consciousness of words as the most responsible of human gifts.[17] I see Blanchot's work as an extended *procès verbal* directed against those who reduce language's social, imaginative, and intellectual character to instrumentalized phrases.

French was less corrupted, in this respect, than German; the French literary heritage had not been, on the whole, drawn into the *Kulturkampf* and betrayed. Even someone as virulently antisemitic as Charles Maurras remained an enemy of Germany and protected the French classical heritage. Blanchot's task, therefore, was a prosaic one, but his analysis of the gift of speech, of its everyday power of contestation—and also his extreme skepticism concerning that power—led him to stylistic experiments, not as daring as those of Paul Celan yet exemplary in their own way.

One of the difficulties in reading Blanchot is easy to describe. Because, according to him, words speak across a distance without eliminating it and preserve, in this way, the individuality or otherness of interlocutors, including their right to withdraw from political engagement, his scenarios, in fiction as in criticism, stage a relentless, as if endless, conversation, with little reliance on psychological characterization, myth, or plot. The plot, in fact, seems to be language itself, or the passion of writing trapped in what Octavio Paz once described as the vertigo of the in between. Yet even if we tolerate Blanchot's at once ascetic and intensely verbose procedure, a doubt remains: Will this "*entretien infini*," this endless conversation, make sense, when the desire to make sense—outraged so often as we recall the Holocaust—is at the heart of what is contested?

Blanchot's word-consciousness does not fall from heaven; it has historical and cultural specificity. Let me mention only its political prehistory rather than its complex literary sources. Blanchot was, for a time, an *enragé* who contributed before the war to right-wing journals prone to antisemitism, especially after Léon Blum became France's prime minister. He mysteriously stopped his militant journalism around the time of Munich in 1938 and turned almost completely to literature and literary theory. Associated later with Vichy's "La Jeune France," he eventually resigned and also refused a leading role in the revived *Nouvelle Révue Française* during France's era of collaboration. He nevertheless contributed a nonpolitical literary chronicle to the Vichy-supported *Journal des Débats* as late as August 1944. It was learning about the camps through Robert Antelme, the author of *L'espéce humaine*, that seems to have been decisive. The story of Antelme's rebirth after his near-death in the camps, together with his reaffirmation of an irreducible humanity and the significance of words outside a power context, will never leave Blanchot.[18]

To value Blanchot's antirhetorical view of language, we must also understand that the question of our speech—of what we can say about the Shoah—has not become less difficult since 1945. Ingeborg Bachmann, in her burdened account (burdened by literary tradition as well as the Shoah) of what she saw ten years after the end of the war in the Ghetto of Rome on the Day of Atonement, affords, if only for a moment, a glimpse of life being renewed. She describes a child that must have been born shortly after liberation calling to the musicians "*Spiel weiter!*" (Keep on playing), not realizing what that phrase meant in the camps.[19] This kind of innocence, with the passage of time, is complicated by the guilt of increased, ever-increasing knowledge: We are fast reaching the point—given the proliferation of books, films, and discourses and aware that despite them genocidal acts continue—where a fatigue enters, one that makes us doubt the human species itself, or the very commandment to remember—to transmit the bad news we compulsively investigate.

In such an atmosphere even the concept of testimony, of bearing witness, whether by the victimized or those who wish to show companionship with them, is in danger of becoming a benevolent and impotent cliché. The pathos of Mallarmé's *"La chair est triste, hélas, et j'ai lu tous les livres"* (roughly: The flesh is sad, alas, and I've read all the books) seems, all of a sudden, understated.[20] There is compassion fatigue, as it has been called, but also a reading fatigue, especially among those sensitive to language, who fear that no word-concept is adequate or will escape erosion and controversy.

"Think of any key concept in the vocabulary of civilized discourse," Terrence Des Pres has written, "and immediately, if its sounding board is the Holocaust, you are in trouble."[21] Such terms as *extreme experience, trauma, terror, disaster, catastrophe, uniqueness*, even *Holocaust* or *Shoah*, are unable to support the work of reflection and self-reflection that tries to understand, to really "grasp," this democidal century—a "grasping" that would ordinarily lead to dedicated personal conviction and political action.[22] Instead, the impasse between the garrulity of trying to say as much as possible and the near-silence of choosing one's words in such a way that others will not despair or be consumed by grief affects every attempt at writing. This happens not only as we confront the Shoah but when, facing renewed atrocities, and not wishing to reject language or abandon life to unreason, we salvage rationality by representing philosophy, literature, and history writing as forms of remedial action.

It is precisely this defense against grief that no longer works—insofar as it makes too hopeful a claim. How can the most rational of our desires be substantiated, that there should be a link between speaking, or expression generally, and progress? In the past, there were those who believed a doctrine *because* it was absurd: Now we have reached a similar stage with the hope we still invest in the effectiveness of reasonable words.

Even commentators like Lawrence Langer, who are eloquent against the presumption that from the Holocaust a specific historical or moral lesson could emerge, cannot entirely forgo the language of hope. Langer wants his essays to contribute to "the incessant anxious dialogue" (an endless conversation?) "about how our civilization may absorb into its reasonable hopes for the future the disabling outburst of unreason we name the Holocaust."[23] The radical character of Blanchot's project—after a certain date—is to find an alternative to the language of historical hope, Hegel's legacy to this day, and which we all, Langer included, seem to need.[24]

—+—

Blanchot's critique is not directed against historical meanings as such, only against their overestimation. He attacks the confusion that makes the study of history in general—not just of the Holocaust—a source of definitive meanings whose influence could integrate a catastrophic past. That we live in the best of all possible worlds is an idea that died long ago with Voltaire's *Candide*. After the Holocaust the question becomes what better world is still possible. In Blanchot, writing, so often associated with action or trying to be justified as an act, begins to accept itself as a passion story, the place where Sarah Kofman's proposition about wording the Holocaust is realized: "Talk one must—without having the power."[25]

Blanchot, however, while rejecting any systematic effort to derive lessons from history, does not give up on finding a rationale for art. He modifies the position taken by Theodor Adorno's famous essay "Commitment."[26] Adorno wanted to shield the Holocaust from profanation, doubting art's capacity to present it without a meretricious stylization; Blanchot is concerned rather with defending art by setting its "passive" integrity against attempts to discredit it once more after so radical a shock. He argues that writers who, as citizens, are ideologically engaged cannot thereby engage literature, too, that is, subdue it to a mimetic-realistic or instrumentalist end—however worthy that end may be. If anything, literature takes back from politics pursued as a religion the power of naming. Poetry, in particular, does not add meaning to catastrophe: On the contrary, in the presence of poetic words meanings withdraw—with the result that words become more opaque and material, more thinglike, and often fascinate qua verbal images.[27] Blanchot once defined the word as "a janus-faced monster, verbal reality which has a material presence and a signification which is an ideal absence."[28]

Yet Blanchot does worry about the unresolved intersection of ethical and aesthetic. Though he insists that writers should not sacrifice their vocation, there may have to be a *"détournement,"* a diversion to politics of the critic's or artist's acquired authority. This must be temporary, however, and for a specific cause, all the more so since war and violence as a political means often turn into ends and displace that cause.[29] Blanchot, moreover, when it comes to the relation between words and world, adapts a key notion from Levinas, that of exteriority.

—+—

Exteriority points to what cannot be internalized; it serves to reject a Hegelian type of mediation in which everything becomes knowable, hence meaningful. Hegel's dialectic is viewed as a form of knowledge lust. But exteriority also points to an external world that is aesthetic in the sense of phenomenal: a world of immediate perception, of colors, sounds, and shapes. The medium of the verbal, says Blanchot, "dreams of unifying itself to objects of which it would have the weight, the color, the heavy and dormant aspect."[30] The word artist is not fundamentally different in this from the painter who acknowledges that colors and shapes exist that seem irreducible to verbal or ethical schemes of meaning. Both arts are driven by "un *moi* insatiable du *non moi*" (a self, hungering insatiably for a nonself).[31]

The effort to appease this hunger leads, however, to a violence of its own—when we substitute words for things or subdue the life in words to purely realistic ends. Blanchot's early novel *Thomas l'obscur* described the revenge of words that turn the tables on the artist and attack him with a devouring intimacy. They are suddenly glimpsed as living beings, even as vampires, who desire to become real through a transfusion of his essence. "He was seized, kneaded by intelligible hands, bitten by a vital tooth; he entered with his living body into the anonymous shapes of words, giving his substance to them, establishing their relationships, offering his being to the word 'be.'"[32]

Thus even words have an otherness to be respected. Words keep things "in the difficulty of what it is to be."[33] "The one who encounters *l'Autrui* [the other-in-his-otherness]," Blanchot writes in the spirit of Levinas, "can only relate to him by deadly violence, or by the welcoming gift of the word."[34] Blanchot's "infinite conversation," then, is not an escape from reality into words but the result of an uncompromising choice: words or violence. Yet words themselves, as I have said, are always shadowed by an intrinsic violence, by their difference from things, their breach with phenomenality. This breach, internal to speech and even more to writing, leads to a dangerous undertow that tempts the writer back into the more organic sphere of embodied and especially politically sanctioned meaning.

The writer, then, must be doubly wary: of words as well as the world. Speech, nevertheless, remains the place where we can best meet in understanding and amity, despite the otherness of the other and the pull toward a speechless violence. "Speech invites man to no longer identify with his power."[35] The opposite happened in Nazism, where the word became exclusively a power instrument, as also at times in Blanchot's prewar phase, in which his journalism turned to a rhetoric of revolutionary or oppositional violence.

―+―

Let me focus more sharply on the moral point made by both Blanchot and Levinas. Hegel's *Phenomenology* had argued that increase of knowledge leads to increase of being, while absolute knowledge, the end of humanity's journey, is nothing less than a fullness in which being and meaning coincide.[36] Levinas rejects, like Blanchot, Hegel's reason-of-history. Hegel's dialectical view of the way history moves legitimized the political realm through the key concepts of nation and cultural progress. But when that realm of public action and discourse devours privacy, it becomes simply a more potent form of oppression. So Czeslaw Milosz's *Captive Mind* is a powerful reminder of how ideals that enforce an interpretation in the name of politics (*raison d'état*) engender an all-encompassing hypocrisy as invasive as the voiceover of propaganda newsreels. This hypocrisy, a pathological form of theater, kills all hope of humor and dialogue, appropriating the past and coercing the future by ideology.

As the expression of a post-Holocaust morality, Blanchot's literary theory is allergic to any such totalizing move. His most dramatic application of this refusal of ideology affects the meaning of death. We consider it tragic when meaning disappears from death and heroic when there is an effort to give meaning to that meaninglessness. Hence the link, in so much thinking, between Holocaust death and martyrdom. Blanchot is among those who question this tragic-heroic link. The Holocaust not only took from its victims the possibility of an authentic, dignified, or beautiful death; the death of that death, as it has been called, takes from us, even now, the conviction that this epoch is over or that a previous innocence can be restored. Edith Wyschogrod says that a primordial mode of being-in-the world, described by phenomenology as a "life-world," suppressed in the camps' universe of death, continues to be part of humanity's collective experience. "*Once the death-world has existed it continues to exist in the mode or eternity as it were, for it becomes part of the sediment of an irrevocable past.*"[37]

Blanchot, possessed by a parallel intuition, defines the Holocaust as an absolute event in which history itself burns up (that is, the Hegelian concept of history), so that "the movement of meaning was ruined."[38] The emphasis here falls on "movement": There is a disorienting finality to the Holocaust, which leads to dejection rather than hope, because no dialectical and sublimating move seems possible.[39]

Making sense of Auschwitz, then, is something impermanent, a simple, repetitive moment of hope, a shimmer unattached to fulfillment. Daniel Libeskind, the architect, has talked of a "Hope-Incision." Though the seductiveness of writing may remain linked to our ability to face the Shoah (to work it through with the help of language), writing worthy of its name is never a power play using a prophetic or historical determinism as its instrument. Blanchot rejects Hegel's "imposture of completed meaning" [*l'impos-*

ture du Sens achevé] and also reverses Christian triumphalism. "Judaism," he asserts, "is the sole thought that does not mediate."[40] His watchword becomes "Watch over [i.e., safeguard] absent meaning."[41]

—|—

There is, nevertheless, one oddly redemptive feature in art as such. Kant, watching in his own way over absent meaning, had emphasized the irreducibility of the aesthetic judgment to a concept: What is perceived and enjoyed aesthetically is disinterested, in the sense that a specific teleological meaning cannot be discerned. Blanchot, focusing on art, emphasizes the persistence of formal elements: stylistic repetitions that illuminate the antiexpressive, inertial features of literary language, and generally its "non-sense" or resistance to change and novelty as sources of meaning.[42] Touching back to poetry as well as philosophy, to Mallarme's hyperbolic "Governments change; versification remains," as well as Hegelian reflections on how language participates in a "labor of the negative," he refuses to declare that literature is on the way to a "new order" of words. He accepts the hazard that gave us the words we have, whose spirituality has been tainted, and whose relation to existence is, in a strong pun of Derrida's, "hauntological."

Thus the formalism of literary language persists, though shaken by the Shoah—and that it persists, that it outlives that event, resilient as grass and flowers covering the killing fields, is scandalous. "The glory of a 'narrative voice,'" Blanchot asserts, prevails whatever the content of our speech. Artistic words always turn wounds into pearls, and thus language and thought will be, after a disaster, as they were before, "exterior" to each other.[43]

How does this insight affect Blanchot's own style? His *Writing of the Disaster*, published in 1980, is not so much a book as a series of fragments. The prose fragment has become a genre by now; points of comparison are Pascal's *Pensées,* on the one hand, and Romantic experiments, on the other. Also Kafka's parables. We encounter a restless style that allows very little closure, something of "l'asperité d'un style sans repos" (the asperity of a style that cannot find rest), which Blanchot used to describe others.[44] Some will say Blanchot's style doesn't add up; others might quote Adorno's axiom, that the fragmentary is the intervention of death in the work.

In Blanchot, writing is linked to "disaster" in the etymological sense, and Judaism provides the prototype by its monotheistic displacement of the stars as deities. Yet writing as star-breaking cannot be systematized, since that would recuperate the negative and convert it, as Hegel did, to a motor for transcendence.[45] Blanchot, then, seeks a different spiritual language ("une langue autre"), one that is neither theological nor a displacement of the theological. The older idiom has been irreversibly tainted by fascism's "spiritual revolution" and inflammatory rhetoric.

Does Blanchot achieve this "other language"? He at least describes what guarantees its possibility. It will be marked by a contemplative streak, the "désinteressé du désastre"—a phrase suggesting that the disaster brings with it a special detachment, one so much part of the disaster that it frees us from it as an obsessive, singular object of concern.[46] The writer's anguish comes, however, precisely from this intellectual freedom: He is torn apart, Blanchot says in an early essay, "by the harmony of his images, by the air of happiness radiating from what he writes. He experiences this contradiction as the unavoidably oppressive aspect of the exaltation that he finds in that writing, an exaltation that crowns his disgust."[47]

It helps to contrast with Blanchot's disorienting style the forceful, Old World simplicity of writers like Améry, Levi, Wiesel, Fink, Shalamov, Klima, and Kertesz, who continue to respect the formula of "new wine in old bottles." They do not problematize the recession of words or the "abyss" between words and thought: the collapse of faith in the progressively greater truth capacity of language. Ernst Simon, in his essay "The New Midrash," sought to show how, after 1933, Martin Buber and others developed a "*Binnensprache*," Aesopian words of resistance based on aggadic midrash.[48] Poets, too, like Sutzkever and Radnoti, mobilize the strength of traditional forms, even if Radnoti, who revives the eclogue, feels compelled to ask: "Is there still a land, tell me, where this verse form has meaning?"[49] The poets who continue to write do so in a no-man's land. Radnoti's despair is clear from a poem excavated with his corpse:

> I lived on this earth in an age
> When poets too were silent: waiting in hope
> For the great Prophet to rise and speak again—
> Since no-one could give voice to a fit curse
> But Isaiah himself, scholar of terrible words.[50]

While Blanchot, conscious that the Shoah has modified narrative competence or intellectualizing arrogance in only minor ways, struggles with language against it, against the seductiveness of narrativity and voice, Radnoti and Primo Levi do not display that obsessive focus. When Levi quotes a passage from Dante's *Hell* in the hell of Auschwitz, he preserves rather than estranges the literary moment.[51] The concern of both Radnoti and Levi is to speak without cursing.

Yet the radical direction taken by Blanchot is paradoxically sustained by them. For if any redemptive structuring of time or language is a passing hope, then literature after Auschwitz will not be essentially different from literature before Auschwitz, despite our anguished consciousness. The terrible beauty born in the wake of the Holocaust is terrible and beautiful because of a sameness, a repetition, an invincibly pastoral or contemplative element. Both types of art, of willing and of defiant consent to traditional literary forms, strengthen Adorno's comment: "The world grown dark makes the irrationality of art rational: art, itself the radically darkened."[52] It is this rationality of art, despite a hopelessness that afflicts us after the Holocaust, which I have tried to epitomize in this essay.

Epilogue (250 Years After Goethe's Birth)

> Only for the sake of those who have no hope is hope given us.
> —Walter Benjamin, "Goethe's *Wahlverwandtschaften*"

Imagine, now, that Goethe, from his place in the literary firmament, saw what happened between 1933 and 1945: the murderous assault of the Nazi regime on the Jews, as well as on others scorned as ethnically inferior, asocial, or unworthy of life, an assault in the very name of culture, of a pure Aryan culture. I do not conjure up a Goethe looking down from heaven because his temperament was Olympian but because he understood the relation between the extremes of happiness and unhappiness, the danger of exaltation together with the fall from sublimity into a disenchantment that must lead to incurable melancholy or savage revenge. "Es fürchte die Götter / Das Menschengeschlecht" [Mankind must fear (coming near) the gods]: The opening of Iphigenia's "Parzenlied," her hymn to the Fates in *Iphigenia in Tauris*, is but one of Goethe's warnings against identifying with "*Herrscher*" mania.[53] Precisely such deification inspired the leaders of a self-styled master race and attracted an enormous number of fanatics and fellow travelers.

Perhaps you will object to my fantasy because whatever it was that Goethe intuited was exceeded by the enormity of the Holocaust to such an extent that he would have been unable to fathom it, or because the Goethean response, in a poem like Iphigenia's hymn, can no longer go to the heart of the matter. Part of me agrees with that assessment. Goethe, who said "there are unbeautiful, terrifying things in nature, with which literature, however skillfully it may treat them, ought neither to concern nor to reconcile itself," and who, though recognizing Kleist's genius, was also repelled by it, may not be—if anyone can be—an adequate witness.[54] But as we pass from generation to generation, and by now the third after the Shoah has come of age, it is impossible to omit from the cause of hope the country from which the destruction originally arose.

As the ravage of genocide is repeated in other parts of the world, it is human nature itself we confront. No god out of the machine can help, as in Aeschylus or Euripides, though an invention like that is prompted by the impasse in human affairs between amnesty and the retaliatory demands of justice. But if we anticipate a lifting of despair, and therefore seek to *study* (I can find no better word) the possibility of hope, it has to come from a renewed understanding of language or art, including Germany's contribution.

It is relatively easy to honor—I do not say to comprehend—Paul Celan, but does the art of a Goethe still move us, can such art prevail despite the Nazi disaster? Reading Goethe today, must we overlook what began to happen only a hundred years after his death? Can we enjoy his wisdom and virtuosity only by confining him to his historical corner, blinkering the inspiration of a creator who is as important to German literature as Shakespeare is to English?

I realize that even Shakespeare's place is no longer entirely secure. Yet his dramas have proved to be more adaptable to a contemporary world that has "supp'd full of horrors."[55] Akhmatova still invokes him, thinking of Londoners during the Blitz: "Time is writing Shakespeare's twenty-fourth drama." But, she adds, "not this, not this, not this,/ this even we aren't capable of reading."[56]

What terror and trauma Goethe knew are not portrayed with the visual force and super-realism of Shakespearean tragedy. For those devoted to literature, however, it may be as important to justify art through Goethe as through Shakespeare. It is precisely because of his reticence, or "klassische Dämpfung," as Leo Spitzer named it—the fact that in *Iphigenia* he evokes catastrophe from the distance of ballad and oral tradition ("Vor meinen Ohren tönt das alte Lied," says Iphigenia [The ancient song comes to my ears])—that my looking to Goethe may be relevant.[57] What might he have said, obliged to star in a "Prologue in Heaven" like the one introducing his own *Faust*? *Iphigenia in Tauris* tries to undo a spell ascribed to the Fates, even if it originated in human nature. The Holocaust institutes once again a break in civilization (*Zivilisationsbruch*) and unleashes a horrendous chain of consequences. This time it is irreducible to the story of an eponymous family on which so much of ancient Greek tragedy is based, the story of Tantalus, Pelops, and his family feud. Yet Goethe, too, seeks to exorcize the Furies, even if his play is almost entirely a learned rumor, a belated pandect of classical themes, and therefore (like Greek tragedy itself) as much recitation as dramatic action. It is, in effect, as pointed in its moral urgency as anything in Shakespeare.

The audience in Berlin that saw *Iphigenia* staged in 1998 was, I am sure, sensitive to its topical appeal, since the play raises the issue of hospitality to foreigners. Was it only, though, my ears that responded to the pathos of the sister's refusal to save her brother and herself before making sure that Tauris would abolish human sacrifice? I cannot vouch for the audience around me, but I thought of the curse the Holocaust had brought upon Germany when she speaks the following words:

> Soll dieser Fluch denn ewig walten? Soll
> Nie dies Geschlecht mit einem neuen Segen
> Sich wieder heben?

> [Must this curse then last for ever? Can
> This people never be reestablished
> through a new blessing?][58]

3. Words Not from on High

"I swear to you it was black," a Holocaust survivor says of the sun rising on Auschwitz. Paul Celan opens his "Death Fugue" with the image of dawn as a "black milk," a humor (in the old sense of a coursing, bloodlike fluid) that determines the mood and even perhaps the inspiration of thinkers touched by that disaster.[1] For those touched, is there a way out of the *univers concentrationnaire* that invades, afterward, the everyday world and gives it permanently a sinister coloration?

There should be a mode of expression to recall what happened, even to make it, despite a certain art-shame, more visible. In Charlotte Delbo's words, "Il faut donner à voir" (they must be made to see).[2] The issue of representability is common enough in discussions of how to face the Shoah. Black milk is a treacherous nutriment, however. Freud's distinction between mourning and melancholia, between, on the one hand, a psychic path (and possibly a communal one) leading through inward or else ritual "work" to mental health, and, on the other, the impasse of interminable grieving—that distinction has become harder to confirm. For there are too many reminders of the Shoah, aftershocks and even near-repetitions. We are bombarded almost daily with images of political misery, terror, and genocidal acts. Our associations, therefore, whether to images or words, are no longer free: This holds true for the survivors but also for a new generation of bystanders, for all who become through the media involuntary and impotent witnesses of a past that seems to return and maintain its grip on the present. Consciousness, however streamy, cannot purge itself any longer of a poisonous residue. Melancholy becomes the Writer.

Vernal moments subsist, it is true; delightful breaks in the weather. Yet even they may not lighten mood or mind. A problematic meaning attaches itself to "free" in "free associations." When one thinks one is free, and that writing has been cathartic by opening the way to a necessary forgetting, for many this happy result augurs an indifference, even a coldness intrinsic to thought and close to the inability to mourn. Fear of *anesthésie émotionelle* returns, and of the aesthetic as a mode of anesthesia.

Our associations remain unfree because of compulsive memories and electronic phantoms, or unfree because a nervous reflex makes us doubt the right to relief. Can we still fashion, then, good words not clouded by disaster? Words untainted by their very sublimity? Adorno is authoritative in alleging that "No word intoned [*getöntes*] from on high, not even a theological one, can be justified, untransformed, after Auschwitz."[3] But what does he have in mind, since "transformation" has a "high" theological or visionary connotation?

No one considered this question of our speech more continuously, insistently, than Blanchot. It may be that feelings of guilt from his inflammatory journalism of the 1930s affected, however indirectly, the postwar writings. It is too easy, however, to play the biographical card. Blanchot was notoriously discreet about his own life. He changed into himself during his lifetime by a creative erosion devoid of memoir. His theme, if there is a unifying one, becomes the search for *un langage autre*. Like Adorno he sought a different, a transformed or thought-transforming speech. A counterlogos would free words to become words of the "other," words of the *Je* that is an *Autre*, yet not a deceptive or preemptive rhetoric, a religious or political propaganda intoned from on high. A counterlogos also to the seductive drift of power-words that exalt not only journalism but literature itself as *mots en liberté*. In the *pensées* that make up *The Writing of the Disaster*, key words give rise to tightly marshaled blocks of thought, sequences that do not betray a clear direction or timeline, that flow without compulsion or *Lichtzwang*, yet seem anything but liberated. While the concept of disaster remains immemorial and generalized, the Holocaust as an *absolute date* haunts many pages.

The sin of this book against Cartesian clarity is, one might allege, its only clarity. But it sins equally against the predominant value-terms of both popular and professional Anglo-American discourse: such motivating words as agency, identity, productivity. There is a kind of Nietzschean transvaluation of values, except that Nietzsche's critique of the cunning of the weak—of their religiously inspired abnegation and passivity interpreted as masking a will to power—is itself transvalued. I often find it more disconcerting to read Blanchot than Nietzsche because he has no afflatus or mock rhetoric: Bareness, or the movement toward it, is all; the usual fictional or accommodating props have been removed. Although the first-person *récits* preceding *The Writing of the Disaster* are novelistic in their setting, they are almost devoid of incident and conventional characterization. (The surrealistic stories written before 1939, an early version of *Thomas l'obscur*, and also the Kafkaesque *Aminadab* are exceptions.) Their literary space remains empty of plot or dramatic action. What action occurs is mainly in the form of simple phrases not from on high. Snatches of an obscurely motivated, even seemingly trivial conversation, uttered by sparsely embodied persons, echo inside a restricted, unidentified locale.

Blanchot's commentary-prose is equally denuded of sequential acts. Improgressive sentences, close to aphorisms, intensify rather than diminish the distance between words and their direct signification. The vessel of understanding keeps breaking into fragments, as if the parts were more signifying than the whole. These essay-books are less containers than empty rooms amplifying a silence in the words spoken. Everything resonates without moving toward a central focus or defined reference point. "The writer no longer belongs to the magisterial domain where to express oneself signifies to express the precision and certainty of things and values...."[4] There is no triumphal *ergo* binding the "I think" or "I speak" to the "I am."

Or to the "you are" or "it is." In this strange landscape, this unreal real of Blanchot's fiction, an asymmetry of relationships emerges that has Levinasian intensity and projects a passion (in the sense of abiding the desire for contact, advent, even revelation) that is as persistent as mourning or as endless as interpretation. For readers in the Anglo-American cultural realm, even for those who have come to appreciate Henry James, this meta-Jamesian conversational probing and internal, meditative elaboration approaches the intolerable as it defeats, without quite abandoning, "l'imposture du Sens achevé."[5] That phrase protests Hegel; the Hegelian dynamic, insofar as it transcends the negative and views history as a providential, end-oriented process, is rejected. For after a disaster, Blanchot writes, time changes direction, and he uses the word *sens* to indicate both meaning and direction. One cannot talk of the Messiah in Hegelian language.

Gnomic as they are, such dicta devalue neither Hegel nor the Messiah: They incorporate a reflection on language which Proudhon, frustrated materialist, declared "full of God" (*plena Jovis*). "Watch over absent meaning" is therefore Blanchot's parole in *The Writing of the Disaster*.[6] Meaning cannot be attributed to history in the absence of messianic hope. But if that is so, must we succumb to a religious and often politically exploited vocabulary that seduces with words from on high?

An irredeemable solitude, a suffering suffered without telos or progress, can only be expressed in terms of passion rather than action. It verges, however, on the suggestion that the human drive for being, for a realization of the "I am," is in the nature of an anticipatory, transfigurative vision. "What is my end, that I should be patient?" Job asks in bitterness of soul.[7] The self wishes to be preserved in order to observe the very suffering that negates it. Or, like Job, to find a witness in itself for itself at the last. Even when persecuted, it strives to be transcendently watchful, enduring rather than escaping the gift of life.

Without denying the promise of community implicit in the very effort of seeking to communicate, Blanchot's hope, not unlike the Pauline version, occasionally breaks through as a desire to be reborn with a pristine vigor of perception, although the human condition is full of pain, uncertainty, equivocation. The writer, having died—in the sense of a molting of his ego—he could spring into a second life and display an Adamic speech "washed in the remotest cleanliness of a heaven...." So that the sun, if seen at all, is seen in its idea. Depictions of the external world are rare in Blanchot, but when they occur they are, as in Wallace Stevens, "notes" toward a supreme fiction. Not just nature, language itself appears as a cosmos that has "expelled us and our images." Yet the innocence of perception called ignorance by Stevens ("You must become an ignorant man again") has grown to be impossible: Blanchot remains burdened by a vigilance coming from knowledge of the Holocaust. A sleep-disturbing ethical insomnia turns day into a night not relieved by any rosy-fingered dawn.[8]

The hazard, then, of this second birth, for which art is the passage-rite, is that one must go consciously into, or through, a dying. The self dies into writing, though not in order to be gloriously embodied on the other side, to enjoy in that place a mystical noon, a permanent moment of ecstatic time purged of all remainders that darken conscience. Nor does it seek to die for the sake of consuming a better product, a heavenly manna, flesh of Leviathan. Rather, it gains through its impossible extinction an instance of life after death, of a capacity for witness neither dimmed nor compromised by the vicious dialectic of mastery and submission.

Blanchot's writerly theory of self-abnegation brings him close to a modernist myth. That myth with its principle of artistic impersonality includes the belief that writing will take the writer out of himself, that he can lose the ability and comfort of saying "I," indeed that his oeuvre will become a *désoeuvrement*. The death of the author, or writing as an endless passion, is the process of giving up authority. Blanchot diverges from the modernist myth, however, in that no substitutes for "I"—no "he," "she," "it," "we"—are allowed to replenish a void created by this refusal to personify. That void is to be suffered just like the self that despairs and cannot die, and unless it dies cannot be reborn. It cannot die because, as Kierkegaard asserts in *The Sickness*

Unto Death, the self is the very "ground of despair, whose worm dieth not, and whose fire is not quenched."[9]

Since the temptation to evade solitude, to fill that void by a proliferation of fictive selves, is so strong, Blanchot's "espace littéraire" becomes a crucial concept. Literary space is the space created by refusing false ecstasies, vitalisms, verbal power-plays. Instead of deploying an arrogant anthropomorphic animism that sustains (traditional) characters with the author's own life, Being itself (*l'être*) emerges at the end of the writer's negative path. His active withdrawal into passivity is comparable to the kabbalistic *zimzum* that clears a space within what is too full. Writers enter that space, or behold it from afar, by accepting their essential loneliness ("Where he is, only being speaks").[10]

The justice of Blanchot's moral and linguistic critique of the modernist aesthetic has not been understood. Perhaps because, despite his emphasis on watching over literary space, his own language is trapped in purgatory, in a twilight of reference. Can he convey what he means except by secularizing a mystical diction? His "langage autre" remains very close to words intoned from on high. Or to the "gigantic murmur" of words under the words, a buzz of subdued associations that almost dissolve the possibility of referential meaning. Yet Blanchot did refuse to compose books, resisting The Book as another illusion from on high.

His thought is silent now. Whether it can pass through death into a book of life depends on each reader.

4. Wounded Time: The Holocaust, Jedwabne, and Disaster Writing

An important attempt to understand the decisive impact of the Holocaust on both fiction and critical discourse is Maurice Blanchot's *The Writing of the Disaster*. Though Blanchot does not equate the disaster referred to in the title exclusively with the Holocaust, he indicates that what happened is epochal, both for human consciousness generally and for the art of writing in particular. He plays on the etymology of "disaster" to suggest a radical disorientation linked to the fall or vanishing of a star. The impasse he faces is that after such a disaster, writing (in whatever genre) must convey an altered state, a wounded sense of time, yet cannot change so radically that it would scuttle either its short-term communicative or long-term transmissive power. The disaster enters his text, therefore, as a prose that reflects "the shock of the unintelligible" yet maintains a normative decorum.[1]

Blanchot's solution is to fashion antisystematic fragments, *pensées* that lack the steadfast "star" of a clear timeline or any synthesis affirming unity of consciousness or the hope of a progressive merging of subjective desire and objective reality. Though these *pensées* refer unmistakably to his own intellectual milieu and are datable that way, most of them remain "impersonified" (as Mallarmé would say). Sometimes this distinctly French mode of literary impersonality, this inertial, anticatastrophic formalism (more radical than T. S. Eliot's famous impersonality theory), results in a word or image bearing an unusual emphasis that can be overlooked—or that overlooks itself, as it were. This happens, for example, in a definition that describes the Holocaust as "the *absolute* event of history—which is a date in history—that utter-burn where all history took fire, where the movement of meaning was swallowed up."[2]

While the contagious metaphor going from "utter-burn" to "history took fire" is conventional enough and encodes the etymology of "Holocaust," the other phrases, emphasizing both history and its conflagration, are more difficult to grasp. There is shock value if Blanchot is saying that history has come to a stop. But that is not what he is saying, unless we differentiate between history as a particular mode of understanding time and time itself. Time does not stop.

What does it mean, then, to take the Shoah into consciousness? The temptation is to claim that it periodizes the flow of time by marking off an exceptional phase, and so dividing before and after. Think of how many "posts" have recently sprung up: post-Holocaust, postwar, poststructuralism, postmodern, post-philosophy, Post-Traumatic Stress Disorder. (Now, perhaps, post-9/11.) Blanchot does not doubt that such a trick of thought helps to focus the traumatic or unintelligible. But the next step, according to him, should be to guard the space or absence created by that sudden incursion of the unintelligible. Guard it, that is, from explanations or consolations seeking to fill a void, from anything that pretends the factors contributing to that moment are over, like a freak storm.

His subtlest point, however, is that responding with a vehement temporal demarcation is part of the disaster. Instead of yielding to "everything is different now," to an epochal before-and-after distinction, this habit of the mind should be challenged. Blanchot's own response is to turn from death, as a final date, toward dying, that is, to contemplate an intolerable unpower or passivity. This goes against our mental nerves, which are trained to be activist. They react to events by working them through or extracting a meaning. Though it may be that a *saeculum* or era is over, this era, like previous ones, was defined by the deceptive notion of an ending. What has come to an end is the notion itself of an end-time.

Blanchot's insight does not remain at the level of methodology or epistemology. The consequences he draws are, instead, insistently moral. For without an end-time, suffering is cut loose from any value system that comforts itself with the thought of a sublime reversal. Catastrophe-creation becomes an obsolete hope, and suffering is no longer a condition of redemption. It is the sufferance, perhaps forever, of suffering, whether we experience it directly or cannot avoid watching the suffering of others. As Blanchot writes, "It is the horror of a suffering without end, a suffering that time can no longer redeem, that has escaped time and for which there is no longer recourse; it is irremediable."[3] The Holocaust, then—and with it the haunting imagery of both utopia and apocalypse—continues beyond 1945 as a possibility too fundamental to be foreclosed by a period term.

Moreover, from Blanchot's quarrel with Hegel throughout *The Writing of the Disaster*, we infer that the important word in "the movement of meaning was swallowed up" is "movement." History may catch fire, but it is not burned up; history's movement is what has been fatally injured. The divisions of time discerned by Hegel, the progressive movement of history powered by the famous dialectic, can no longer be invoked. There is at most what Adorno labeled a negative dialectic: a contestatory temporal rhythm or flux that recalls Nietzsche's "eternal return."

Blanchot's insight is far from being a limited polemical response targeting the Hegelian illusion. It cuts to the heart of the effort to find an explanation in history for the destructions recorded by it. All attempts to discern the shape of time, in the form of microchronic or macrochronic speculation, are in danger of being disqualified. Does knowledge still provide a sort of comfort, as in Pascal's famous saying that man is a reed who is crushed, but a thinking reed that knows what is happening? "O you who know," is Charlotte Delbo's subversive reply in *None of Us Will Return*, "Did you know that suffering is limitless / that horror cannot be circumscribed / Did you know this / You who know."[4]

I was reminded of the notion of timeless suffering while reading about the horrifying massacre of the Jews of Jedwabne, Poland, in Jan T. Gross's *New Yorker* article of March 12, 2001, a prelude to his book on that subject, *Neighbors: The Destruction of the Jewish Community in Jedwabne, Poland*. The details are so crude and cruel, so utterly inhuman, that one wonders, despite the modern commitment to expose and publish, whether anything redemptive, or even historically necessary, could come from knowing about this episode.

The author effectively marshals the eyewitness and court depositions on what happened in barely eight hours on July 10, 1941. Indeed, he succeeds remarkably in setting the episode into the context of World War II and the successive occupation of this part of Poland by Russia and Germany. Yet it is clear, even from the *New Yorker*'s condensed, journalistic version of Gross's book—which focuses on a survivor's account of April 1945 (the only one from that time), testimony from trials held in 1949 and 1953, and later interviews—that the author wishes to do more than sort out the precise sequence of events and the identity of the murderous posse. He rectifies in the manner of a historian an impression that the responsibility for the atrocity can be laid mainly at the feet of the occupying German army, especially its commander. For the mayor and the town council, only too willing to kill Jedwabne's Jews, seized on the commander's oral permission that they had eight hours—according to one deposition—to do what they wanted. They immediately set out to slaughter by the primitive means at their disposal (stones, bricks, knives, axes, and clubs) all their Jewish neighbors and, when that proved too large a task, drove the remainder into a barn and burned them alive. Between one thousand and sixteen hundred perished.

To remove what is at best a half-truth, a self-protective distortion on the part of the perpetrators or others wishing to ease the reputation of Poles, hardly exhausts the reasons for publishing this harrowing account. The headlines of the *New Yorker* article make that clear. They come as a triple layer that starts with "Annals of War," proceeds to "Neighbors," and adds, "One day in 1941, half the population of a small town in Poland murdered the other half. Why?"[5]

Journalism as a mode of reporting, even when the subject is an event dating back many years, is characterized by conflicting trends: sensationalism, on the one hand, and rendering the sensational intelligible, on the other. So, as in a macabre detective story, an irrational eruption in the form of an unexpected corpse functions like a grisly question mark that stimulates a lengthy search for a solution, one that uncovers more corpses.

The account itself begins with a date and location: "In January of 1949, security police detained fifteen men in the town of Jedwabne in northeastern Poland."[6] This composition of place is an utterly conventional narrative opening, yet it makes sense if it elicits questions in the reader, especially after the rest of the story, with its many specific dates, has been absorbed. Why the hiatus between the end of the war and the trials of 1949? Why a further hiatus between those trials and today's fuller disclosure? What is the significance of the town's being in northeastern Poland?

These questions are easily answered by the historian, but the up-front specificity of date and place remains overdetermined. It tells us this did not happen "once upon a time" and in some country of the mind. The historian must insist on the instant of happening, on these dates and not others; moreover, the spontaneity of the massacre itself is part of the riddle. Yet dates and actual place-names also limit by their very concreteness the effect of what is told: It happened then and over there, and what happened is "history."

This containment of the event turns another containment into a bitter irony. The German commander, as reported, objected to the butchery taking more than eight daylight hours. Why he objected we do not know. Was it because of habitual Germanic or military precision, was it a taunt to humiliate the Polish killers, or did he wish to make the conquered Poles feel entirely controlled? Were those eight hours of murder insignificant in his mind compared to the Nazi vision of a thousand-year Reich?

A fictional telling not only could explore these motives but would not need a double-edged rhetoric of specificity. Fiction's "once upon a time" suggests "once and always." Jedwabne's condensation of time, moreover, the fact that the slaughter was organized and evolved so swiftly, in the space of a day or less, adapts it intrinsically to a precept of classical tragedy. The restriction of place to a few square miles and of time to that single day, augmented by the fact that up to 50 percent of Jedwabne's adult population of male non-Jews—as well as quite a few people gathered from the nearby countryside—participated in the massacre, leaves one with the feeling of a natural disaster gathering suddenly and striking randomly. That the pogrom was a face-to-face, close-up killing projects a devastating and unintelligible image of human nature.

Not that Jan Gross neglects to seek explanations. He refuses to rail, like Claude Lanzmann, against "the obscenity of understanding."[7] He clears away, for example, false or unproven allegations that the Jews brought the disaster on themselves by collaborating with the Soviet regime or betraying the Polish resistance. He brings evidence, in fact, that inverts the "well-established cliché" of the closeness of Jews and communists. In a radical revision of popular historiography, or folklore, he suggests as a hypothesis that "anti-Semites rather than Jews were instrumental in establishing the Communist regime after the war."[8]

Yerushalmi's well-known book, *Zakhor*, has posited an absolute incompatibility between memory—in particular, the Jewish collective memory—and modern historiography. Jan Gross, it seems to me, disproves the dichotomy by producing a powerful *yizkor* (memorial) book based on strict historical methods. And he revives the proverb that truth is stranger than fiction. The one difference here between fiction and history centers on *probability*: While the historian has to prove that an incident, however incredible, happened, the fiction writer must convince us that it happened without the self-limiting authority of established fact.

Probability is no small matter. Incidents like Jedwabne, like many such in the Holocaust era, are so hard to believe that while local knowledge of them survived, outsiders in contact with that knowledge could not suspend their disbelief. It took Jan Gross four years to follow up on what he heard. In an important chapter of his book he urges historians to take a new attitude toward oral sources, in effect to think of them initially as truthful rather than false.

The first superscript of the *New Yorker* essay, "Annals of War," is also a contextualizing move that emphasizes factuality and prepares us for a partial motivation of the pogrom. (Crimes must be motivated to have probability; that there are victims is not enough.) The massacre took place in wartime, shortly after the launching of Operation Barbarossa, Germany's invasion of the Soviet-occupied part of Poland. Some Jews, it seems, but also some non-Jewish Poles, had indeed welcomed the Russian troops and even collaborated. But whatever motives or passions were served by the false rumor of extensive Jewish collaboration—greed for Jewish property certainly played its part in the massacre—many inhabitants of Jedwabne mentioned that an already existing, if latent, antisemitic resentment was ignited.

Gross emphasizes, however, the exceptionally good relations of Jews and their neighbors in Jedwabne, even while acknowledging certain exceptions, such as threats of a pogrom every Easter. The second headline of the article indicates that something improbable happened, something hard to believe had we not seen the astonishingly swift disintegration of neighborly relations in the multiethnic towns of Bosnia.

Yet moral astonishment is implied rather than explicit, perhaps because it might seem naive (the most intimate relations can also turn into the most hostile) or because the modern historian tries to present rather than moralize. To be a moralist would require the ironic and self-lacerating skills of another Pole, Czeslaw Milosz, as in his poems "A poor Christian looks at the Ghetto" and "Child of Europe."

The third headline does spell out a moral anguish, a "Why?" that cannot be suppressed. The Raul Hilberg doctrine of having Holocaust historians or political scientists tell how what happened happened—that is, keeping to facts and uncovering the functional, administrative reasonings and mechanisms operative in organizing mass murder on that scale, rather than speculating on intention—never quite succeeds in suppressing that "Why?" as we descend to the bloody particulars. It is only in the form of a general, metaphysical question that it leads to impotence of thought or to inane answers by those who claim to speak for God and blame the victims (usually for their infringement of orthodox Jewish law) as well as the perpetrators (who figure, implicitly at least, as instruments of God's retribution).

Every few years another shockwave from the past reaches us. The Polish case, in its complexity, shows how much was suppressed to this very day. The "Why?" surfaces again, as much as an irrepressible cry as a call for historical explanation. The historian can turn that cry into a rational narrative of Nazism's mobilization of irrationality as it escalates from persecution to genocide. Yet making the exterminating process intelligible by dividing it up into functional solutions at the local level, solutions motivated by ideology, or ethnic and religious hatred, or a perceived military necessity, explains neither the face-to-face murderousness nor the rare acts of goodness. And, since the story of Jedwabne reveals once more how the historian's resurrection of the past continues to open the wounds of the Holocaust, it is no wonder art responds to the suppressed cry in its own way. If the numberless victims burned in barns or shoved into mass graves hurt too much to fit the measures of poetry, the accumulation of cruel facts also scuttles almost every attempt at a bearable narrative, let alone one still trying to make sense of a people's collective biography.

This does not mean that the Matter of the Holocaust is impossible to depict. The problem is one of evoking an original response, of freeing rather than freezing our feelings and speech. Neither the subtlest nor the most graphic imaging of the disaster guarantees such a response.

Fiction at its best leads to a recognition scene. "Do you know me?" is the question haunting *King Lear*, a superbly royal but also ironic question, since the king clearly did not have knowledge of himself. Shakespeare's play stays longer for the absent answer than any other writing about the human condition. The finest history writing does something equivalent. Jan Gross asks the Polish people to know themselves, to focus on this agonizing quest for self-knowledge. One unusually explicit moral reflection links this quest to the future of Poland: "If at some point in this collective biography [of Poland] a big lie is situated, then everything that comes afterward will be devoid of authenticity and laced with fear of discovery. . . . Like several other nations, in order to reclaim its own past, Poland will have to tell its past to itself anew."[9]

Milosz is a precursor of that authenticity. He confronts his postwar consciousness of the Holocaust in lyrics that shuttle between Poland and America. He challenges the morality of the bystanders (including himself), especially those tempted to deny the claims of memory in the very name of communist dialectics: "He who invokes history is always secure./ The dead will not rise to witness against him."[10]

History is written by the victors, yet episodes the poet cannot *not* know, like the burning of the Warsaw Ghetto or massacres like Jedwabne, compel him to honor the dead and become a witness against false witness. If Milosz keeps addressing himself as well as his fellow Poles and us, it is to remove indifference and expose a living wound in need of being healed:

> You swore never to touch
> The deep wounds of your nation
> So you would not make them holy
> With the accursed holiness that pursues
> Descendants for many centuries.[11]

The truth may be holy, reconciliation may be holy, but the wound itself is never holy.

5. Elie Wiesel and the Morality of Fiction

> "Doesn't the Talmud say that after the coming of the Messiah, the dead will rise from their graves and crawl all the way to the Holy Land?"
> "Not our dead, Pedro. Our dead have no graves."
> Pedro turned to stare out the window.
> "We are their graves," he replied after a long silence.
> —Elie Wiesel, *Twilight*

The eulogies on the occasion of Elie Wiesel's Nobel Peace Prize announce an ethical and inspirational ideal. It seems clear and uncomplicated. "From the abyss of the death camps," we read, Elie Wiesel "has come as a messenger to mankind—not with a message of hate and revenge but with one of brotherhood and atonement. Elie Wiesel is not only the man who survived, he is also the spirit which has triumphed."[1] But in his acceptance speech the honoree refuses to shift the emphasis entirely to the living or to a triumphant message that elides the continuing cycle of revenge and hate. It is not conventional modesty alone that makes him reply, "No one may speak for the dead, no one may interpret their mutilated dreams and visions."[2]

Yet speak for the dead is precisely what he does—in *fiction*. Dreams and visions: This is where poet and novelist enter and where, through them, the multitudes who perished continue to make their claim. Jews were to be despoiled not only of their life but also of their spiritual influence. No one would remember their dream of righteousness, their fidelity to a law that underwrote an intricate mixture of mercy and legal rigor. All of Elie Wiesel's writings fulfill a pledge: "I will defeat our murderers by attempting to reconstruct what they destroyed."[3]

Wiesel refers in his speech to those who died in the Holocaust. "I sense their presence. I always do ... The presence of my parents, that of my little sister. The presence of my teachers, my friends, my companions."[4] The full weight of those words is felt only after reading his novels. They portray survivors and their children who cannot forget the dead. The past within them is always about to dissolve the present. Their interior monologue is often so intense, so self-haunting, that they no longer know where they are, as the milieu shifts confusingly. Are they in Brooklyn, or in Galicia, or searching for a mass murderer in a German town after the war?

Wiesel's protagonists are burdened by thoughts that include revenge as well as feelings of unworthiness that they should be alive, or alive in the place of another. But they seek to turn a disabling into a creative melancholy. They hold to a moral order, a teaching more than two millennia old. To quote Psalm 19, it makes the simple wise, rejoices the heart, and produces a "clean fear of the Lord" (*jinat adonai tehorah*, verse 16). Yet what if this fear—this awe—is now unclean?

For the *tremendum* of the Shoah has not only implanted hate for the perpetrators but also bitterness toward God. The fear of the Lord takes its origin today not only from precepts of a just moral order, or from a sense of impurity as we approach the precincts of holiness, but also from the impossibility of theodicy. "The devil himself," Hayim Nahman Bialik once said, "is incapable of imagining a vengeance that would redeem the blood of an infant."[5] If mankind is made in the image of God, what kind of God does His creation reflect? *The Forgotten* expresses in the bond between father and son an enigma with theological overtones. The son is placed in the position of having to undo a curse, or dispel a secret. In Freud's concept of family romance, it is the mother whom the son wants to rescue; here it is the father who has to be redeemed. (The younger women, in these novels, are generally self-willed, sensuous presences, intent on seducing the brooding survivor back into life.) The very word "Father," in *The Forgotten*, conveys a fundamental relation, like Martin Buber's "I-Thou"; to be exact, that word turns into a despairing vocative seeking to establish a relationship once more, one that would save the Father from an encroaching amnesia more devastating than the traumatic return of memories. It is an amnesia that makes the reader fear for God as a Father, as if God Himself were losing his mind and forgetting creation. Can God get Alzheimer's?

Who is being addressed, when we read the following in *Twilight*:

Father, I saw everything, I heard everything as I lay there among the corpses. The corpses protected me, Father. I waited until nightfall to climb out of the pit. I ran away from the dead, from their staring eyes, their tangled bodies. I ran like a wild animal until I found a stream where I washed the blood from my face, my hands, my clothes. I looked like a slaughterer. I moved only at night. I saw the mass graves, the ones in Stanislav and in Kamenetz-Podolsk. I understood that the same fate was awaiting all Jews, make no mistake. I had to tell you this, Father. Now that you know, what will you do? What will we do?[6]

The mythical descent of the living to the realm of the dead is a daily reality in the memory of survivors. In a series of brilliant inventions, Wiesel shows they cannot forget; they can only go mad, or become a living Yizkor book, reenacting legendary characters in a sad *commedia dell'arte*. Or, as in *The Fifth Son*, they confuse the dead and the living: The child taken away usurps the child that struggles for its own, independent life.[7] We who were born afterward say easily enough, let there be new life, and even they say, let there be new life, but the dead still inhabit both generations too intimately.

How, then, will a novelist, who is their messenger, separate the living from the dead; how will he disentangle the survivors, or their children, or young people in general, from "mutilated dreams and visions"?

In *Dawn*, whose frame is the fight against the British in Palestine, the terrorist's quest is to get beyond fear, clean or unclean.[8] But Elisha's memory, in the long wait for the dawn when he must execute a British hostage, retraces his journey from victim to terrorist in terms of a dialogue with the dead. The simple plot dissolves into a chorus of phantoms. There is always a moment when the narrator enters a conscious dream, a dream that recapitulates the lost vision of those who have died. Then "Time does not matter, only the tale does."[9]

Memory should become, Wiesel has said, an "irresistible power," one that gives the dead their due, that tells their story—rather, brings them back to tell their story, even if it was buried with them in an unknown place. Only then is there a chance for catharsis, and so, perhaps, a "clean fear." But his writings show how difficult that purification is.

In *Twilight*, Raphael, whose name signifies healing, commits himself to a clinic, in the manner of a would-be psychiatrist to a training analysis. Many characters in these novels try on madness and so run the risk of becoming mad. Raphael needs this halfway house in which the inmates identify with biblical characters. The novelist shuttles by montage between the destroyed communities and the living dead of the clinic. A strange fire, a different holocaust, claimed Nadav and his brother Avihu. "I am nothing but a handful of ashes. My face is made of ashes. My chest is filled with ashes. And yet, the fire has never gone out."[10] A moment before listening to Nadav, Raphael was in his father's house, as Aharon Lipkin plans to escape from a Galicia under German rule. Now, through Nadav, he is reminded of another father, the biblical Aaron, who disappears into sadness—the sadness of a leader isolated by the need to make decisions.

Characters like Nadav are mainly voices, memory transfusions from the Bible. "If there were such a thing as song personified," Raphael says, "it would be Nadav.'"[11] Can the reader accept such poetry, the irruption of ecstasy into extreme suffering?

"'Don't touch me,' says Nadav. 'One must never touch the dead.'"[12] That is a priest's horror of impurity returning. The one not to be touched is, ironically, the person trying to live normally. Nadav and Avihu, the children of Aaron, offered "strange fire" and were consumed. Is not our effort to justify God after the Holocaust (an effort disguised as theories attempting to justify fiction after—or about—the Holocaust) also a strange fire? We simulate a phoenix in the ashes. When love and joy return, they prove unstable; even in a freed Jerusalem the restored dream falters. "The sky is not filled with stars but with funeral candles . . . the eyes of death, the eyes of the dead stolen by death from the living."[13]

Part of me, I admit, resists such pathos. It prefers the broken speech of survivor testimony: "Je n'ai pas eu peur. J'ai déshabillé des morts. J'ai vu tous les jours des morts, la mort c'était pour moi comme fumer une cigarette" (I felt no fear. I stripped the dead. I saw corpses every day; death for me was like smoking a cigarette).[14] Or the concise style of Wiesel's *One Generation After*: "The victims elect to become witnesses."[15] Yet another part of me is drawn in; who else, with the exception of Shmuel Yosef Agnon as inspiring and daunting precursor, incorporates so much Aggadah in his fiction? Wiesel, without removing the focus from the fate of the Jews, finds within his tradition, from Bible and midrash to Nahman of Bratslav and modern Yiddish storytellers, figures and scenes that bring the tragedy home to everyone. Through the process of novelistic discovery, this teller of tales—and he is preeminently that—prepares us for the future. It is not a triumphant future but rather, quite simply, one that gives a voice to all victims, from Kolyma as well as Auschwitz, non-Jewish as well as Jewish, honoring the many mutilated visions that afflict us because of an unabated, even unabashed, racism.

Fiction is a mode of silence, under the constraint of eloquence. Words overcome a sense of their guilt and are wounded by that success. An imaginary dialogue in *One Generation After* is explicit on that score. "'*What are you doing now?*' 'I am a sculptor. And you,' 'I write.' 'The way you say that . . .' 'What do you expect? Millions of human beings had to die so that you might become a sculptor and I, a story-teller.'"[16] A voice out of the whirlwind, which is our own voice, commands us to be silent, to lay Job's finger on our lips. How do we learn to stutter again?

I need not add that the Matter of the Holocaust, more than other matters of epic devastation, holds an entire civilization, the words and images that constitute it, accountable. After the hate speech we have known and that continues to incite murder and genocide, what good words are possible? You may call such reflections morbid, but I do not say we should succumb to them, only that they shadow us even in our best moments, our most creative moments.

There are those, like Karl Kraus or Shakespeare's Thersites or the Juvenalian satirist, whose indignant rage is so strong that no euphemism survives. But they tend to generate, therefore, more hate speech, rather than a purgative and renovating awe. Mixed with carnivalesque laughter or biting wit, as in Brecht or Beckett, savage speech sometimes does release us. Yet Wiesel, despite the impossibility of theodicy or of euphemism concerning both human actions and God's inaction, husbands a tradition that preserves the good name. The dead cannot praise; the Holocaust dead cannot even be laid to rest. The morality of his fiction as fiction is to achieve a *gilgul* of the uprooted, traumatized, and dispossessed, as in *A Beggar in Jerusalem*. Working against the grain of modern realism, he even attempts a sympathetic portrayal of the *Judenrat*. Yet blessing the memory of the dead or the conscience of the survivors has its bitter antithesis in accusation: in a satanic or righteous malevolence, shown by Sam in *The Trial of God* or by the anonymous accuser of Pedro in *Twilight*.[17]

No one reads Wiesel without admiring his versatile storytelling in all the genres: novel, drama, parable, essay, midrashic or Hasidic exemplum, novella, autobiography. Yet the specter of the impotence of words, even of the divine word, is always present. I want to illustrate this presence, in conclusion, by two episodes that have no direct link to the Shoah, though today they cannot be read outside of that context.

The first is a personal reminiscence about the young Elie, who asks his rebbe not to attend his bar mitzvah. The reason: "To speak with you present would be like playing teacher in front of my teacher." His rebbe refuses the request. He is not expecting the boy to be a master, only to prepare to accomplish "his duty as messenger and witness." "To the astonishment of my parents and friends," the story concludes, "I went through the ceremony without a speech."[18]

What does that speechlessness indicate? A failure of nerve, an adolescent's exaggerated desire for perfection? The anecdote leaves something unsaid. Immediately before it another story is told, about a disciple who approaches a Hasidic Master with the confession that he has lost his faith in man and God. What should he do? When the reply comes, not unexpectedly, "Go and study," the disciple admits he opens the Talmud and stays on the same page for months on end. He is paralyzed. Instead of an answer, Pinhas of Koretz tells the disciple about his own episode of paralyzing doubt. "I tried study, prayer, meditation. In vain. Fasting, penitence, silence. In vain. My doubts remained doubts, my questions remained open. Then, one day, I learned that Rebbe Israel Baal Shem-Tov would be coming to our town. Curiosity led me to the house where he was praying. When I entered he was finishing the *Amidah*. He turned around and the intensity in his eyes overwhelmed me. I knew he was not looking at me alone, yet I knew that I was less alone. Suddenly, without a word, I was able to go home, open the Talmud and plunge into my studies once more."

"Without a word" reinforces the wordless intensity of the look of the Besht when he finishes the *Amidah* and turns around. The *Amidah* has a prelude: "O Lord, open Thou my lips, and my mouth shall declare Thy praise." This is, in a way, the signature tune of the Master of the Good Name. It asks God for two things: to enable us to speak and to speak blessings—words of praise and acknowledgment but also words characterized by a clean fear. I glimpse here less a *ba'al kol* than a *bat kol*, an echo of God's voice that resounds even in silence. The *bat kol* is all that remains when open vision and prophecy depart from Israel; it is usually portrayed as a heavenly voice but also as something the anguished soul experiences accidentally—for example, by opening the Bible and stumbling on a passage that has the effect of a cautionary voice, even an oracle. The accident is invested with providential force.

In Wiesel, the classical Jewish heritage has become such a *bat kol*; we respond to Elie Wiesel, to his parables and fictions, because we continue to sense a precariousness within his eloquence. In part this precariousness comes from a mystical streak that knows the debility of words and wishes to change them into something more embodied, like the wonderful gaze of the Baal Shem-Tov. According to the mystics, as we approach the Divine Countenance, "the world is transformed into a face, a thousand faces. Words turn into faces, as does light, as does fear, as does prayer."[19] The poet-novelist too seeks this transformation.

But the hazard of Wiesel's writing comes also from another source. He has said that survival during the Holocaust was accidental, for the divine word was stifled during that time.[20] It is as if his fiction turned to Bible, Talmud, and Jewish lore out of a concern that their muteness might continue. There is mystery in the fact that they have not fallen silent before, that Jews continue to identify with a spiritual heritage tied to so much pain and horror. Would it not be better, as *The Oath*'s sad and witty plot suggests, to cut the link between Jewish memory and Jewish suffering by giving up the role of memory, of transgenerational witness?[21]

Yet even that desire for silence demands to be recognized and transmitted. The teller of tales is haunted by ghostly characters that want to rest yet cannot do so until his pages provide a requiem.[22] In Agnon, tale and diction fuse:

A vanishing Yiddish world is evoked without false vitalism by the intricate vitality of the author's Hebrew, which Emmanuel Levinas has called a "resuscitated language, beginning again with its own trace."[23] Wiesel, steeped in the same world, which has now receded still further, and writing (after the first version of his first novel) neither in Yiddish nor Hebrew, struggles against silence to achieve a compensatory eloquence in a diasporic language.

At the end of *A Beggar in Jerusalem*, the narrator feels unable to insert a wish, as custom demands, into the *kotel* liberated by the Six-Day War. He hesitates to sign the paper in the name of his parents; and the novel's dream-*gilgul*, its wish-fulfilling reconstruction of orthodoxy, breaks down. Recovering, however, he then affirms the dream in their place, affirms the Name through the names of the dead. Are not Elie Wiesel's writings always a wish placed in the wall of a ruined Temple? They keep the hope alive that fiction will delay, rather than hasten, the demise of the *bat kol*.

6. Afterword to *Lodz Ghetto*

Reading this book is a haunting experience.¹ It is as if we had an open line right into the ghetto. By careful choosing, the editors bring us voices crying from the archive rather than documents buried in it. A whole community becomes present to us, from the Eldest of the Jews, with his proud yet pathetic speeches, to the anger and self-pity of a young girl demanding a life denied to her. The 128 substantial excerpts are full of astonishing humor and self-criticism: Nothing escapes observation. There is no need for me to describe how these voices, arranged by the compilers' art of chronological montage, compel us to deeper and deeper levels of sympathy, as we follow them in their variousness, querulousness, vacillation, wit, outrage, human perplexity. Unlike the traditional Remembrance Book, however, which can include events and stories from pre-Holocaust days, this anthology limits itself strictly to the five years and four months of the Occupation, during which time, as Ringelblum observed of his own community (he organized "Oneg Shabbat," a secret project preserving the story of the Warsaw Ghetto), the Jews were forced back into medieval conditions and a world (world?) no one from the outside could enter.

The internal perspective of these stories about life and death in the Lodz Ghetto, culled exclusively from eyewitnesses, creates plot, drama, tension, tragic irony. The drama and tension have to do with hopes of outliving the war and the deteriorating conditions of a community kept on starvation rations and ravaged by disease. The tragic irony comes from the fact that we know what the inhabitants could not know: Their hope of surviving was a false hope. There are vivid sketches of daily life that do not spare the inhabitants, pungent caricatures of the *Yekes* (German Jews), descriptions of a landscape of death more eloquent than any photo, scenes of family life with sacrificing women, and dramas centering on half a slice of bread. The plight of the sick and the children is inscribed everywhere. The record of this individual and communal effort to survive is overwhelming. One becomes ashamed of one's own voice, and wishes to do exactly what the compilers of this book have done: to quote, and avoid commentary.

Fifty years after the beginning of Lodz's agony there are questions that trouble us. What does this book commemorate? What can we learn from such comfortless stories? Can anything in our increasingly documented and detailed knowledge of the Holocaust redeem what happened? Of course, even should we be unable to find a redemptive meaning, it would still be our duty to remember. But the burden is shifting from historian to reader. We are at the point where the historical and memorial activity, while it must continue (for there is still much to be done), may not neglect the issue of interpretation: of how to say more, after reading this, than *never forget*.

The collective memory, which preserves the traumatic event in a bearable way, is not concerned with troubling moral questions but with reviving the community's faith in itself. Our rituals, too, the commemorative services we hold, aim at that result: They emphasize survival and bind up the wounds of loss. Yet, to ritual and to research a third, more personal response should be added. It would allow us to discuss the *shame* (Primo Levi's word) that afflicts us when we read these materials. It is a shame afflicting our image of human nature and does not spare anyone. It chastens the redemptive drive of the collective memory.

The self-administration of the ghetto under Rumkowski resulted inevitably in Jews oppressing Jews, with a Jewish police that did its job only too well. Where else do we find, on such a massive scale, Jews doing the work of the Nazis in the hope that the ghetto would outlast the war and that a portion of its people—the strongest, or those most favored by the Rumkowski administration—might survive? The entire scheme of self-administration appears demonic in retrospect: The Germans compelled Jews to act as their agents and execute soul-searing, soul-besmirching orders. They threatened worse if there was no compliance and raised Rumkowski's hope that each deportation would be the last. His speech on September 4, 1942, when the Nazis have once more betrayed his hopes and demanded the delivery of twenty thousand Jews (bargained down from twenty-four thousand, he tells us, and limited to children below the age of ten, but a quota that will fall mainly on the children and the sick) is an astonishing piece of rhetoric. "In my old age I must stretch out my hands and beg: Brothers and sisters, hand them over to me! Fathers and mothers, give me your children!" (328). The end of his speech reveals that he still believes, despite this catastrophe, in the rationality of his plan.

One needs the heart of a bandit to ask from you what I am asking. But put yourself in my place, think logically, and you'll reach the conclusion that I cannot proceed any other way. The part that can be saved is much larger than the part that must be given away. (331)

It is hard to see how Rumkowski's desperate gamble was less catastrophic than if cooperation with the Germans had been refused or resisted. There were deeply divided attitudes in the ghetto toward this man who felt obliged to lead his people *into* slavery. He is reviled as a corrupt administrator and exalted as a father of his people; his reputation, as is reported here, can shift with the availability of potatoes. But at the moral center something else emerges, more frightening by far than doubts about a dictator installed by the Nazis and trying to manage. The naked truth is that Rumkowski's plan, unless the war ended quickly and the Nazis were removed, was bound to result in the death of the sick and of children below working age. A clinging to life remained in the ghetto, but there was not enough moral oxygen to breathe. In this *huis clos*, this manmade hell created by the Nazis, most choices were not choices—whatever was done would cause death, injury, humiliation. Even acts of "spiritual resistance," as they tend now to be called, such as cultural activities kept up in these surroundings—performances of Beethoven, religious worship, schooling, the writing of the Chronicles—are morally dubious if they instilled a deceptive hope that weakened other kinds of resistance. By 1942 the Jews of Lodz were all death-bound: The Final Solution had been set in motion. The "logic" to which Rumkowski appeals at the end of his speech is no longer there, if it ever was.

There are many negative lessons, then, which can be the subject of painful moral debate. A single phrase in those bureaucratic German documents also assembled here makes the heart freeze as we realize the world it stands for. How is confiscated property from the ghetto to be legally classified? It belongs to the state because it is "ownerless." Legally the ghetto's Jews were dead persons to the Nazi administration. They just did not exist as human beings. One wonders again what forces of coldness, what inhumanity, what propaganda, could bring the Nazi administrators and their followers to this point.

After a while, among the victims too, the heart grows cold. There is the phenomenon of the *Muselmänner*, who go about like zombies, no longer feeling, no longer caring. Even those who cling to life notice a deterioration. To see, day after day, starving children, to know that the sick are ripped out of hospital beds in the night.... So many dead, everywhere. "There are no coffins. The corpse lies between two boards, packed in old scraps of paper. It is held, like a dead fish, in a net that is carried on two slates and let go over the grave.... The sheet-metal wagons keep delivering the dead into the hall, the nets keep taking them out of the hall. The earth fills itself with dead.... As numerous as grains of sand in the ocean, stars in the heavens" (273).

In the same mortal year 1942, Oskar Singer invents the category of *Litzmannstadt death*. "Morality cracks," he writes in his notebook, "but ethics remains." Certain institutions like the family do not collapse, though they are severely altered; death, too, is altered. "We can no longer die as other people do. We no longer have the possibility of a noble end. Litzmannstadt death is an alien, ugly death" (299).

The moral and descriptive power of these impressions, even when they parody Scripture, as in the comment on the dead "as numerous as grains of sand" (which mocks God's promise to His Chosen People) begins to answer my question: What comfort can we take from this record of desolation? In the "foreign land" of this ghetto world, the writer does not lay down his pen. He cannot praise God or most of his fellow Jews, but he can still describe what he sees and perceives—holding to a standard provided by the tradition, even if he quotes it against itself.

There is an incredible resilience in these testimonies, which comes only partly from a respect for life under any conditions. The private notebooks are sensitive to the slightest sign of normalcy and open up to a beautiful day or a picturesque detail. So great is the discontinuity, the departure from normalcy, the separation of the ghetto from the world—also, incongruously, from the war, for this War Against the Jews has superseded the other—that any sign of constancy is greeted. That is why the journals abound in marvelous caricature of different types and groups. *Something* has remained unchanged. But this discovery is often mingled with the opposite mood: How could the outside world (insofar as the ghetto has an outside) remain the same? How could God Himself remain the same? (He rarely enters this book, however, except in the form of Bible quotation.) The conflicting moods meet in Shayevitch's poem *Lekh Lekho* ("Go forth," Genesis 12:1), in which the poet identifies with Abraham as he prepares his own daughter Bimile for "the unknown journey" of deportation:

> The evil hour has arrived,
> When I must teach you, a little girl,
> The terrible *parshe* of *Lekh Lekho*.
> But how can we compare it
> To the bloody *Lekh Lekho* of today? (227)

There is a sort of comfort in that bitter, homiletic application: A traditional paradigm is maintained. But the poet's mood turns, as he images in a passage both blasphemous and humorous the desecration of his own writings, so full of holy paradigms:

> Tremble, tremble, holy volumes ...
> Someday, in the dawn, someone will rise
> And in just his pants
> Will cut square pieces from you
> For toilet paper,
> And will grimace, that the writing
> May, God forbid, hurt him. (226)

The witnesses—private diarists, official chroniclers, experienced artists—intend their voices to survive, even if they and the community perish. Despite a temptation like Job's to "blaspheme God and die," they exercise restraint and remain *observant*. It is the reader who may feel like drawing up a dossier against God: They have no use for such fictional and self-indulgent exercises. We commemorate them, their testimony, their clarity of voice and mind. I wish I could say more, for instance that we confront here a great and purifying tragedy, one that could make us respond with woe and wonder. But though the totally ghettoized perspective of the eyewitnesses creates a concentrated picture, a place and action as unified as the neoclassical stage, and though that stage is as crowded as a Shakespearean play, the tragedy here is that there is no tragedy. We do not have heroes to identify with. Rumkowski has a touch of madness and pathos, but he does not represent the community. Nor can the Holocaust ever be the subject of tragedy without shame's being added to the root emotions of pity and terror. Primo Levi has said that this shame can never be purged, that there is no catharsis. I end by quoting Oskar Rosenfeld, whose notebook suggests a different understanding of the tragic that should be set against mine. It points to God, even to a gnostic insight, yet avoids accusation:

> This tragedy has no heroes. And why [call it] tragedy? Because the pain does not touch upon something human, on another's heart, but rather is something incomprehensible, linked with the cosmos, a natural phenomenon like the creation of the world. One must begin again with the Creation, with *B'raishit* [the first word of the Bible]. In the beginning, God created the ghetto. (276)

7. Unbearable Truths

Providence moves in mysterious ways.[1] Albert Speer was Hitler's favorite architect, commissioned before the war to transform Berlin into "Germania," a grandiose capital worthy of the German Empire. Having become one of Hitler's intimates, he was given an additional task during the war. Appointed Reichsminister in February 1942, he achieved the revitalization of Germany's armament industry, in part by assembling a huge slave labor contingent. (Under Speer's ministry, according to one researcher, close to 4,800,000 foreign workers were recruited or torn from their homes.) If he had been condemned to hang—a fate meted out by the Nuremberg Tribunal to Sauckel, in charge of Labor Allocation within his ministry—posterity would have lost valuable information about the highest circles of the Third Reich. Denying all awareness of the terrible conditions in the labor and concentration camps and portraying himself as an administrator who was privy to neither Hitler's plans for war nor, later on, murderous actions in the East against the Jews, Poles, and Russian POWs, Speer escaped the gallows and received a twenty-year sentence.

Before his release in 1966, Speer smuggled twenty-five thousand letters out of Spandau Prison and before his death in 1981 published three books on the Third Reich. Gitta Sereny, in her seven-hundred-and-fifty-page biography, also makes use of many unpublished documents, including Speer's letters after his release and his report for the Allies on Hitler's entourage. She does not neglect the extant literature but draws liberally on her three years of extensive interviews with Speer, supplemented by those with his friends, former friends, his attorney at Nuremberg, and family members.

Despite the mass of data Sereny collects in order to recreate Speer's milieu—especially interesting is her account of life close to Hitler in the Führer's mountain retreat, the Berghof—her masterful synthesis never loses its focus. The truth referred to in Sereny's title is Speer's knowledge of

Hitler's criminal designs, in particular the inhuman treatment of the foreign labor force and the extermination of the Jews. The word "struggle" carries, however, some pathos, and readers may not be as sympathetic as the author is to the picture of Speer struggling with the truth or, more precisely, against denial.

Speer's change begins in the last months of the war, when he realizes the true character of the man he served blindly and too well, as Hitler tries to take Germany down with him, ordering a scorched-earth policy everywhere, including in his own country. Speer resists and even countermands Hitler's attempt. Like so many Germans, he had identified Germany with Hitler but now is forced to save Germany from him. Yet Sereny's book is mainly about his claim not to have known what one of her chapter titles names "The Unbearable Truth."

There are actually two such truths, closely related: the systematic and partially executed extermination of the European Jews and the evil nature of Hitler ("the horror in him that now stands revealed," in Speer's own words [140–141]). Forced to face the facts at Nuremberg, the result was shock and total disenchantment. "Nothing can compare to the intensity of his feelings for Hitler, of their relationship," Speer's long-time and still loyal secretary told Sereny. And she associates herself and all Germans with that intensity and its betrayal:

> "If Hitler had this solution of the 'Jewish question' in mind from the start, if that solution could ever *enter* his mind, then everything he was and did was an abuse of our confidence, our loyalty, our faith. Because then there was *never* any national integrity, any nobility in the movement, in the sense in which we believed we were living it. My God," she said, "if this was in his mind," she stopped and went on, "then there was *never* anything pure about it. It means that we were betrayed to the very depths of our beings." (703)

I have quoted this "ordinary German" (my allusion is to Daniel Jonah Goldhagen's *Hitler's Willing Executioners: Ordinary Germans and the Holocaust*, which is often an important counterstatement to Sereny) because Sereny's book is preoccupied with the question of what Speer, and Germans generally, knew about the fate of the Jews. She presents pages upon pages of testimony to the effect that, unbelievably, Germans from all ranks and professions, while often aware of the persecutions in Germany itself, had no knowledge of the systematic killings by shooting and gassing in the East. She even remains unsure how much Speer knew before Himmler's infamous speech to Nazi leaders at Posen in October 1943. It disclosed that not only were Jewish men being systematically murdered but also all women and children. Speer was in Posen on the day Himmler gave the speech but claimed (backed up by affidavits from friends) that he had left before the incriminating talk. After weighing all the evidence, Sereny decides: "There is simply no way Speer can have failed to know about Himmler's speech, whether or not he actually sat through it" (401).

Despite telling the Nuremberg court that he had never visited a labor camp, Speer did inspect Dora, one of the most hellish, in August 1943. This camp, established to manufacture rockets, was under the total control of the SS, having been set up by agreement with Himmler. The latter undertook, Sereny writes, "to guarantee complete secrecy about the rocket production if the work would be entirely produced by concentration camp prisoners, all of whose contact with the outside world would be eliminated" (403). Sixty thousand men were deported to Dora, of whom thirty thousand died. Speer was "appalled" by what he saw there and ordered the building of a barracks outside the tunnel—which the workers up to that time had never left (406).

But the mystery remains of how Speer could have hidden from the truth for so long—a mystery that implicates, of course, many other Germans, ordinary or in high places. Sereny records in meticulous detail Speer's continuous self-examination and self-exculpation. Insofar as this correct but cold man shows any emotion, it is concerning the Final Solution. There is no evidence that he harbored strong antisemitic feelings: No remarks escaped him in this regard, and, just as he seemed not to care about the political opinion of his employees, he allowed several persons with partial Jewish ancestry to work in enterprises he controlled. In all his books, interviews, and letters he identifies Nuremberg as the place that revealed the truth and shocked him profoundly.

Yet Speer's awakening, which continues during the prison years, remains a limited one. The position of this skewed genius, whom I am tempted to see as the prime specimen of an educated and professional class in Germany that actively collaborated with the Nazi regime, is that he must share responsibility for what happened, but if guilt means prior intent and knowledge, he is not guilty except by taking that guilt on himself. He does, after Nuremberg, denounce Hitler as a criminal, yet the nearest he comes to admitting direct knowledge of the Holocaust is in an affidavit sent in 1977 to a South African Jewish organization to help it fight revisionism. "To this day," he affirms, "I still consider my main guilt to be my tacit acceptance [*Billigung*] of the persecution and the murder of millions of Jews" (707).

Sereny entitles her last chapter "The Great Lie," for the evidence that Speer must have known about the Shoah is overwhelming. Through his capacity to blind himself, all the more astonishing in one endowed with enormous intelligence and administrative genius—he was said to "see around corners," and he survived both court intrigue and counterproductive decisions by Hitler himself—Speer was able to continue his work with zest and to prolong the war, according to some estimates, by an entire year.

I am both fascinated and put off by the author's skillful mise-en-scène of a great white-collar criminal. By quoting generously from interviews and using Speer's personal correspondence, by seeing even the period of power and Führer adoration through the lens of such later sensitive and self-reflective documents, Sereny restores the human qualities of a cold and authoritarian personality, whose name, according to the ancient curse, should have been erased rather than consolidated by this *tombeau*.

Since Speer did lie and saved his neck by that fact, why do we need a book so massive and careful, indeed caring, about him? The evidence against Speer, together with his main line of defense, could have been presented in a much more efficient, hard-hitting way. (The matter recalls the difference between Churchill and the Americans on war criminals: Churchill wanted to take a dozen or so of the worst and summarily shoot them; the Americans, in particular, insisted on a judicial proceeding.) Sereny gives Speer every chance to explain himself; she also seeks out the testimony of friends, coworkers, subordinates, and even those who drifted away from him. Every conversation is personalized, the arrangement leading up to it and the (usually elegant) setting in which it takes place are specified, and the flow of what is said—pauses, emotional breaks or eddies—all contribute to a sense that everything here is part of the truth. Something quietly aesthetic or redemptive, therefore, infuses Sereny's portrait. I am left with the feeling that Speer was an actor rather than an agent: someone destined to fulfill a certain role, someone sent to make guilt of this kind intelligible.

Could the author have fallen under Speer's spell to a certain extent? Does she, like Raphael Geis, who was imprisoned for a time in Buchenwald and (quite improbably) became Speer's spiritual advisor, yearn for a forgiving kind of closure or even reconciliation? Is it possible that she leans, when all is said and done, toward Speer's strategy at Nuremberg of depicting an idealistic Germany that was hoodwinked by Hitler and the extreme patriotism he aroused?

These possibilities pass through one's mind. They may be, of course, defensive reflexes of a reader impatient with Sereny's skillfully interwoven documentary plethora, "the many voices [that] . . . have to be heard," her respect for what Geis called the difficulty of categorizing human beings (13).

The thing that is certain is that Sereny's biography shows in its very texture and method what was lacking in Speer: a compassionate use of intellectual power. Though the book is too long, it is valuable as the portrait of a person who, like Hitler himself, could only use that intellect instrumentally and was virtually incapable of combining it with love. Moral and emotional incompetence, Sereny suggests, characterized both Hitler and Speer. In Speer's case, there were occasional breakthroughs, including "this tie to Hitler, the deepest—perhaps the only real—emotion he had ever felt" (704).

—+—

I would like to supplement Sereny's focus on what Speer knew about the Holocaust by raising a related and equally difficult issue: What do we learn from this book about the motivation of the perpetrators or highly placed civilian leaders? The axiom of the humanistic biographer, "Nothing human is alien to me," comes under severe pressure when applied to those responsible for crimes against humanity. The reason is that these crimes rebuff the quality of understanding that characterizes a biography like Sereny's. To understand such crimes, to find a motivation for them that still conforms to the idea of humanity we constantly propose to ourselves, is not possible. Either we change that idea and call ourselves something else, give ourselves a different species-image, or we retain that image, outlaw the crime, and renounce a humanistic approach to it—that is, the possibility of benefiting from seeking to understand it. In that sense, there is no "legitimacy of forbidden knowledge," and Justice Jackson was right when he declared at Nuremberg: "The real complainant at [this] bar is Civilization" (546).

The following typical Himmler statement made in 1943 to the Hitler Youth is all too clear as doctrine or ideology yet falls outside of our concept of what is human by its absolute refusal to consider the humanity of the victims. It declares in the name of a cultural ideal and the struggle for national survival that we can withdraw from designated populations all understanding and compassion:

> Whether [Eastern] nations live in prosperity or starve to death interests me only insofar as we need them as slaves for our culture, otherwise it is of no interest to me. Whether ten thousand Russian females drop from exhaustion while digging an antitank ditch or not interests me only insofar as the antitank ditch for Germans is completed. (311)

Basically everything human is alien to Himmler except the Aryan *Volksgemeinschaft*, and so all others can be wasted as a means toward achieving German hegemony. Even were it to be shown that a statement like this falls within the range of intelligibility—by citing Vico's principle that whatever human beings do ("history") can be understood by them—I would still consider it tainted knowledge, like that derived from inhuman experimentation on humans.[2]

The reflections gathered in Sereny's book about Hitler's charisma, hypnotized German trust, and the power of denial or "determined ignorance"—in Speer personally, with his extraordinary capacity to compartmentalize, but even at Führer Headquarters generally—these certainly convey a kind of illumination and may be useful to strengthen foresight and post warning signs about future behavior. But in terms of what *motivated* the inhuman doctrinal actions of the Nazis and their followers, we remain in darkness. Sereny's search for a knowledge to prevent further outbreaks of genocide cannot do more than show the banality of the perpetrators—moral weakness given stature by power. When Speer admits he was blind by choice to the deportation of the Jews from Berlin and concerned only with making sure his department's interest in their property would be respected, she adds:

> Speer had always loathed bureaucrats and despised their greed, but they were a marginal concern for him, as was the persecution of the Jews. The sad truth is that he didn't care about the Jews then, any more than he would later care about the millions of forced laborers who slaved for him. When he needed something, he went after it, irrespective of human cost. (223)

That is clear enough, but what kind of a "truth" is it? Why doesn't she simply turn in disgust from this ruthless, opportunistic, if brilliant, mind?

Consider also how Sereny motivates Himmler's speech to SS officers and other leading national and provincial officials assembled at Posen by speculating:

> Hitler charged Himmler with making the most faithful in the party privy to guilty knowledge.... Himmler's orders from Hitler *would have been* to draw everyone in the upper ranks of Nazis into the net, so that no one could henceforth dare to break ranks, claiming innocence or ignorance. (388–389, italics added)

All the leaders, she suggests, were to be trapped, like Speer was, into a lifelong lie (*Lebenslüge* is Alexander Mitscherlich's characterization) by this disclosure.

The glimpsed motivations, then, are banal as well as pernicious, and we cannot, I have argued, discover deeper ones by way of empathy or humanistic research. The imputed reason for Himmler's speech must be distinguished, moreover, from the rationalization of the Judeocide in his speech. Though criminal knowledge can be used to intensify bonding or complicity, the secret divulged by Himmler points to the relation of knowledge and power, not knowledge and guilt. It is as if this forbidden knowledge were empowering in itself, as if it promised the bearers of the secret that "ye shall become as Gods" (Genesis 3:5).

An important essay by Saul Friedländer, "On the Unease in Historical Interpretation," emphasizes that Himmler's explanation of the unlimited killings was instrumentalist only in part (Jewish women and children might produce a new race of avengers): His sinister disclosures are also characterized by an elation, a sense of sublimity, related directly to "the staggering dimension of the killing . . . the staggering number of victims." The difficulty presented to our understanding is not, then, that the spectacle of power produces a dangerous state of elation—something of that is easily felt when we watch footage of Nazi mass rallies—but that this exaltation is linked in Himmler to a "compelling lust for killing on an immense scale."[3]

Sereny's efforts to turn Speer into a parable are not unjustified, however. For Speer blocked out rather than shared Hitler's inhuman doctrines and orders, and it is this power of denial, never entirely overcome even in his belated struggle against it, which creates the morality tale. That he lived a lie and was an opportunist on a grand scale cannot be redeemed by Sereny's magnanimous treatment. But that this lie should become an unbearable truth is precisely the stuff of which fictions are made. The life-lie and its necessity obsess Ibsen's dramas, while the Oedipus of Sophocles is driven to discover and then assume the guilt of his unconsciously committed crime.

It may be that fiction—though less referential, factual, and probative than historical research—can guide us toward a limited form of understanding in this sensitive area of knowing and not-knowing. Its theme is often a traumatic or potentially traumatic self-knowledge, one that cannot reach full consciousness without becoming life-threatening. After reading Sereny I am tempted to think of Speer's *Lebenslüge* in this light: the discovery of a truth that reveals his life to have been a lie, yet a discovery so unbearable—both because of the earlier, blind exhilaration and now the brutal facts—that he is forever an accomplice of that experience. When his daughter Hilde, on her seventeenth birthday, finally asks him directly how he could have been so long part of an evil system, he makes the following reply: "The tasks Hitler had confided to me, first in architecture, then in government, his 'friendship,' the passionate conviction he radiated, the power his favor conferred on me, all this was quite simply overwhelming and had become so indispensable to me that to hang on to it I would probably have swallowed anything" (636).

Speer's struggle with truth comes after a dramatic reversal of knowledge and fortune, but there is no resolution to it as in the Oedipus story. He continues to live in prevarication and partial denial; his unusual intellectual resources go as much to evading the truth as to acknowledging it. What is most affecting in Sereny's book—which does not therefore cease to be historically accurate—is consonant with a conflict familiar to us from some of our most influential works of fiction.

8. Breaking with Every Star: On Literary Knowledge

> Even the starry union is a fraud.
> Yet gladly let us trust the valid symbol
> For a moment.
> —Rilke, *The Sonnets to Orpheus*

> So, there we are (again) per aspera—not with the stars—the stars, thank you very much!—, but close to words, which come from hands and can be grasped by the hands.
> —Paul Celan

I feel honored to have been asked to give this lecture in memory of Peter Szondi and to mark the thirtieth anniversary of the Comparative Literature Institute whose first director he was. I was unsure initially whether to accept. Might not the task be more appropriately carried out by one of his students or close associates, who are in this audience? They have facilitated the publication of all his writings, which is a remarkable service, a contribution to scholarship and to the development, specifically, of a literary hermeneutics distinct from, though entirely conscious of, the philosophical traditions within which it arose. But more is at stake than continuity of tradition within a "critical university." In a period when it could well be asked, "Wozu Akademiker in dürftiger Zeit?" (What use are academics in times of need?), Szondi's writings remind us of an exemplary teacher and public intellectual who took seriously his profession's place in the life of his university, of Germany, of Europe.[1]

It is not posthumous flattery to point out how rarely we come upon his combination of qualities: erudition, philosophical and historical culture, pedagogical patience, and, beyond these, even resisting these, that is, refusing to allow them to be virtues in themselves, a steadfast love for literature, including whatever was valuable on the contemporary scene. I know "love" is an emotional word, one he would not have used, and I certainly don't mean that he considered the study of literature as in any way a transcendent activity. On the contrary, he understood art as aesthetic education in the broadest sense: No illusory hope or sympathetic magic is suggested, but a gradual, temporal process implanting the conviction that human freedom from personal compulsion and arbitrary authority is a possibility.

In this qualified hope for an emancipation, Szondi is fully of the Enlightenment. Yet he differs from its methodizers or administrators in searching for a pedagogy that does not rely on mechanical operation. Method, as he shows in essay after essay, is a form of modesty. Sometimes that modesty feels like sadness, because there is no bravado in him, no flaring up as is characteristic of the very objects of his care, the great writers he seeks to understand. Nevertheless, something remarkable in his fidelity to literary and aesthetic education comes through. He takes the part of language, even—or especially—in the sphere of daily politics, where language suffers by being compromised through instrumental half-truths and promotional formulations.[2]

If I emphasize, then, Szondi's literary focus, it is not to escape back into an enclosed academic or aesthetic domain and so to risk simplifying his legacy. But I cannot overlook what has happened in the years since his death. I fear that the art of reading that he enhanced, of close and reflective reading, which is also an art of naming, is in danger of being displaced once more by the seductive bytes of new academic positivisms as well as scholarship struggling to be politically relevant.[3] It helps us, in the face of both temptations, to recall his characteristically modest caution: "Es gibt eine Realität der Dichtung, die sich nicht mit der empirischen Realität deckt, aber darum noch nicht zur folgenlosen Unwirklichkeit wird" (There exists a reality of poetry, which does not coincide with empirical reality, but does not therefore become unreal and without consequence).[4]

That *is* always the challenge, of course: to demonstrate the reality of art. This effective reality—*Wirklichkeit*—is what we feel active in poets like Hölderlin, Mallarmé, and Celan, even when a cryptic element remains, when the darkness or density of their poetic words obstructs our impatient desire for light. A *libido sciendi* (Nietzsche: "Lust des Erkennen," "Wahn," "Wissenstrieb") pretends that clarity and total intelligibility are unquestionable ideals and so risks "overdeveloping" the poetic negative. But literary knowledge, which is at once the knowledge transmitted by literary works and the knowledge we bring to such works in order to understand them (the word "Erkenntnis" in Szondi's famous essay "Über philologische Erkenntnis" is hard to render into English, but it points to recognition, not just to cognition)—literary knowledge, then, is both more and less than a "Wissenschaft" in the strict sense transferred from the natural sciences and applied by Husserl, for example, to philosophy.[5]

The formal result of a specifically literary coming-to-knowledge will always remain twofold. The interpretive essay, however illuminating it is, cannot replace or marginalize its object, the literary text. Interpretation fails when it pushes literature aside and says, in effect: Now that we have attained a more directly communicative knowledge with your help, you are expendable. At its extreme, this attitude might envisage getting rid of mediating texts altogether, substituting for them a naked thought process or a symbolic logic not dependent on the seriatim and integral reading of such "external" sources. Literary knowledge insists on the stubborn dualism of text and commentary. Interpretation cannot be end-stopped.

Szondi makes the point cogently by using the hermetic poem as a limit case. Though that kind of poem can be elucidated by means of keys that philological and interpretive expertise provide, "muß es doch in der Entschlüsselung als verschlüsseltes verstanden werden, weil es nur als solches das Gedicht ist, das es ist" ([I]t must nevertheless be understood as something that remains enciphered even when it has been deciphered, because only as such is it the poem it is).[6] So criticism too, though its aim is the opposite of hermetic, should outlive its clarity and remain readable after it has done its job. It has, at best, a consistency, even a constancy (*Beständigkeit*) of its own: It is marked by what used to be called *intentio*, an intensity of attention directed both toward its object and back to itself.[7]

I have mentioned Szondi's erudition, but what is more remarkable is his attempt to tame learning. In a historicizing age he engages the historicity of understanding as a fact rather than as a problem and does not try to resolve its aporias in the manner of Gadamer. His focus on a specifically literary analysis seeks to make scholars more reflective about the way *Historie* (positivistic historical scholarship) blocks the literary understanding as well. His emphasis on hermeneutics goes in the same direction: To understand art means to renew art as well as one's understanding. This is what assures "die unverminderte Gegenwärtigkeit auch noch der ältesten Texte" (the undiminished presence of even the oldest texts).[8]

Now literary texts are obviously marked by their time; they can be treated as documents and brought into the present by retrieving their historical content. The literary critic does not differ from the historian in an absolute way; he too is moved by what Celan called "die Frage nach dem Uhrzeigersinn" (the question concerning the meaning of the hands of the clock).[9] Yet aesthetic objects not only reflect history; they are themselves history, still radioactive with it. They form an institutional sequence of their own, and, breaking through historicized time, discredit periodizing clichés. Though subject to changes in interpretation and esteem, such works remain alive as long as they produce a "perpetuated understanding," an "uninterrupted conversion of knowledge into recognition" ("perpetuierte Erkenntnis," "[die ununterbrochene] Zurückführung des Wissens auf Erkenntnis").[10]

All such categories, however, still vest the vitality of literature in what it does to the intellect: how it deepens or advances it. The question of the limits of reason does not arise except as it points to a resistance or otherness to be overcome. The Kantian perspective, in which concepts do not adequately account for the aesthetic in nature or art, remains only as a vague methodological caution. But in practice Szondi's hermeneutic optimism about understanding, "Verstehen," is used to argue for a modern type of "Verständlichkeit" (intelligibility): It is focused on poems whose intelligibility is in question not because they are from the distant past but because, radically contemporary, even too near, they disclose how thought and language overlap. There is no "Einfühlung" psychologism in Szondi, no attempt to identify intimately with individual genius or the spirit of an age. Nor does his art of explication "administer the unintelligible"—an accusation directed against theology by Enlightenment critics and cited with relish by Nietzsche.

Instead, by revealing the poet's commitment to words Szondi seeks to convey a fundamental shift that transforms those words into more than the outward of thought. In this he comes very close to Derrida's grammatological concept of *écriture*, of the view (often misunderstood) that what is written has priority. The status of ideas changes with Derrida: The classical and commonsensical view had given them precedence, judging writing to be a kind of *aide-memoire*, the ornamental or persuasive expression of a more universal, platonic or inward, reality. Now writing claims a signifying force of its own, deconstructive rather than mimetic. Szondi asks whether the exclamation "Hyperbole!" that begins Mallarmé's "Prose" signifies "die Figur der Hyperbel, den Akt des Übertreibens, oder werden beide in eins gesehen, die Hyperbel als Bewegungsfigur des geistigen Aktes? . . . Die Antwort auf diese Frage verbietet der Ausspruch Mallarmés, Gedichte würden nicht aus Gedanken, sondern aus Wörtern gemacht" ([Is it] the rhetorical figure of hyperbole or the act of exaggerating, or both viewed as one, with the hyperbole serving as the image representing the mental act? . . . We are forbidden to answer this question by Mallarmé's pronouncement that poems are not made out of thoughts but out of words).[11]

Yet the issue of literary knowledge as a special kind of insight does not find its complete exposition in Szondi's writings. I can only guess that he thinks of such insight in terms resembling those of Benjamin: It is an energy as well as a form of knowledge; it breaks through time like certain memories or revolutionary events; in Benjamin's words, it is "a discovery linked in a most singular way to recognition."[12] Without a special theory of his own, Szondi fosters a *concordat* between the *Kenntnis* (expert knowledge) necessary to approach radically poetic words and the *Erkenntnis* that would come from understanding them. Learning and literary culture, it seems, are reconcilable. The epistemological problem of how literary knowledge is possible and the scientific problem of how verifiable it is result in a special kind of *Entstehungsgeschichte* in which the interpreted work remains the formal beginning and end of discovery. Indeed, Szondi's most consummate close reading, that of Celan's "Engführung," reverses genesis and structure by respecting that poem's manner of proceeding ("Führung"), allowing it to determine the process of understanding and preventing in this way foreclosure of its maze of textual meanings. His work on Celan is more rigorous and sustained, in its notice of nondisambiguated multiple meanings, than anything since William Empson.

―――――+―――――

I will now explore what kind of reality may be ascribed to literary knowledge. That reality shows itself mainly "within the loop" by way of the impact of poet on poet, or poet on reader, and insofar as figurative language produces a shock of recognition. It is important to elucidate this energy of figurative language and the curious fact, related to it, that certain dead symbols continue to prevail in the Enlightenment despite all efforts to purge them as "nonsense" or word-magic.

Among those dead symbols are the stars. Over time, they have signified the portals of the unknown, the heavenly host, the souls of the departed, guardian spirits, also unremovable constancy, mathematical truth, the immutable, the eternal. Modern verse from Mallarmé on seems even more fixated on them than Romantic or older poetry. Of course, such division between old and new is as arbitrary as any modernity-claim. The stars are always being displayed and displaced—from the time of the first canonical sky-poem, the opening of the Book of Genesis.

There the greater as well as lesser lights are *created* and so subordinated to a creator. "The heavens declare the glory of God," in the words of Psalm 19, or as the Vulgate has it, "coeli enarrent."[13] But let us look at this psalm more closely. In a move that has mystified translators and commentators, the metaphor of the speaking heavens in the first two verses of the psalm is recanted in verse three: "There is no speech, there are no words; / Their voice is not heard." What kind of deconstructive move is that; dare we regard the biblical spirit of iconoclasm, here turning against a metaphor, or reminding us that it is not to be taken literally, as already modern? Yet the poem recovers its "oriental" zest quickly enough in the next verse, and with the famous image of the invigorated sun leaving its chamber like a bridegroom the *chupah*, the tent where the marriage was consummated.

The psalm's second part strikes up a separate theme. It celebrates not the visible cosmos but "The law of the Lord [which] is perfect," "The commandment ... [which] is pure, enlightening [*meirat*] the eyes." Tradition consecrated this joining of what might have been two separate poems by discerning a transition from one kind of evidence to a second and transcendent kind. The first is the "light of nature," at once the light coming to us from nature and the *lumen naturale* in us, the inborn spark of reason that can infer from nature the existence of a Creator-God. The second is the supervening light of revelation, from Scripture rather than nature. A formal discontinuity on the level of theme is resolved this way, but the theological implications surrounding the disputed affinity of these two kinds of light have tremendous doctrinal consequences in the history of Christianity.

In Judaism too, though systematic theology (even when practiced by Maimonides) was only grudgingly tolerated, there is an abiding concern for how natural images influence a potentially idolatrous imagination. This concern extends from actual images to verbal icons (Celan's "Augenstimmen") and then to the impact of voice itself as naked, persuasive, promissory. Thus after the two sets of seven verses whose difference I have described, Psalm 19 concludes with a one-verse coda: "Let the words of my mouth and the meditation of my heart be acceptable before Thee, / O Lord, my Rock and my Redeemer." This expresses, it seems to me, more than a pious reflex.

In the context of the psalm as a whole, that verse is a self-reflective step after the bold imagery of the opening section (bracketed by line 3) and the praise of Scripture-Law (Torah) in the following section. It is anticipated, moreover, by another apparently conventional religious thought: "Who can discern errors? / Clear Thou me from hidden faults." We cannot tell precisely what errors or faults are meant: As is well known, the *Sitz im Leben* of the psalms is never very specific. Whatever their cultic origin in coronation or acclamation ceremonies, the psalmist speaks as a representative of the human community. This personal though nonspecific quality of Psalms contributes to the sense that an inward turn is being expressed—perhaps by a culture lacking developed expressions for internal moods or thought processes. If there is such an inwardness, it is continuous with the struggle against idolatry, a struggle reminding us not only that the stars, the heavenly bodies, are creatures (*res creatae*) but that words too, the words of this very psalm and the hidden speech of thought itself, require scrutiny for idolatrous error.

My point is not primarily a historical one, in the sense of seeking to locate the emergence of conscience or self-consciousness in its relation to ritual. Nor is it thematic, a supplement to the history of literary topoi that might take us from these star-words to Mallarmé's sky-poem "L'azur" or his inverted image of the night sky as (white) poetry on a (black) page. All these are valid, interesting connections. But the *literary* question raised by Psalm 19 concerns the fact of speech itself, and strong, imaginative speech in particular. According to the psalm, that speech has to be given back, or bend back, to God: Its glory must reflect His glory. Words are no different from the heavenly bodies in that respect. Within this biblical poetry, noted for its figurative strength, a countervailing thrust is found that puts the words being uttered in question.[14]

What keeps the stars from becoming dead symbols is not, I am suggesting, a primitive or sentimental awe alone but also their association with hyperbolic words: the kind of words that seem to have an independent existence, that hang glittering in the firmament of discourse, startling, autonomous phrases that religion thinks it must subordinate, like Scripture the Book of Nature. Yet, as I hope to have shown, there was already a conspiracy of Scripture and language, because—and one does not have to be a Hegelian to appreciate this—words negate the immediacy of nature and institute a symbolic notation that is "naturally" iconoclastic. That notation distances sensuous ideas without denying them and so makes space for thought: paradoxically a *literary space*, one that transfers the power of those images to the fictive word.

―+―

> The art is lost, and correspondence too.
> ―John Donne, *The First Anniversary*

> L'immense grappe brille à ma soif des désastres.
> ―Paul Valéry, *La jeune parque*

What happens at the present time to this literary space, which maintains a connection between poetic words and stars?[15] Language is a form of life that allows, to quote Hegel, "an immediate self-conscious existence," but it also exhibits an increasingly skeptical questioning of its own figurative or quasi-sensuous character.[16] Somehow the pathetic fallacy does not depart from modern poetry. The fiction of a sympathetic cosmos, that there was a time when the starry connection existed, continues to be influential, if only as a fiction.

So Nerval's opening sonnet in *Chimères* laments the death of "ma seule etoile" (my only star), which turns him into "le ténébreux,―le veuf,―l'inconsolé" (the dark,―the widower,―the inconsolable).[17] Poetically, the death of that star seems as traumatic as the death of God in Richter's famous fantasy. And before the word "correspondence" designated a purely secular mode of communication, it pointed (as still in Baudelaire's well-known lyric) to mysterious conjunctions or constellations.

Star imagery haunts both Celan's poetry and that of Nelly Sachs. In Celan, however, there is a repeated suggestion that the sympathetic link between poet and language has suffered a radical breach, or is grown cold as coldest air. Despite that, or rather, in its despite, "Sternunfug setzt sich fort" (starry nonsense continues).[18] Speech and reality seem now to proceed along separate tracks, in a duplicitous, contrary doubling, or (to permit myself one pun) in the form of an "Unfuge," so that, for example, Celan's "Sprach, sprach. / War, war" ("Engführung" [The Straitening]) parodies the fiat, makes of it a perpetual dry run.[19] For Maurice Blanchot, similarly, literary space cannot be dissociated from an ill-starred literary intensity that wrecks "what it makes known, burning the thought which thinks it and yet requiring this thought in the conflagration where transcendence, immanence are no longer anything but flamboyant, extinguished figures—reference points of writing, which writing has lost in advance."[20]

Blanchot remembers here the sober revel of thought in the final stage of the odyssey of spirit as Hegel's *Phenomenology* describes it. "Das Absolute Wissen" ("Absolute Knowledge") does not fall into its own abyss but comes out of itself after having embraced the total historical memory of mankind, all the oppositions and mediations it has had to endure. There is a return to phenomenality. Blanchot reinterprets this rebirth of phenomenality out of what Hegel names the "night of self-consciousness" by associating it with the way writing limits interiority. "Writing excludes the limitless, continuous process just as much as it seems to include a nonmanifest fragmentation, which in its turn, however, presupposes a continuous surface upon which it would be inscribed, just as it presupposes the experience with which it breaks."[21]

I turn now to the way Nelly Sachs and Celan view the connection (or disconnection) of star and inscriptive word. Let me begin with the obvious remark that though Celan is linguistically far more daring than Sachs, he still maintains a convergence of noun-form and symbol. Whatever the play of meaning, some stable namings persist: *Stern, Feld, Nacht, Baum, Auge, Stunde, Stimme, Geburt, Gelände, Blick, Licht*. Indeed, the more difficult it is to follow a poem's sequential or narrative meaning, the more we grasp at these constants. At the same time, we are often deliberately frustrated by Celan, since his nouns are not all that stable: There are many more peculiar and fragmenting noun formations (as well as other "Partikelgestöber") than in Nelly Sachs. She is closer to Rilke, who called the stars "unsäglich" (not sayable) in the ninth of his *Duino Elegies*, though only to ground speech more firmly: "Haus, / Brücke, Brunnen, Tor, Krug, Obstbaum, Fenster,— / höchstens: Säule, Turm" (house, bridge, fountain, gate, pitcher, fruit-tree, window— / at most: column, tower). "*Hier* ist des *Säglichen* Zeit, *hier* seine Heimat" (*Here* is the time for the sayable, *here* is its homeland).[22]

Rilke's catalogue is comforting. It suggests that even though the *Duino Elegies* begin by associating beauty and terror, they remain this side of sublime or sinister and often yearn for a solid principle of order, a yearning that the First World War's disorder only intensified. One might have thought, following another World War, and the Holocaust, that an *écriture du désastre* would finally take over, a writing that, in the words of Blanchot, would "break with [every] star."[23] But this certainly does not hold for Nelly Sachs. Though her lyric fluency, her wealth of metaphor, may not be as torrential as Rilke's, the stargazing is, if anything, more unembarrassed and recuperative.

In *Flucht und Verwandlung* [*Flight and Metamorphosis*], Sachs, while recalling Rilke's personal myth of "Verwandlung," differs from him by avoiding self-reference and recreating an older, "Wunderhorn" naiveté of style.[24] Her "Träume aus Wunden" establish a surprisingly cool linguistic surface.[25] When she writes in her poem "Einer,"

> Einer
> wird den Ball
> aus der Hand der furchtbar
> Spielenden nehmen
>
> [Someone
> will snatch the ball
> from the hands
> of those who can hardly play]

the words remain transparent despite a basic indeterminacy. We suspect but cannot be sure that these players are the immortals themselves: the Fates, or similar mythic figures. They play their terrible games with us, or we ourselves are the players, under their influence. This astrological perspective is confirmed by the second stanza:

> Sterne
> haben ihr eigenes Feuergesetz
> und ihre Fruchtbarkeit
> ist das Licht
> und Schnitter und Ernteleute
> sind nicht von hier

[Stars
have their own laws of fire
and their fertility
is the light,
and reapers and gleaners
are not from here].²⁶

The poet makes the stars *sayable* despite Rilke's admonition, and the lucidity of her words is itself a contained fire. She is refusing to pass "outside sidereal space," outside "Desire, [which] is still a relation to the star."²⁷ The "fire-law" she evokes is not repressive but generates light and reverses "furchtbar" into "fruchtbar" ("fearful" into "fruitful"). The stars, linked to her words, intimate a transcendent fate.

The question for the reader is what access there may be, here and now, to that starry law. In restoring a sense for hidden possibilities, is Sachs weakening Rilke's secular emphasis ("Hier is des *Säglichen* Zeit") in favor of a mysterious "correspondence" between heaven and human destiny? Does her claim that "reapers and gleaners / are not from here" move toward a dualistic vision that widens the distance between the wounded and the transfigured world, rather than recalling a natural supernaturalism—the aura, however fleeting, that may suffuse earthly things?

Weit draußen
sind ihre Speicher gelagert
auch Stroh
hat einen Augenblick Leuchtkraft
bemalt Einsamkeit

[Their storehouses
are far away
even straw
in a flash of luminous power
colors loneliness].²⁸

It is tempting to interpret that "Weit draußen" as an inverted version of Rilke's "Weltinnenraum" (world-inner-space), because the stanza ends on a note that is both redemptive (the luminosity of straw, as in the fairy tale of "Rumpelstiltskin," reaches our world from that other world) and inwardly consoling ("colors loneliness"). The poet withdraws from dualism, though not from solipsism. The next-to-last stanza allows "Einsamkeit" to flow into the repetition of the poem's first word:

Einer wird kommen
und ihnen das Grün der Frühlingsknospe
an den Gebetmantel nähen
und als Zeichen gesetz
an die Stirn des Jahrhunderts
die Seidenlocke des Kindes

[Someone will come
and sew the springbud's green
onto their prayer shawl
and as a sign
on the century's brow
the silken locks of the child].[29]

Who is that "One" if not a figure of hope, of messianic expectation? Though "Einer" is a casual word, as ordinary as straw, the poem surcharges it momentarily to express not only advent but unity—in the Jewish sense of *yichud*, the oneness that guards against duality or division in God.

Yet, as in Psalms, the consolation offered is not attached to a particular faith. The images are no more Jewish than Christian. "Einer," in fact, has an evangelical simplicity rather than a ritualistic gravity. There are, nevertheless, specific historical overtones. "Feuergesetz" may include an allusion to what surrounds Sinai and the giving of the Law. "Gebetmantel" (prayer shawl) is associated with Jewishness, and "Seidenlocke" may re-sound as "Seitenlocke," a mark of the orthodox Jew. The modulation from "Stern" (star) to "Stirn" (forehead) is not uncommon in poetry, but the figure of sewing a spring-bud on the prayer shawl could bring back the memory of a different sign that Jews had been forced to wear. Yet there is, here, a deliberate vagueness, or better, a *suggestiveness*, inherited from the poetics of the Symbolist movement.

As a Symbolist symbol "Einer" is indeterminate enough to designate the poet as well as one of the Fates or some fateful—messianic, prophetic—figure. The same holds for the "Spielenden": Linking the imagery of the first stanza to the theme of the child and the (relative) simplicity of all these words, we are led to ponder the difference between two sorts of "play," that of the child with an open future and of the child with a foreclosed destiny. Given that choice, it is clear what side the poet is on. But she may not have had that choice except in the charmed space of her lyrics. These, on the edge of night, of becoming Hymns to the Night, keep their voice cool and steady, like lullabies.[30]

Despite some stylistic similarities between Sachs and Celan—in particular, the short, quasi-absolute phrases with which they often begin and which are not always absorbed into sentence structure—each poet's relation to word-surface is quite different. The idea of a "nonmanifest fragmentation" does not apply to Celan any more than does the "Ungefähr" of Symbolist poetics.³¹ His verbal pattern is close to a jigsaw collage, and it often assembles pieces of speech more jaggedly than in the following:

> Ein Holzstern, blau,
> aus kleinen Rauten gebaut. Heute, von
> den jüngsten unserer Hände
>
> [A wooden star, blue,
> from small diamond shapes built. Today, from
> the youngest of our hands].³²

This hand-made star must guide us through transitions obscurer than those of Nelly Sachs. As first presented, the star is a simulacrum fashioned by a child—or, if a metonymy for poetry, by a new generation of writers. The star's blue (intensified by the assonance of "aus," "Rauten," "gebaut") may have emblematic significance but could also resist it by evoking a fauve or nonsemantic clarity—the kind that expels historical or sentimental meanings.³³ But the aim of Celan's fictions is not that of restoring natural images clouded by anthropomorphic sediments. Rather, it is to image the jeopardized word itself as a survivor of its contamination:

> Das Wort, während
> Du Salz aus der Nacht fällst, der Blick
> wieder die Windgalle sucht
>
> [The word, while
> you fell salt from the night, the eye
> again for the wind-gall searches].³⁴

The formal parallelism of "Das Wort" and "Holzstern" creates a small sky-poem which here displaces the star and exhibits the Word instead, during—enduring—a bitter night. Is this an anti-idolatrous move, as in Psalms?

If so, it is also a move against "the Word" considered as a transfigurative icon. Nelly Sachs created new star-words, made them *säglich* again (not only speakable but saga-like). She does not leave her tradition; she reinstates herself in it, and quite impersonally so. But Celan makes us participate in the personal travail of such a reinstatement. It is not a matter of finding words for an unspeakable reality: Words are themselves part of that reality, so that he has to find his way to words before finding the words. Hence the syntactical awkwardness of the second stanza, which obtrudes the "Du": symbol of desire for the "ansprechbar," for the recovered possibility of direct address.[35]

If poetry remains oriented toward the stars, it is because the constancy of the poet requires a sublime object, a Stella for his Astrophel, however cold the sidereal space of desire has become. Yet even when poetic words fall upward, they remain the work of human hands.[36] The uplift of hyperbole and hypostasis ("Das Wort" of stanza 2) cannot make poetry fall out of language or the human. We seek a conversation with language itself; as Celan says in his Bremen speech, today our whole being is involved in this, "wirklichkeitswund und Wirklichkeit suchend" (wounded by reality and seeking reality). The efforts of poets, he also says, are "überflogen von Sterne, die Menschenwerk sind" (canopied by stars of human manufacture).[37]

Celan's next stanza, then, should not surprise:

—Ein stern, tu ihn
tu den stern in die Nacht

[—A star, put it
put the star in the night].[38]

The poet's request—to us, to himself—is to put a star back into that night, as the work of human hands, as an artificial, hopeful, tactile, verbal compound. The colloquial "tu" emphasizes the hands-on character of the act, and sounds strangely like an attempt to say "du." The hands address.[39]

What is surprising is how these and the final verses create an alternate simplicity to that of Nelly Sachs. The question for both Celan and Sachs is how language can be restored, and the fidelity to poetry maintained, despite a contamination that went so deep that, usually, Celan's manifest fragmenting of words compulsively reenacts the problem. Can words become a terrain without deadly associations—given the "thousand eclipsing darknesses of death-bringing speech" ("die tausend Finsternisse todbringender Rede"), given the traumatic historical reality that makes Szondi burst out, in the midst of his careful and gradual elucidation of "Engführung": "Ein Gelände des Todes und der Trauer ist dieser Text" (this text is a terrain of death and mourning)?[40] Poetry is, after all, neither a jigsaw puzzle nor a coloring book, nor one of those children's games which are solved by drawing a representational line that connects numbered dots.[41] "The Word" of stanza 2 is, after all, encompassed by a stormy night, in which salt is precipitated like lightning.

Yet each poet organizes the innocence of words in a different way. Nelly Sachs writes in the anxiety of hope: that someone will take the word-game out of her hand and make it more than play. Her poem is a space in which, "zauberkundig," she barely suspends the childlike expectation for a redemptive, crowning event. For Celan there is no pattern that goes from figure to fulfillment or toward a truth ("Wahrsagung") that transcends language.[42] His "Holzstern" may be as blue as the sky or the color of hope—yet as a blue-cold surprise it makes us think *and* not-think of the Holocaust. Only the youngest hands can elide wounding associations.[43]

"Wirklichkeitswund und Wirklichkeit suchend."[44] To conclude, let me make explicit what I have learned about literary reality. Szondi puts in a large claim on behalf of Celan, based primarily, though not exclusively, on "Engführung": "Die Dichtung ist nicht Mimesis, keine Repräsentation mehr: sie wird Realität. Poetische Realität freilich, Text, der keiner Wirklichkeit folgt, sondern sich selbst als Realität entwirft und begründet" (Poetry is not mimesis, no longer representation: It becomes reality. Poetical reality, to be sure, text, which does not follow up on the real world but conceives and founds itself as reality).[45] I am uncomfortable with that claim; it seems too abstract, even for a poem as daring as "Engführung," and too unproblematic for the Celan in whom every phrase has its antiphrase. This poet's wanderings, his "Wüstensinn" or desert sensibility, his "geh … geh!," do not found anything. They lead to a night emptied of starry words, to the uprooting *lekh lekha* ("Get going!") that ordered Abraham to break with every star—except the word of the promise.[46]

Szondi is right, however, that in poetry of this uncompromising cast the words are always ahead of the reader—as they are of the poet, whose very purpose is to "fall into" them, and who does this in two quite different ways. Celan commits himself to language as if it were fate: no ideas but in words. But he also "falls into the word" in the colloquial sense of interrupting, of provoking a harsher and truer conversation.[47] This is one reason for his interruptive and contrapuntal style. The plea "Ein stern … / tu den Stern in die Nacht" must be read against the divine promise cancelled by the genocide: "And He brought him forth abroad, and said: Look toward heaven, and count the stars … So shall thy seed be."[48]

Celan's renewal of the word, within these eclipses and broken promises, is indeed remote from mimetic pleasure, even as simple as that which produced the wooden star. The hypostatized Word of the second stanza also cannot be an object of imitation and falls back into language. Too sublime, too much of a star, it is replaced by a speech-movement that becomes personal and understated and ends by enclosing itself in parentheses. This constriction illustrates perfectly Celan's precept: "Geh mit der Kunst in deine allereigenste

Enge" (Go, take art along with you into your narrowest, uniquely personal enclosure).[49] The poem's concluding lines take that precept to mean: "falle ins Wort" (interrupt). Celan's

> Kam ein Wort, kam,
> kam durch die Nacht,
> wollt leuchten, wollt leuchten
>
> [Came a word, came
> came through the night,
> wanted to shine, wanted to shine]

should be placed beside his vulnerable wish for a starry word, however manufactured.[50] The wooden star is a substitute, even, perhaps, a natal star replacement:

> tu den Stern in die Nacht
>
> (—In meine. In
> meine.)
>
> [put the star in the night.
>
> (—In mine. In
> mine.)].[51]

9. Learning from Survivors: The Yale Testimony Project

I

An important reason for oral testimonies of the Holocaust is to allow survivors to speak for themselves. We should not speak for them; rather, we have a duty to listen and to restore a dialogue with people so marked by their experience that total integration into everyday life is a semblance—though a crucial and comforting semblance. One of the first things we learn from the taped memoir is that the survivor's language has an uncalculated poetry that won't fit in with most poetry as we know it, let alone most prose.[1]

I become aware, that is, how much of a monologue my own talk tends to be and how important it is to let the voice of others come through. Not only because I am a single person and they, the survivors, are many; not only because, as I have mentioned, their very inarticulateness can be eloquent, affected by the extreme experience they—often for the first time in a public context—recount; but also because we who were not "there" always look for something the survivors cannot offer us. Though as a group survivors undergo the same pressures of mythmaking as we do, or a temptation not to speak the worst, the testimonies in the Yale Video Archive cannot be collectivized: They disconcert us and alarm even the interviewers. Face to face with that world, it is our search for meaning which is disclosed, as if *we* had to be comforted for what *they* suffered. For us, who were not there, the classical axiom holds that "Nothing human is alien"; for them, "Nothing human is entirely familiar." The sense of the human has always to be restored.

Nor can we rejoice, as modernists have done, in the perspectivism of these witness-accounts, that is, in the interesting difference marking each story off through point of view and resonant detail. For the stories are also disastrously alike, repeating the same trauma, the same catastrophes. The Holocaust history that emerges from these personal accounts does not support the moralizers among us. If we learn anything here it is about life when the search for meaning had to be suspended: We are made to focus on what it was like to exist under conditions in which moral choice was systematically disabled by the persecutors and heroism was rarely possible.[2] That it occurred, in quiet acts of resistance or extraordinary ones like the Warsaw Ghetto revolt, is close to miraculous.

II

The term "oral history" to describe the Video Archive's effort suggests that although what is brought into view are individual testimonies, their purpose remains the documentation of a collective fate, the depiction through converging witness-accounts of an event unparalleled in its murderous scope and with continuing, far-reaching consequences. Without the vast paper trail, of course, generated by perpetrators whose triumphalism was at once punctilious and absolute—without this mountain of evidence assembled and interpreted by academic historians, we would not be able to construct an adequate picture. Yet it would remain the picture of a self-documenting machine, of bureaucratic memos and orders of the day, of railroad schedules and administrative decrees, tons of masking jargon, or in Hannah Arendt's words, "elating clichés."[3] The victims would not be heard and would remain a presence only through humiliating or atrocious photos. Attention would continue to be displaced from them to a fascination with evil, power, and indifference—to the enigma of the killers and the bystanders.

We occasionally find in the response of professional historians an attitude that shows commitment yet is also surprisingly narrow. They say: These memoirs cannot be primary materials for history. For oral history is even less reliable than letters and diaries. Your belated testimonies seem to be spontaneous but are highly mediated: At such distance from the event memory fades or plays tricks or is contaminated by what the survivor has heard or read. When it comes to Holocaust history, moreover, the requirement to be exact is even more important, since slanderers that call themselves revisionists will pick on every discrepancy.

These objections have some validity, and I will return to them. Yet we do not have to accept the opinion that oral and written history must coincide totally, with the oral part auxiliary to some great Book of Factual Truth. Certainly there are difficulties in remembering particular facts or thoughts as one moves away in time from an event, but may there not be compensations, including that very density or mediatedness of perception that the historian sees as problematic?[4] Obversely, can we be sure that the discourse of written history, so revised and contradictory, sometimes in matters of fact but always when it comes to interpretation, is any less mediated? Because "history" is written by one person, however well informed, does not mean it has a truth-value transcending the heterogeneous chorus of voices, the being made of many beings, that is so present and alive in literary memoirs or oral documentation.[5] Recently, moreover, the conviction has grown that local knowledge, which speaks from inside a situation rather than from the outside in an objectifying manner, can provide a texture of truth that eludes those who adopt a prematurely unified voice. Social criticism is best done, as both Clifford Geertz and Michael Walzer have observed, by a "connected critic."[6]

Even if pure spontaneity is an illusion—especially forty to fifty years after the event—it is bad faith to simply substitute the dry tones of the academic historian for the voice of witnesses. Few historians, actually, would deny this, and few nonhistorians would deny value to a written history that leads us through the mazes of confusing particulars by sifting all sources, including personal memories. We need that conscientious overview called history because, as Thomas Friedman wrote in the *New York Times*, covering the Demjanjuk Trial: "The memory of evil, no matter how extreme, has its limits."[7]

Despite these limits, evil is a greater force in etching details on our memory than the good or ordinary life. The details themselves, of course, are by no means all about evil. Some camp inmates, knowing they faced annihilation, made their minds a scroll and recorded everything. Others were highly selective, or the choice of detail was done for them by personal factors that infuse and individualize their testimony. But the general accuracy of recall is astonishing: It has been suggested that in the absence of material remnants of their previous life (such as photos or personal items with associations), survivors treasured each fragment of memory. Deprived, moreover, of funerals and formal rituals, the very pain of their memories might often have become an identity mark important to the work of mourning, and which, necessarily incomplete in the camps, extended itself into the time after liberation.[8]

Oral memoirs, then, do not try to turn survivors into historians but value them as human witnesses to a dehumanizing situation. The person who tells the story is important, as well as what he tells about. We cannot allow only images made by the perpetrators to inhabit memory. The interview situation is social in that it recognizes the survivor and acknowledges what has been endured. It has been said that "testimony has both a private dimension, which is confessional and spiritual, and a public aspect, which is political and judicial. The ... word *testimony* itself links both meanings."[9] The records we are gathering intend to open the book of the survivor's mind: They are, at once, formal depositions, informal chronicles, expressive memoirs, and testimonies that look toward the establishment of a legacy. In a world increasingly deprived of oral tradition, they keep something of it alive. Those who collect these testimonies form small communities of transmission and help alleviate the isolation of the survivors, as well as their own.

The distinction, in any case, between oral and written history fades out as we recall that nothing was meant to come from Auschwitz, written or oral. Auschwitz as a negation of Sinai was to be absolute. In its own terrible and unexpected way, however, the universe of the Holocaust did bring together, in a chain of places that were one place, the Jews of the diaspora. They beheld, as one victim put it, a black dawn. "I swear to you, it was not the sun, it was black."[10] A somber revelation of infamy comes to us still from that attempt to eclipse Sinai. I agree with those who say that to remember after Auschwitz is different from remembering before Auschwitz. Something has changed: We cannot "do history" as usual.

III

Through personal depositions, in a simple room that is not a courtroom, and heeding the ancient injunction "Thou shalt tell," thousands of survivors and bystanders have refracted the abstraction "six million" back into the fate of one person and then another, of one family and then another. Through this procession of individual testimonies the memory of evil—and sometimes of good—is made to extend its limits. Some barriers or limits remain, of course.

One limit comes from within the individual, whose physical survival had to be followed by a renewed contract with ordinary life, a psychic thrust into the future permitting relief and forgetfulness. Yet a remarkable degree of precision remains, because the memory of evil is first and last the memory of an offense, independent of the massiveness of the injustice suffered. So, at one point, a somber expression falls over the face of a witness, as he describes his schooling, just before his story reveals what causes that change of aspect. Even now, today, the pain of being hit by the teacher for the first time, just because he was a Jew, comes over him. (Jean Améry has described how devastating that "first blow" can be.) It is hard for me to forget, on another tape, a sudden ghastly grin as the narrator hesitates, then relates the sudden disappearance, practically overnight, of the entire gypsy population of the camp. The two events, the teacher's blow and the fate of the gypsies, may seem incommensurable, yet that they are not part of a statistical or impersonal narration, that we see the individual change as memory returns, makes them equally unforgettable. We understand better Jean Améry's protest against "the cold storage of history." "No remembering has become a mere memory....

Nothing has healed....Where is it decreed that enlightenment must be free of emotion?"[11]

IV

Yet when scars are exposed and emotions are given so direct a representation by a thousand voices, do we not invest that group and the further thousands each person stands for ("I am my town archive," one of them remarked) with a grim privilege? Is there an assumption, however tacit, that Jewish Holocaust survivors have a monopoly on suffering? And even if there is no such assumption, does the collective effect of their testimony tend in that direction? I hope not, but here a need for interpretation shows itself because of the immediacy of what is recalled.

There is something too forceful in every confession, irrespective of content. The difference between confession and testimony has still to be defined: I can suggest that the insistence on personal experience in *testimony* is not meant to silence us but to record and value a collectively endured history. The authority of testimony is linked to an immediacy that reinforces rather than displaces what can be generalized. It does not come from the singularity or even extreme character of what was undergone. For injustice has a universal structure: It arouses feelings of sorrow and indignation that can be shared, even when the actual experiences cannot.

Though it is the case that the Nazi-inspired Holocaust was unique in both conception and implementation—it instrumentalized the killing of all the Jews through camps and factories whose formal product was death—this horrible truth simply numbs both intellect and heart. We can respond to death only as we remember life: the livingness of a person, an hour before, or yesterday, how such a one looked, loved, spoke. To view these witnesses on the screen is not to exclude other suffering but to be reminded of every injustice, great or small, that wastes human life.

This point has particular importance because other persecuted groups could come to feel that Jews are seeking to exceptionalize the Holocaust at the expense of their own historical or continuing suffering. Toni Morrison's dedication of her novel *Beloved* to "Sixty Million and more" asks us to recall the sorrows of enslaved African Americans since the Middle Passage, their forced transportation to America in inhuman conditions.[12] So it is crucial to stress that the claim of exceptionality refers to the implementation of an ideology that singled out the Jews for extermination solely because they were Jews. All were to be killed, whether by shooting, gassing, or working them to death—including the children. It is this fact, not numbers, which made the

Nazis' war against the Jews an exceptional act of genocide, one we define by the special if inadequate term "the Holocaust."[13]

Black people, twinned with Jews in Nazi caricatures, were also considered a degenerate race in this sick ideology. Nazi racialism, presented as a science, established a pseudohierarchy of races: The Aryans were the masters, while those very low on the scale, Slavs, Blacks, etc. were doomed to be enslaved. The Jews, particularly dangerous because they might "pass," were to be driven out or killed; the conference at Wannsee in January 1942 confirmed and coordinated this policy of extermination.

V

I have said that the immediacy of these first-person accounts burns through the "cold storage of history." They give texture to memory or to images that otherwise would have only sentimental or informational impact.[14] The difference between holocaust and everyday experience remains, but now—as also in the way literature rouses the sympathetic imagination—emotion and empathy accompany knowledge. In fact, these personal narratives, though less shocking and fixating than many photos, could overwhelm viewers or arouse inappropriate defenses. This is especially true of the young: If they feel too vulnerable, if they draw the conclusion, however unconsciously, that their parents' protection is not reliable, they may defensively identify with whoever is more powerful.

Older persons too occasionally betray discomfort. Are you not, they ask, invading the survivor's privacy? The question arises even when it is known that each witness has come forward freely, perhaps after years of hesitation, and that, generally, the only pressure exerted is by the children of survivors who feel testifying is important, both for their parents' sake and the future. Those who express this reservation feel *their* privacy invaded by such intimate and painful recitals.

Why do we not complain about powerful and painful scenes in film, drama, or novel? Are these not equally an invasion of privacy? The reason is simple though not particularly praiseworthy: We fall back on the thought that this is fiction, a maneuver like closing the eyes when we can't look anymore, or averting one's face internally. With survivor testimonies that sort of evasion is more difficult. If we wish to know what happened, to be in touch with realities, then we cannot turn away. When that same wish is shown to be hollow or halfhearted, then there is discomfort, even anguish.

Fiction, then, is quite different in its effect. Our awareness of it as mimesis, as a reconstruction or recreation, encourages a more speculative and dialogic attitude: We can criticize or talk freely with ourselves and others about it. While survivor testimony elicits its own kind of dialogue, it is only partly a dialogue with *us*. The survivors face not only a living audience, or now accept that audience rather than insisting on the intransitive character of their experience. They also face family members and friends who perished: In English the first book of oral documentation of the Holocaust, David Boder's interviews of survivors in displaced persons camps soon after the war, bore the title *I Did Not Interview the Dead*.

It is the witnesses who undertake that descent to the dead. Though they address the living frontally, often using warnings and admonishments, they also speak (at some point in the testimony this is usually made explicit) for the dead or in their name. This has its dangers: To go down, as Virgil said, may be easy, but to come up again (*revocare gradum superasque evadere ad auras*), that is the hard task.[15] "I am not among the living, I died in Auschwitz and no one notices it," Charlotte Delbo wrote.[16] So they remember the dead, remember that they too were in these Houses of the Dead, yet they are not ghosts but truly back here addressing and instructing us. All this I cannot deal with except as it bears on the authenticity of a mode that may have the strength, if anything can have it, to counteract apathy as well as forgetfulness: an apathy that comes from emotional exhaustion but also from the media's false vitalism, or its repeated, competent, routinized, and glossy display of extreme situations.

It is important not to sanctify witness accounts but to see them as a representational mode with a special countercinematic integrity.[17] When film is used for realistic purposes we remain aware that it is film: a simulacrum, something impersonated, artificial, and with the closure of traditional narratives. Documentaries too have a way of buffering realistic extremes: They are presented, and the narrator's patter induces a kind of distance.[18] Even sensational images—archival footage depicting humiliating parades, deportations, executions, charnel houses—often induce us to create a defense by thinking of all this as "events in the past." The past insulates those anonymous victims. But in video testimonies (or "testimonial video" generally) there is nothing between us and the survivor, nor, when an interview really gets going, between the survivor and his recollections.[19] The effect, therefore, can be extraordinarily intimate—it is hard not to cry. Those tears, when they come, are compounded of sorrow and rage: On the one hand, as Primo Levi has described his feeling at the moment of liberation, we would like "to wash our consciences and our memories clean from the foulness that lay upon them"; on the other, "nothing could ever happen good and pure enough to rub out the past.... [We feel] that the scars of the outrage would remain within us forever, and in the memories of those who saw it, and in the places where it occurred, and in the stories that we should tell."[20]

It is this very intimacy, then, as well as condensations or contingencies of recall, and what Lawrence Langer has called a "confusion of tongues"—the clash between the assumptions and vocabulary of the present world of survivor and interviewer and the word-breaking realities of the concentration camp universe—that make each testimony a text in need of interpretation. Students of the arts have learned that sympathy and a degree of identification need not exclude a thoughtful, analytic response.[21] In the classroom especially, given the charged nature of the testimonies, an introduction, a discussion, and a follow-up in the form of readings are appropriate. The reactivated connection between survivors and their experience, which the interview helps foster, the courage shown by survivors in allowing themselves to recall a living death, should not place a contagious emotional burden on the viewers. Dialogue, not paralysis or secondary trauma, should be the result. Historical knowledge can reenter and all sorts of hard questions about the How and the Why.

Let me give a single example of how indispensable interpretation is. A Belgian girl finds refuge in a Catholic home and recalls her excitement when her father visits for the first time since their separation. The incident is so fraught with emotion that she wishes to do more with it in recollection than is possible. The result is a contradiction in the narrative: She tells us that she hid behind the door because she did not know who was coming, and she tells us she hid because she was so happy and wished to surprise her father. The contradiction, surely, is understandable; not only its emotional but also its imaginative side should be acknowledged. Since the dominant fact here is that she is in hiding, doubling the motive shows not only her mixture of fear and expectation but discloses the underlying theme of hiding within hiding.[22] The normal situation (the child jumping out to surprise her father) contrasts with the abnormal circumstances and suggests a deeper withdrawal.

VI

The issue that looms so large in the objection to oral memoirs, especially those recorded some time after the event, is memory's susceptibility to be modified: by books, hearsay, or wishful factors. This issue should be faced. Testimony requires vigilance and the kind of methodical wariness we must bear toward all narratives, spontaneous or patently artful. There are always conditions that surround and influence the *prise de parole*.[23] Primo Levi divides the survivors into different classes of witnesses, whose knowledge was limited by their status in the camps or the moral burden of that status. He concludes: "The history of the Lagers has been written almost exclusively by those who, like myself, never fathomed them to the bottom. Those who did so did not return, or their capacity for observation was paralyzed by suffering and incomprehension."[24]

"Human memory," he also writes, "is a marvelous but fallacious instrument." This is the topic sentence of his first chapter in *The Drowned and the Saved*. Levi there apologizes for the fact that his book is "drenched" in the "suspect source" of "distant memory." Yet none of this prevents him examining the past with a vigor born of a need for communication contracted in Auschwitz and that remains with him even forty years after Liberation.[25] Many survivors mention their recurrent fantasy of finding someone to hear them out after Liberation—a fantasy that, in most cases, was not satisfied and contributed to their silence after an initial outpouring of narratives.

Just as the close study of scribal methods discovered such typical errors as dittography (skipping from a word in one line to the same word in another line, and omitting everything between), we observe parallel though more interesting lapses in the memory-work of oral testimony. Aside from inaccurate names and dates there is the Rashomon effect, possibly caused by the pressure of private associations; there are condensations similar to those described by Freud in dreams; there are colorful mistakes ("I took off my golden ears," says a woman, when she means the earrings that bought her, in the ghetto, a couple of eggs for her birthday); there are simplifications that can be described as metonymies (every Auschwitz survivor seems to have gone through a selection by Mengele, as if he manned that post forty-eight hours a day); and there are moments that recur so frequently that they seem to be archetypal, whether literally true or not. Witnesses, for example, often quote a friend or relative who charges them, as the dying Hamlet does Horatio, to tell his story. This last tendency, in particular, produces a "collective memory," a story typical enough for most to identify with. It is like being shown a group photo taken long ago and seeking to discover oneself in it. One is tempted to say "That's me," even though the image is so dim or different that one cannot be sure.[26]

Survivor testimonies do not excel in providing *vérités de fait* or positivistic history. They can be a source for historical information or confirmation, yet their real strength lies in recording the psychological and emotional milieu of the struggle for survival, not only then but also now. It is no secret that when interviewers meet to discuss their work, they exchange interesting anecdotes about difficult cases. The survivors' identification with their lost companions can become an overidentification and produce a confusion between different if convergent destinies. The voice of the dead still calls the survivors to fulfill a promise. There have even been appropriations of the stories of those who perished, as if they were one's own story.

Another type of overidentification that affects the process of recording comes from viewers (or even interviewers) who are too protective. They do not always allow the survivors their voice. While interviewers acknowledge, of course, the terrible things that happened during the time of victimization, they often balance that by the fact of survival, which is then represented as more than accidental, indeed as a heroic outcome. There is nothing worse in this respect than talk shows where the host oohs and aahs over the terrible past and the brave, so remarkable person who can chat about it here on the show. Even at more sophisticated levels this search for heroic meanings is a need of the overidentifying listener rather than of the survivor. It is far from innocent, for the temptation to "launder" the behavior of people under extreme stress, and the lasting mark left by that stress, suggests that in terms of moral response we have not yet learned enough from the Holocaust.

By such laundering, by such defensively ennobling comment, we are expressing an anxiety that the survivor may be tainted. Primo Levi again speaks truly when he writes of the "awful privilege" of his generation that they have grasped the incurable nature of the offense imposed like a contagion on the human spirit. "It is foolish to think that human justice can eradicate it. It is an inexhaustible fount of evil; it breaks the body and the spirit of the submerged, it stifles them and renders them abject; it returns as ignominy upon the oppressors, it perpetuates itself as hatred among the survivors, and swarms around in a thousand ways, against the very will of all."[27] To take away this kind of honesty from the witnesses is to treat them as patients rather than agents. But in telling their stories survivors are indeed agents: not heroic, perhaps even allowing the worst to remain unsaid, yet the strength required to face a past like that radiates visibly off the screen and becomes a vital fact.

VII

There have been three periods when survivors of the Holocaust recovered their voice and an audience materialized for them. The first was immediately after the war, when the camps were disclosed. That period did not last: A devastated Europe had to be rebuilt, and the disbelief or guilt that cruel memories aroused isolated rather than integrated the survivor. What has been aptly called a "latency period" intervened.[28] A second opening was created by the Eichmann trial in 1961, and a third came after the release of the TV series *Holocaust* in 1978. *So many lost their lives, will their life story too be taken away?* was the complaint. Any survivor could tell a history more true and terrible in its detail, more authentic in its depiction.

Thirty-five years after Liberation, moreover, the survivors and refugees living in America were fully settled, with grown families and a third generation in the offing. It was late: Now if ever was the time to talk; they were no longer hesitant to be recognized and to pass on their experience as a "legacy."

A grassroots project developed in New Haven, when sensitive neighbors found they knew next to nothing about the survivors in their midst. By the time Yale offered its support, the Holocaust Survivors Film Project, initiated in 1979 by Laurel Vlock, Dr. Dori Laub, and William Rosenberg, had pioneered the video testimony concept and deposited two hundred witness-accounts. The Video Archive for Holocaust Testimonies at Yale was founded in 1981 and opened its doors in October 1982.

There is no reason why oral testimony projects like Yale's could not also collect the memories of other groups: those of Vietnam veterans, for example, or the historical experience of African Americans, Native Americans, or immigrants. The growth of journalistic television cannot substitute for oral history because of its brief attention span; it cannot replace careful and sustained listening. The events in Bosnia should not have to wait thirty years to be documented in detail by the survivors.

If we had stopped to resolve all the questions surrounding our effort—including that of the exact value of oral history as history—we would never have proceeded beyond the first experimental tapes. But these proved so affecting, and the survivors were so supportive, that the film project continued, relying on a nondirective interview that encouraged spontaneity.

The principle of giving survivors their voice has been a sustaining one. Also that of giving a face to that voice: of choosing video over audio, because of the immediacy and evidentiality it added to the interview. The "embodiment" of the survivors, their gestures and bearing, is part of the testimony. It adds significantly to the narrative dimension. There was also our judgment that, in terms of education (though not in terms of politics and propaganda), Radio Days were gone. Audiences now and in the future would surely be audiovisual.[29] We decided to make video recordings of public broadcast quality, to build an Archive of Conscience on which future educators and filmmakers might rely. These living portraits are the nearest our descendants can come to a generation passing from the scene.

Let me emphasize that we are not filmmakers. We are gathering original depositions, as one gathers important manuscripts. (Many who testify did not have the chance for a higher, or even uninterrupted secondary, education: This oral history, then, does more than duplicate or confirm what is already written down.) From that collection, which is being analyzed and indexed, quotations are put together in montages of fifteen to fifty minutes that are suitable for all audiences except young children.

I do not deceive myself into thinking that we have developed the perfect interview. There may be no such thing: The quality of oral history is influenced by the human chemistry between interviewer and interviewee and even by the day and place of filming. We have learned to accept that element of chance. One sometimes hears questions that seem wrongheaded or intrusive, yet surprisingly it does not always matter: Once initiated, the flow of memory is so strong that such questions are swept aside or lead to a startling result. In a good interview the initiative remains with the person interviewed. The survivor's readiness is all, together with a conviction about the importance of giving public testimony and trust in the group that is providing the occasion. The interviewing process, in fact, creates an ad hoc community, and whether or not finally telling the story relieves traumatic stress, that communal dimension is certainly a comfort.[30]

Our extracts have an educational purpose: We put them together assuming that young adults are part of the audience and that pedagogy is crucial. After Claude Lanzmann—and his *Shoah* does divide the history of Holocaust representation into Before and After—after Lanzmann, it is hard to think of communicating to children anything of that genocidal hell that made a point of killing children. When Helen K., a witness recorded by Yale, says, "I cannot believe what my eyes have seen," she refers to children being exterminated, and—if anything could be worse—waiting in line day after day for that. But the Video Archive does not set out to be an anatomy of genocide or a relentless assemblage of each step in the extermination process. Using the interview in a compassionate way we gain a description of the everyday and psychological milieu of those caught up in the Holocaust, not excluding their life before or after the war in different countries.

The Holocaust is "eventful" history; it may even be an event that has ruptured our sense of what human nature is. Many expressive details of these witness-accounts belong, however, to the relatively noneventful, nondramatic story of men and women returning to ordinary life after extreme circumstances and working their memories through.[31] It is the entire person who is asked to speak, not only the one recalling terror and time of trial. In this, above all, the historical or sociological value of the testimonies is clear.

Yet we refuse to "program" the interviews, declining to guess what special interests future generations might have. The welling-up of memories is crucial, rather than the imposition of a particular research interest, however important the latter may be for the overall picture. I will not claim that the interviewers do not have their own strong motivation and therefore an agenda.[32] They too, after all, belong to a specific *milieu de mémoire*: They create, in effect, a bridge or channel of transmission between generations by this timely, communal work. But in preserving a memory based on memories, on individual and multiple narratives, they renounce an omniscient perspective and allow the testimonies freer impact.

    I have described what the testimonies are, as a mode of representation, a distinctive genre combining new and very old elements. My experience in viewing the testimonies is similar to that of Lanzmann, while making his film. "There was an absolute break between the bookish knowledge I had acquired and what these people told me. I understood nothing anymore."[33] I hope that everyone who views the testimonies will agree that breaking the silence is, for those who endured so dehumanizing an assault, a painfully affirmative step, in part because of their very willingness to use ordinary words whose adequacy and inadequacy must both be respected.[34]

10. Public Memory and Its Discontents

I want to raise the issue of how to focus public memory on traumatic experiences like war, the Holocaust, or massive violations of human rights. You might think this is not an issue at all, that we are, in fact, too absorbed in such painful matters. I have often heard objections that say that the study of the Holocaust, in particular, is displacing among Jews a tradition of learning two thousand years old. There may be some truth to that charge; it is easy to become fascinated with cruelty and violence, with the mystery of such extreme inhumanity. But we cannot turn away from the world in which this happened, and the question of what impedes our focus is complicated by the very efficiency of modern media, their realism and representational scope.

The substantial effects of film and telecommunications are having their impact. An "information sickness," caused by the speed and quantity of what impinges on us and abetted by machines we have invented that generate endless arrays, threatens to overwhelm personal memory. The individual, we complain, cannot "process" all this information, this incoming flak: Public and personal experience are not being moved closer together but further apart. The arts, it used to be said, aspire to the condition of music; now the "total flow" of video seems to dominate. Can public memory still be called memory, when it is increasingly alienated from personal and active recall?

Among the symptoms of this malady of our age are philosophic discussions about the existence or nonexistence of a "posthumanist subject," a conference on "The Uses of Oblivion," and the fear, openly expressed, that "our past will have no future in our future" (David Rieff). Even as our senses are routinely besieged, the imagination, traditionally defined as a power that restores a kind of presence to absent things, has its work taken away and is in danger of imitating media sensationalism. It becomes, as Wallace Stevens said, a violence from within pressing against the violence from outside. In the midst of an unprecedented realism in fiction and the public media, there is reason to worry about a desensitizing trend, one that keeps raising the threshold at which we begin to respond.

How do we keep our sensitivity alive, when such vivid and painful events become our daily fare? How do we prevent denial or indifference from taking over? We have known for a long time that there is great suffering in the world, suffering impossible to justify. Such knowledge must have been with us at least since the Book of Job was written. But we also know, from the time of Job's so-called friends to that of Holocaust negationists, that suffering is explained or rationalized against all odds.

Today we have entered a new period. Until recently, perhaps until news from Bosnia reached the screen, we clutched at the hope that had the indifferent masses in Germany or America known what was going on in the concentration camps, known with the same graphic detail communicated today by TV, surely the atrocities could not have continued. There would have been an outcry of the popular conscience and so much protest that the Holocaust would have had to stop.[1]

Yet right now we are learning a new truth about human indifference. As the media makes us bystanders of every act of violence and violation, we realize that this indifference or lack of focus was not so incomprehensible after all. For we glimpse a terrible inertia in ourselves and can even find reasons for it. We register the fact that no event is reported without a spin, without an explanatory or talky context that buffers the raw images, and we realize that pictures on TV remain pictures, that a sort of antibody builds up in our response system and prevents total mental disturbance. Even while deploring and condemning the events, we experience what John Keats called "the feel of not to feel it," as we continue on with everyday life.[2]

It is not my intent to add to our already considerable sense of guilt or powerlessness. My point is that the media places a demand on us that it is impossible to satisfy. Paradoxically enough, their extended eyes and ears, so important to informed action, also distance the reality of what is perceived. Terrible things, by continuing to be shown, begin to appear matter-of-fact, a natural rather than manmade catastrophe. Zygmunt Bauman has labeled this the "production of moral indifference."[3]

For our sensibility, however compassionate, is not superhuman: It is finite and easily exhausted. Sooner or later coldness sets in, whether we admit to it or not. We remain deeply engaged, however, because official morality does not cultivate that coldness. This is an important difference between our situation and that of Germans under the Nazi regime. Today viewer reaction splits schizophrenically into responding passionately to images of global misery and an exhausted self-distancing. Those images, for all their immediacy, become too often electronic phantoms.[4]

A desensitization of this kind (Robert Lifton calls it "psychic numbing") was already noticed by Wordsworth near the beginning of the Industrial Revolution.[5] He complained in 1800 of a "degrading thirst after outrageous stimulation," which was blunting "the discriminating powers of the mind" and reducing it to "a state of almost savage torpor." People were losing their ability to be moved by ordinary sights and events, by "common life," because of "the great national events which are daily taking place, and the increasing accumulation of men in cities, where the uniformity of their occupations produces a craving for extraordinary incident which the rapid communication of intelligence hourly gratifies." Wordsworth created, in response, a minimalist poetry, a "lyrical" ballad that reduced the narrative or romance interest to near zero, and urged the reader to "find a tale in everything."[6]

Since Wordsworth's time psychic numbing has made considerable progress. The contemporary problem is not Bovaryism or Quixotism—seeing the real world (defensively) with an imagination steeped in romance—but looking at whatever is on the screen as if it were unreal, just an interesting construct or simulation. Actuality is distanced by a larger-than-life violence and retreats behind all those special effects. Herbert Marcüse discerns an "obscene merger of aesthetics and reality."[7] So it is not surprising that Robert Rosenblum, the art historian, should defend what he calls Warhol's "deadpan" by claiming that it reflects a "state of moral and emotional anaesthesia which, like it or not, probably tells us more truth about the realities of the modern world than do the rhetorical passions of *Guernica*."[8]

But if the present has now less of a hold, if abstractness and psychic numbing have indeed infected us, how can we remain sensitive to the past, to its reality? Spielberg's *Schindler's List* won its acclaim in part by getting through to us, by lifting that anxiety—though not without deploying spectacular means.

Consider a related problem intensified by the media: whether we can trust appearances. Because our technical power of simulation has increased but forgetfulness has not decreased—the speed with which events fall into "the dark backward and abysm of time" has, if anything, accelerated—the greatest danger to public memory is *official history*.[9] Even the dead, as Walter Benjamin declared, are not safe from the victors, who consider public memory part of the spoils and do not hesitate to rewrite history. Or re-image it: Milan Kundera in the opening episode of *The Book of Laughter and Forgetting* recalls how a discredited Communist leader was airbrushed out of a famous historical photo. So readily is history falsified and public memory deceived.

You may have seen a movie that is set in Argentina under the military dictatorship. It could also have been set in Eastern Europe during the time of Soviet domination. Puenzo's film, *The Official Story*, tells a tragic and typical narrative of public deceit and personal discovery. It is the story of a mother who learns that her adopted child was stolen from a "disappeared" Argentinean woman. At first she does not suspect the truth, but a small doubt punctures the basic trust she has in the system: That doubt grows and grows, the search for the truth grows and grows, until—as also in *Oedipus the King*—a hidden past is revealed. But, tragically, her resolute pursuit of the truth breaks up the family and endangers the child.

What I have described comes close to being a universal kind of plot, as old as the historical record itself. What is the difference, then, between past and present? The contemporary difference can be summed up in a famous phrase of Emerson's: "We suspect our instruments."[10] The very means that expose untruth, the verbal or photographic or filmic evidence itself, is tainted by suspicion. All evidence is met by a demystifying discourse or charges of manipulation. The intelligent scrutiny to which we habitually submit appearances becomes a crisis of trust, a lack of confidence in what we are told or shown, *a fear that the world of appearances and the world of propaganda have merged through the power of the media*. To undo this spell and gain true knowledge would then be more tricky than in gnosticism, which distrusted nature and tried to gain a knowledge of the true god behind the god of nature.

What I have just argued is that there is a link between epistemology and morality: between how we get to know what we know (through various, including electronic media) and the moral life we aspire to lead. My account has been rather pessimistic: It implies that the gap between knowledge and ethical action has not grown less wide for us. The pressures to be politically correct, to say and do the right thing, have increased, but neither our thinking nor our actions have adjusted to the challenge so clearly stated by Terrence Des Pres, who said that, after the Holocaust, "a new shape of knowing invades the mind," one that opens our eyes—beyond the Holocaust—to the *global* extent of political misery.[11] In a democracy, moreover, and once we are in the electronic age, while there is more realism, there is also the liability that goes with that: a gnawing distrust of public policy and official memory. The free speech that is one of the foundations of truth in the democratic marketplace of ideas leads to a continual probing, testing, and even muckraking that has an unexpected effect on the integrity of the public life it was intended to assure.

Indeed, the more that official history is disputed by scholarship or media journalism, the more an insidious and queasy feeling of unreality grows in us. What are we to do, for example, with all the speculations about Kennedy's assassination that parade as investigative journalism or docudrama? It is as if the political realm, and possibly all of public life, were inauthentic—a mask, a Machiavellian web of continuous deception.[12] This negative insight also undermines the specific gravity, the uniqueness of lived events, and encourages a deep skepticism about the world—or a relentless, compensatory search for what is fundamental and unfalsifiable, a something that often takes the form of nationalistic or religious fanaticism.

My aim in raising this issue of the relation of morality to knowledge in a democratic and electronic age is, frankly, moralistic. I seek to draw some conclusions, not only to describe as clearly as possible a contemporary dilemma. Terrence Des Pres, again, states that dilemma with the precision of a proverb: "Thanks to the technological expansion of consciousness, we cannot not know the extent of political torment; and in truth it may be said that *what others suffer, we behold.*"[13] The triumph of technology has created two classes that can coexist in the same person: those who suffer and those who observe that suffering. This fact cannot be touted as moral progress, but there is one gain from it: Given our new eyes for the pain of others, and given that "we cannot not know," all monopolistic claims about suffering no longer make sense.

—+—

"What others suffer, we behold" is like a second fall from innocence, a second bite of the fatal apple. It removes all excuse by taking away our ignorance, without at the same time granting us the power to do something decisive. Often, therefore, we fall back on a religious feeling, as President Reagan did at Bitburg, though in his case it served the bottom line of NATO policy. At Bitburg, Mr. Reagan's reconciling memorial perspective equated fallen German soldiers, including Waffen SS, and the civilians they killed, many of them Jewish victims. This "dead" perspective short-circuits reflection on a torment Des Pres called political because of its manmade rather than inevitable nature.

Even when the politics are not so obvious, skeptical contemporary thought sees them everywhere: in religion, in memory, in art. But that insight too has no activist or redemptive value. It simply confirms Des Pres's hellish vision of universal political torment. When we ask, haunted like Tolstoy by such suffering, "What is to be done?" no image of action proposes itself as entirely credible. Rather, the ethical impasse breeds desperate and Manichean solutions, post-Tolstoy fundamentalisms, whether religious or political.[14]

A related reaction is cultural revolution and its instrument, the politicized memory. In flight from human and hermeneutic complexities, this kind of politics saturates everything with ideological content and claims redemptive power for a purified vision of the past. I have previously mentioned the role of official history, based on a highly selective memory promoted by the apparatus of state. It manipulates memory like news.

Now it is true that a war is always going on to modify memory, and we all wage it in ourselves first: Who does not remember moments of altering (or rationalizing or shading) experiences painful to self-esteem? When waged publicly, however, such warfare leads to an institutionalized and bogus recollection, a churlish denial of the history of others (covering up, for instance, at Theresienstadt and Auschwitz, the Jewish identity of most of the victims), or an artificially inseminated perspective. A single authorized narrative then simplifies not just history but the only *active* communal memory we have, made of such traditional materials as legends, poetry, symbols, dances, songs, festivals, and recitations, the sum of which help define a "culture," when combined with various interpretive traditions.

Art as a performative medium—art not reduced to official meaning or information—has a chance to transmit *this* inheritance most fully. When art remains accessible it provides a counterforce to manufactured and monolithic memory. Despite its license, art is often more effective in embodying historically specific ideas than the history writing on which it may draw. Scientific historical research, however essential it is for its negative virtues of rectifying error and denouncing falsification, has no positive resource to lessen grief, endow calamity with meaning, foster a vision of the world, or legitimate new groups.[15] But art remains in touch with or revives traditional materials that satisfy our need for community without repressing individualist performance.

We start indeed with a cultural inheritance, yet that cannot be fixed as immutably as doctrine is in theology. Memorial narratives asserting the identity of nation or group are usually *modern* constructs, a form of antimemory limiting the subversive or heterogeneous facts. Invented to nationalize consensus by suggesting a uniform and heroic past ("O say, can you see . . ."), they convert "great memories" into political theology. Cults and myths do not go away in modernity; on the contrary, revolution, national rebirth, and the drive for political legitimation make blatant ideological use of paradigms from the past. So Marx objected in *The Eighteenth Brumaire* to the French Revolution's masquerade: its archaic revival of symbols from the Republican phase of the Roman Empire.[16] This tendency, taken to its extreme, views the culture of a community not as its "nonhereditary memory" but as a pristine essence to be repristinated, a foundation with biological or mystical force that determines history.

What is viable, then, in the notion of collective memory tends to be artistic rather than nationalistic, and unless we keep in mind this link between art and memory—recognized when the Greeks made Mnemosyne the mother of the Muses—national or ethnic politics will reduce culture to a tyrannous and frozen difference, a heroic narrative demanding consent.

—+—

A sense of the nation as vital to cultural memory arose in Romanticism. Throughout Europe artists and scholars tried to free literature from the yoke of "foreign" classics by retrieving (and counterfeiting if necessary!) a native tradition. This literary nationalism was often a reconstruction, motivated by visionary nostalgia. "A people who lose their nationality create a legend to take its place," Edwin Muir wrote about Walter Scott's attempt to carry on a tradition that had lost its continuity.[17] Even a strong nation-state like England sometimes did not seem English enough: Keats preferred Chatterton's Rowley poems (a forgery) to Chaucer because their English diction had less of a Norman admixture. The ideal culture, according to Romantic historicism, was produced by the spirit embodied in a people, a spirit of the folk (*Volksgeist*) that expressed the true, distinctive voice of each nation among the nations.

Collectors and antiquarians hunted for old stories, songs, and ballads: relics of a past now disappearing too quickly and to which popular or archaic strength was imputed. A lively interest arose for anything regional rather than cosmopolitan: the buzzwords were "local attachment," "local romance," even "local superstition." Hence Wordsworth's "Hart-Leap Well," a self-consciously recreated ballad, typical of a return to stories represented as an emanation of particular places—places impressed on the collective memory and still part of the imaginative life of ordinary people.[18]

These legends about place (close to genealogical and etiological myths) stretch back to the Bible and seem to reflect traces of a popular memory. Being topocentric—subordinating time to place—they also lessen our anxiety that the ancient rapport between singer and audience, or artist and community, may have broken down. Unlike the Athenians, Alasdair MacIntyre declares, "We lack ... *any* public, generally shared communal mode either for representing political conflict or for putting our politics to the philosophical question."[19] This panicky view shows how deep the nostalgia for a collective memory runs. Since it is indeed difficult to humanize modern urban spaces, to invest them with a historically charged sense of place, the picture arises of a storyless modern imagination moving from nonplace to nonplace, and even enjoying the anonymity of highways, airports, large hotels, and shopping malls. It looks as if each sacred memory-place (*lieu de memoire*) is emptied out to become what Marc Augé defines as a nowhere-place (*non-lieu*).[20] In reaction new myths arise: Michael Kammen in *Mystic Chords of Memory* wonders at "the remarkable way in which local events can be conceptualized to conform to paradigms of religious tradition or to the totally secular needs of a modern state struggling for existence."[21]

Before I discuss three recent literary ventures that respond to the challenge of reattaching imagination to the collective memory, or creating a communal story under modern conditions—conditions described in the introductory part of this essay—let me add a few words to define contemporary *public* memory in its difference from the traditional *collective* memory.

Maurice Halbwachs, killed in Buchenwald, viewed the collective memory as a "living deposit" preserved outside academic or written history. "In general," he writes in his posthumously published book, "history begins only at the point where tradition ends, at a moment where social memory is extinguished or decomposes.... The need to write the history of a period, a society, even of an individual does not arise until they are already too far removed in the past" for us to find many living witnesses.[22]

Although these lines were probably composed in the 1930s, they already seem dated, for today we feel a need to record everything, even as the event is occurring, and the media not only make this possible but encourage it. It is this nervous effervescence that marks modern experience and the rise of public memory in distinction from collective memory. The loss or subsumption of the past in the present, a present with very little presence beyond the spotlight moment of its occurrence—which wearies itself out of the mind by its violence or is almost immediately displaced by another such moment, sound bite, instantly fading image—this self-consuming present, both real and specious, vivid and always already a trace, is curiously like the collective memory in that it has, to quote the historian Yosef Yerushalmi, "not the historicity of the past but its eternal contemporaneity." (Yerushalmi offers the example that in Jewish liturgy the Khurban—destructions of the First and Second Temples—are conflated, as if they were the same Khurban, and the Holocaust is often assimilated as the third Khurban.) Of course, public memory is also utterly different: It strikes us as a bad simulacrum, one that, unlike the older type of communal or collective memory, has no stability or *durée*, only a jittery, mobile, perpetually changing yet permanently inscribed status.[23] Hence my opening question on what could focus public memory on the traumatic events it is busy recording.

Halbwachs's observation that we are motivated to write things down only when they are in danger of fading entirely can be made relevant to his own project: Today the collective memory is in this danger. Doubly so: It is weakened because public memory, with its frantic and uncertain agency, is taking its place, and because a politicized collective memory, claiming a biological or mystical permanence, tries to usurp the living tie between generations.[24]

With this remark we return to literature. One reason literature remains important is that it counteracts the impersonality and instability of public memory, on the one hand, and, on the other, the determinism and fundamentalism of a collective memory based on identity politics.[25] Literature creates an institution of its own, more personal and focused than public memory yet less monologic than the memorializing fables common to ethnic or nationalist affirmation. At the same time, because today the tie between generations, the "living deposit," or *passé vécu*, as Halbwachs calls it, is jeopardized, creative activity is often carried on under the negative sign of an *absent memory* (Ellen Fine) or *memoire trouée* (Henri Raczymow).[26] A missed encounter is evoked, through a strenuous, even cerebral exercise of the imagination, as if the link between memory and imagination had been lost.

I turn first to Toni Morrison's *Beloved*. Its epigraphs suggest not only a comparison between the political suffering of Blacks and Jews but also that the pathos and the covenant have passed to the former. One epigraph is a dedication: "Sixty million and more." The second alludes through a New Testament quotation to the concept of the Chosen People: "I will call them my people, which were not my people; and her beloved, which was not beloved" (Romans 9:25).

It is no exaggeration to call *Beloved* that people's *zakhor* ("Remember!"). Where in Black history is there something comparable to a genealogy of begats or the millennia of myths, chronicles, scriptures, and scriptural interpretations that characterize the collective memory of the Jews? (Concerning the begats, Julius Lester reminds us on the dedication page of *To Be a Slave* that "the ancestry of any black American can be traced to a bill of sale and no further. In many instances even that cannot be done," and John Edgar Wideman prefaces *Damballah* with "A Begat Chart" and a "Family Tree.")[27] African-American memory remains to be recovered. But more important still, *where is the conviction of being loved that makes memory possible?* What kind of story could have been passed on, or who stayed alive long enough to remember a suffering that destroyed those who might have recounted it, a suffering that allowed no development of person, family, or ethnic group? "Anyone Baby Suggs knew, let alone loved, who hadn't run off or been hanged, got rented out, loaned out, bought up, brought back, stored up, mortgaged, won, stolen or seized."[28]

Between Baby Suggs, or Grandma Baby as she is also called, and Beloved, the little girl killed by her mother, there is no growth or normal history or significant genealogy. The child whose life was aborted at less than two years old and who preternaturally reenters the mother's house as a young woman (now able to talk and carry on conversations of the most affectionate kind) is a ghost from folklore who expresses hauntingly the unlived life, a love that never could come to fulfillment except in this fantasy form. Morrison's startling use of the *revenant*, the spirit figure that returns in many a romantic ballad (a genre that itself needed "revival"), challenges us to a suspension of disbelief. Not so much, I would suggest, disbelief affecting the preternatural return of Beloved—for that partly pagan, partly Christian myth has "a foundation in humanity," as Wordsworth would have said[29]—but disbelief concerning the atrocities suffered by Black Americans, that ghost which we have not entirely faced.

African-American history discloses, then, in a novel like Morrison's, a special difficulty concerning its "absent memory." The subject of that history, the Black community, is so scattered by suffering, so "disremembered and unaccounted for," that the story to be passed on "is not a story to pass on," and Morrison can only represent it by a ghostly "devil-child," a fantasy-memory of the love or election this people has not known. In search of that reversal of fate, *Beloved* becomes a Song of Songs, the Shulamite's scripture.

My second example of absent memory is very different. The postmodern work of art, to which I now turn, cultivates that absence and does not seek to recover the very possibility of memory itself—of "rememory," as Morrison names it. Raymond Federman, for example, tries to do without resonant names and local romance in *To Whom It May Concern*, though he too, like Morrison, subverts an unfeeling realism. He uses gimmicks (as he admits) to fight "the imposture of realism, that ugly beast that stands at bay ready to leap in the moment you begin scribbling your fiction." He renounces realism even in a novel that recalls the great roundup and deportation of Jews from Paris in July 1942 and its impact on two children who escaped. His self-defeating venture takes courage from experiments starting with Sterne and Diderot, which portray life as an infinite detour rather than a punctual drama or epiphany: as something less than heroic, composed of accidents, small gestures, and simple, even insignificant words. Thus the *non-lieu* gains a sort of authenticity. "The grim story of Sarah and her cousin should be told without any mention of time and place. It should happen on a timeless vacant stage without scenery. No names of places. No decor. Nothing. It simply happened, sometime and somewhere."[30]

Federman is indebted to the New Novel that evolved in postwar France and such films as *Last Year at Marienbad*. They depict memory as a mode of seduction—as a narrative of past encounter suggesting that the human condition is so empty or forgetful, so deprived of sacred space (*lieu de memoire*) and therefore so needy, that it cannot be redeemed except by the construction and imposition of an imaginary history. This deliberate recourse to a perhaps fictional past returns us, of course, to the province of the collective memory, except that *Marienbad* seeks to erode the latter's historical and nationalist pretensions (the Versailles-like decor in the film is meant to be only that, a decor) in favor of the private, imaginative needs of one man and one woman. Federman, like Resnais or Robbe-Grillet, refuses to give his characters more memory than they have. The wound of an absence remains. In this he speaks for an entire postwar generation that lost parents or relatives, while they themselves missed the brunt of the war. "They suffered from not suffering enough," he writes of his escaped children.[31]

My last example is a genre that in documentaries like *Eyes on the Prize* or Lanzmann's *Shoah* or the witness accounts in Yale's Video Archive for Holocaust Testimonies is also oriented toward an "absent memory." Personal testimony has long been a significant part of both religious and secular literature and is usually considered a type of autobiography. Videotaped oral testimony, however, is partly a creation of modern technology and so has a chance of influencing that environment. As history it seeks to convey information, but as oral witness it is an act of remembrance. And as this spoken and more spontaneous mode, which can be recorded without being written down, it contributes to a group biography through highly individual yet convergent stories. The collective memory thus becomes a collected memory (James Young), at once a private and a public legacy, and through video itself counters video's dispersive flow.

Each testimony is potentially an act of rescue, as the Israeli poet Haim Gouri observed when covering the Eichmann trial: a rescue "from the danger of [survivors] being perceived as all alike, all shrouded in the same immense anonymity."[32] Moreover, by recording an experience collectively endured, by allowing anyone in the community a voice—that is, not focusing on an elite—a vernacular and many-voiced dimension is caught.[33] Memory collected this way is too plural and diverse to be politicized or sacralized. I can characterize the genre of these testimonies best, and the Archive of Conscience they are building, by saying that they accept the *presence* of memory, however painful, rather than its absence.[34]

The amnesia that invades characters in postmodernist fiction (think of the difference between Beckett and Proust), creating a limbo in which the tape of memory starts and crashes, again and again—this amnesia may reflect a public memory that has become primarily space instead of place, anonymous, and occupied by shifting and impersonal networks of information. As memory, then, it is purely virtual if not absent. In oral testimonies, however, a burdened recollection asserts itself and fashions a complex relation to the rupture between the positivism of historical experience and the symbolic stores of collective memory. Not only do memory's informative and performative (or ritual) functions try to unite again, but time present, in these testimonies, becomes more than a site of loss or nostalgic recuperation: more than the place that reveals that our capacity to experience has diminished or that the past must be forgotten to be survived.[35]

Even if memory, as Rimbaud said of love, has always to be reinvented, this does not alter the truth that some kinds of memory are better than others. Though Plato suggested that writing would be harmful to recollection, it proved essential for transmitting thought, both in manuscript and print. Writing a thing down meant passing it on, for a communal or generational recipient. But who is the addressee of the new electronic writing, with its capacity for nearly instantaneous reception and transmission? Every TV program is implicitly addressed "To Whom It May Concern," which begs the question of who *must* be concerned.

Videotaped oral history is an important compromise, because it comes on the cusp between generations, addresses those still growing up, and at a time when the collective memory is fading into the quasi-timeless, panoramic simultaneity of public memory. From Abel Gance and Walter Benjamin to Jean Baudrillard, this impact of technology on memory-institutions such as art and history has been a subject of intense reflection. I have emphasized the difficulty, moral as well as cognitive, of responding to the images before our eyes in a critical or affective manner when the audiovisual mode becomes ineluctable and bypasses or floods time-bound channels of personal memory.[36]

I have also suggested that there is such a thing as memory-envy. It shows itself in writers who seek to recover an image of their community's past—a past deliberately destroyed by others or not allowed to form itself into a heritage. Memory-envy also touches a generation that feels belated: the "generation after" that did not participate directly in a great event that determined their parents' and perhaps grandparents' lives. Memory is lacking in both cases as a basis for the integrity of a person or group. At the level of the collective, moreover, memory-envy can take the form of foundation narratives, myths of origin that fortify group identity. Some of these decisive but also imposed identity-fictions must be labeled false memories.

Increasingly, politicized and simplified aspects of the collective memory take over from an actual artistic heritage. We still have the arts, and literature in particular, to recall that each of us is a being made of many beings and that the heritage of the past is pluralistic and diverse. But as the collective memory weakens, political religions (Eric Voegelin's name for totalitarian regimes) falsify the complexity of the past and cultivate an official story that seeks to reawaken ancient hatreds. This falsified memory, with its foundation myths, or fundamentalist notions of national destiny and ethnic purity, is the enemy. We cannot allow it to masquerade as history, as is happening with the Pamyat movement in Russia, the attempt to rehabilitate Tiso in Slovakia, and nationalistic nostalgia, whether in Bosnia or the Middle East. The outbreak of unreal memory can be fought, but only if younger bystanders, whether artists or scholars, bring testimony of their own, ballads of their own, before our eyes. And only if, like the Caribbean poet Derek Walcott, they accept the scarred rather than sacred, the fragmented rather than holistic nature of what he names "epic memory," which has to be recomposed—performed—again and again. For oral tradition, however monumental its aspiration, remains an art of assemblage. To reconstruct "this shipwreck of fragments, these echoes, these shards of a huge tribal vocabulary, these partially remembered customs," needs a special love. "Nothing can be sole or whole / That has not been rent," Yeats's Crazy Jane tells the Bishop. "Break a vase," says Walcott, "and the love that reassembles the fragments is stronger than the love that took its symmetry for granted when it was whole."[37]

11. Shoah Literature: The Universal Aspect

I want to move away from the recent emphasis on historical and generational differences and back toward transgenerational, transnational, and even universal aspects. One way of doing so is to concentrate on the difficulty of defining (or defending) the *generic* importance of imaginative literature, with Shoah literature as an exemplary case. Can fiction dealing with the Holocaust be justified, despite the fact that contemporary as well as later witness accounts yield more than enough pity and terror? Does that fiction have a truth of its own to supplement, even if it cannot match, the unrelenting detail and barely tolerable depictions produced by testimony and historical research?

The Shoah has revived, through its very shock and specificity, a distinction always evoked by creative writing: that between truth and "truthiness" (Oprah's word for verisimilitude), between "vrai" and "vraisemblable" (Jorge Semprún) or "vrai" and "veridique" (Charlotte Delbo).[1] Aharon Appelfeld confirms the importance of that distinction, as it arises from a deadly realm where everything tended toward the unbelievable rather than, as is sometimes claimed, the unrepresentable. Though his subject is the Holocaust, Appelfeld does not dilate imagination but restrains it. "Everything was so unbelievable that one seemed oneself to be fictional.... If I remained true to fact, no one would believe me.... I had to remove those parts that were unbelievable from 'the story of my life' and present a more credible version."[2]

Briefly stated, literature's truth must induce belief, or at least a willing suspension of disbelief. Aristotle's *Poetics* stipulates that art must have probability, a word that points not to a statistical criterion but to the human heart, to a wisdom based on human nature. The trouble in the extreme case of the Shoah is that the events constituting it are so callous and inhumane that they may produce sentiments of incredulity rather than probability. However irrefutable the evidence, the offense to memory is so great that we practice various evasions. We become, as Lawrence Langer says, deflective rather than reflective.

Knowledge in this domain, whether derived from history or from literature, is deeply hurtful because it slanders our humanity, our species-image. One cannot expect, therefore, that the young, and even the mature, will easily overcome their disbelief, some sense of exaggeration and propaganda. How believable as nonfiction fiction is the opening of Jakov Lind's "Soul of Wood": "Those who had no papers entitling them to live, lined up to die."[3] Lind steals the tonal matter-of-factness of fables to make us think it is a fable. For a moment the awfulness of the reality is suspended. As both teachers and critics, we have to recognize that in addition to the negationists' malicious denial there is also a doubt that is not malicious, and we try to find means whereby, in the face of that period's extremity, a willingness to hear and respond can be developed instead of denial or deflection.

—+—

Let us, then, begin to deal with this issue by not underestimating either the intelligent distrust or the psychological defenses roused when people are confronted by the extraordinary brutalities of genocide and the enormity of the attempt to exterminate every Jew, or other person in a designated ethnic, racial, or religious group. An additional shock comes on learning about the complicity of so many professionals and educators—"Hitler's professors," as Max Weinreich called them—who colluded with *Rassenwissenschaft*, the pseudoscience of race and ideological basis of the killings.[4]

The problems of reception in this area are enormous. Even if, in dealing with defenses against a devastating knowledge and a blatant breach of civilized values, art is capable of evoking a powerful emotional and intellectual response, this will not be effective unless we are prepared to accept such a response also in the *classroom* and place it in the service of research and reflection. But does academic hygiene presently permit literary study to be more than a specialized training in reading skills and a utilitarian rhetoric seasoned by empathic expressions of horror and regret?

This "more than specialized training" need not imply a diversion from literary competence by an overlay of political, ethnic, or moral sentiments. It suggests, rather, a return to qualities that keep literature a necessity for culture. We may hesitate to apply to literature about the Shoah formalistic categories of analysis. Yet it was precisely the simplicity and relative coolness of such categories that strengthened their value vis-à-vis the great tragedies of ancient Greece and allowed Aristotle in his *Poetics* to establish universal criteria. It is illuminating, for example, to read Renata Lachmann on Danilo Kiš and glimpse in his oeuvre an operative poetics that makes one think Holocaust literature may contain works of art that have a chance of being compared with the most significant productions of the past.[5]

Indeed, despite the pain aroused by its subject, Holocaust literature requires a measure of detachment in the critical observer as well as the author. How else can it be transmitted and keep us returning to events that, being too real, tend to be repressed or tabooed? "In Auschwitz," Hans Jonas declared, "more was real than is possible."[6]

Not that the literary arts ever had an easy time confronting what is impossible, including impossibly real. Their *serio ludere*, however, their serious play, may lend a sort of credence, a semblance of probability, to almost anything. In seventeenth-century France, Boileau gave his reluctant admiration to art for fashioning "monstres agréables." He is careful, at the same time, to make a distinction. While accepting the monster-marvels of pagan fable, he objects to their admixture with sacred Christian verities. One set of impossibilities could be played with and moralized; the other was isolated as a mystery too sacred for fiction.[7] Today purists argue that the Shoah should be kept free of any sort of imaginary treatment, especially when depicting its most terrible phase, for which we still use the tainted euphemism "Final Solution."

The Shoah, it must be emphasized, confronts us with monstrosities that evoke feelings of improbability stronger than those arising from impossibility. They are stronger because, while we accept hippogriffs, batmen, spidermen (or women), assorted vampire villains, and other venerable or newfangled monsters that transgress the laws of nature—accept them as long as they instill a truth of the heart—we do not accept transgressions perverting that truth. To build a New Order, as Nazism aimed to do, on a raison d'état that embraces murder, torture, and enslavement, to justify and even take pleasure in these, is to mutate the image we have of our species.

Terence's famous dictum—often inspiring art—that "Nothing human is alien to me" is challenged by the Holocaust's limit-experience.[8] The atrocities committed are so grave that the human image cannot be saved. Writers are reduced to employing stylization, indirectness, or impotent if ironic voiceovers. So Paul Celan's "Der Tod ist ein Meister aus Deutschland" ("Death is a master-artist from Germany") mimics Nazi boasts celebrating a sinister achievement.[9] The masterpiece created by a nation of "Dichter und Denker" (poets and thinkers) was mass murder ennobled and systematically carried out. By means of the concentration camp's alternative world, Nazism reinforced its self-image as master race and imposed the most shameful form of death on those it declared to be subhuman.

Controversy, then, about the possibility of a truly realistic portrayal of the Holocaust will continue because the artists involved have to project a view of human behavior different from what the mind can accept and the heart tolerate. Yet mobilizing the imaginative force latent in their medium, they seek to overcome these difficulties of reception. That is why Imre Kertész remarks provocatively: "The concentration camp is imaginable only and exclusively as literature, never as reality."[10]

I am suggesting that Aristotle's criterion of probability has been injured by the Shoah; this, moreover, may have caused collateral damage to fiction generally. It is harder than ever to define fiction's type of truthfulness. (Think of the implication of a new literary category called a "nonfiction novel.") Also harder to apply is a related criterion, that of decorum.

Literary decorum can be understood as an art of distancing. That is, of creating space for a nonescapist thoughtfulness in both author and audience. Decorum in art is not an abstract quality or a byproduct of social etiquette. When Kertész enters the quarrel about Roberto Benigni's *Life Is Beautiful*, which he defends as a fable with its own raison d'être, he is also defending the rights of fable, even of comedy, and so relies on a sense of that genre's decorum.

Now *Life Is Beautiful* is not a great film, and some of Benigni's comments on his own work are inane. The movie's second part, about the deportation and the camp, cannot be compared, as he claims, to a tragedy. It remains within the parameters of comedy; at best it might be called a tragic farce. We have to reject Benigni's comment. The film, relying on comedy's subversive logic, does not ask us to believe that the father's benevolent deceit masking the camp's reality could have succeeded: While defying credibility, the unreal scenes Benigni invents are only as outrageous and incredible as we know the real death camps to have been. The father's game, moreover, saves the euphemistic vision that keeps hope alive in the eyes of a child. What is staged by Benigni is "a kind of terrible childishness," a desperate remnant of hope or trust.[11]

The decorum involved, therefore, is that the film hews almost till its end to a venerable definition of comedy as a story with perilous complications that do not terrify, that do not provoke fear of death. The comic genre assumes that even if the clown dies, the worst returns to laughter—"Holocaust laughter," as Terrence Des Pres courageously named it some years ago.[12] Comedy's gymnastics and gyrations, its confusions and improvisations, by recalling human resilience as well as human folly, relax and vitalize its audience. We seem suddenly to have many lives, many chances to escape from the noose of the plot.

In general the amount of license permitted depends on the chosen literary genre. In older theories of decorum, subject matter and type of style were correlated. Tragedy demanded a high style, though Shakespeare's genius got away with interspersed "low comedy" episodes. The pure high style, as in neoclassical French tragedy, did not permit coarse words or coarse episodes, let alone the direct depiction of death on stage. A scene like that in *Hamlet*, where Prince and Gravedigger test their wits against each other, so that not only mortality but an uncontrolled, perhaps uncontrollable verbal dexterity levels high and low—"equivocation will undo us," the Prince remarks—that kind of scene is unthinkable under the rules of the *genera dicendi*.[13] Today, breaches of stylistic decorum or a mix of genres are standard fare, so it is not possible to prescribe an exclusively high-serious treatment for certain events.[14] Hence an emotional as well as ethical reason for the wish to insulate the Holocaust from fiction.

Some of the most interesting stories, in any case, like Carl Friedman's *Nightfather* or Motek's imaginings in David Grossman's *See Under: Love*, have a built-in comic effect based on children trying to make sense of secretive hints or on words and events remaining unintelligible because their frame of reference is missing. This comic incongruence is especially noticeable in second-generation fiction about the Holocaust.

Comedy, moreover, does not necessarily moderate outrage. Yet it can serve to describe childlike perceptions that continue to be recorded by writers of the survivor generation who were children when disaster struck.[15] If "the suction hole of unreason," characteristic of Holocaust atrocity, disables the standard logic of storytelling, and we cannot make decently rational what is obscenely irrational, then a childlike perspective or the acceptance of a grotesque logic are both not just powerful defensive reactions but renderings of an accommodation to what was the only reality the youngsters knew and had to survive.[16]

There is, in short, a generational factor, but it is not decisive. The same goes for the ethnic factor, when we consider the element of the comic, or grotesque, that already enters Tadeusz Borowski's *This Way for the Gas, Ladies and Gentlemen* (1946). Here too a camp inmate (not fictive, however, as in Benigni's movie) retains some tenderness and humor, even if his life is imperiled all the time. True, as a non-Jew Borowski is not automatically condemned to death; for him too, nevertheless, a misstep, a Kapo's word, and death follows. The possibility, also, of maintaining an innocent vision or a pre-Holocaust state of mind is totally excluded: compared to *Life Is Beautiful*, Borowski's stories are much more complex, shifting with surprising ease from straight-faced irony to disgust at aesthetic idealization. The tone is essentially that of an observer who maintains a measure of autonomy as he sees the human comedy acted out even in a deadly milieu.

I turn now specifically to generational issues affecting literature and witness accounts in the postwar years. Here too—unfortunately this time—a universal dimension enters, a malignant or "schlechte Unendlichkeit" (bad infinity). For the Holocaust has not turned out to be the genocide to end all genocides. In fact, at this point in time, insistence on its uniqueness produces bitter awareness of a repetition. The historical circumstances or motives of each genocidal occurrence are different, the scope and duration are different, but the extreme brutality and suffering are overwhelmingly the same.

The fact, also, that the Shoah was extensively recorded, given the arrogant documentation of the perpetrators as well as a courageous "*schreib un verschreib*," the "Write it all down!" said to have been addressed to the victims by the historian Dubnov, distinguishes the Shoah from previous genocides. Through the writings of eyewitnesses and "secondary witnesses" still in touch with eyewitness testimony, we learn something about the lasting resonance of a collective trauma of this kind.

Still in search of criteria, I come back to Aristotle, who said that "poetry" was more universal than "history." This judgment can be tested by reading two poets, close in age, yet whose historical situation is quite different. Since both have achieved a certain exemplarity, there surely is a universal as well as generational element in the literary response to Shoah literature.

Irving Feldman is a secondary witness: a native of the United States, not a survivor then, yet conscious of the enormity of what happened. Dan Pagis, two years younger, and who died in 1986, came to Israel as a survivor from the Bukovina camp shortly after the war. He developed into a distinguished literary scholar as well as poet.

When we read in Feldman's "To the Six Million,"

> Survivor, who are you?
> ask the voices who disappeared,
> the faces broken and expunged.
> I am the one who was not there....

and

> Should I have been with them
> on other winter days in the snow
> of the camps and the ghettoes?
> And on the days of their death that was
> the acrid Polish air? ...

> Here on the struggle-ground, impostor
> of a death, I survive reviving[17]

we recognize the inheritor of a void who "revives" the dead as ghostly interlocutors. So many families were decimated in the Holocaust that the injury suffered becomes an injury to recollection itself. The identity quest that follows can become dangerous, even pathological, as a suicidal Esther illustrates in Henri Raczymow's *Un cri sans voix* (*Writing the Book of Esther*). More generally, there is a need to research Jewishness, to try it on, as it were, so that Austria's Robert Schindel, for instance, both exemplifies and resists the complex psychic state Alain Finkielkraut has characterized as the "imaginary Jew." "To tell the truth," Schindel confesses, "My roots are foreign to me."[18] Yet the effort of remembrance in the generations-after, in what has been named postmemory, retains its persistence precisely because it is not a memory based on personal and direct witness. An artificial recollection recovers details about, and even identifies with, the life and death of those who disappeared.[19]

Feldman's secondary witness leaves a clear mark on his poems. Historical research, with its cumulus of documents and facts, cannot by itself fill an emotional void. Fiction (or faction) remains essential for a reparative quest that wishes to bring home to others that an entire culture was decimated, together with millions of individuals. It is through feats of the artistic imagination that we come into the presence of absent figures culled from the emptiness and on whom art, often aided by miraculously preserved chronicles of the *hurban*, bestows an identity: that "solidity of specification" which alone satisfies a modern realism, according to Henry James.[20]

Feldman's "To the Six Million" is unusual because it has few topical references and does not lean on authenticating fragments from eyewitness texts, as is customary in many postmemory poets.[21] His poem is a general lament whose most telling moments come when it incorporates verses from the Song of Songs that underwrite Feldman's own feelings of loss. Like the Shulamite in search of the "one whom my soul loves," the poet strays through the emptied streets of his imagination, seeking to find what he cannot find. It is incongruous, this analogy between the poet's post-Holocaust quest and that of the Shulamite, but also powerful, recalling another, more sacred identification of her voice as collectively Israel's own.

Dan Pagis's "The Roll Call" is also focused on absence and emptiness. Evoking in a strangely whimsical way the camps' daily torture ritual of the *Appell*, the speaker suddenly subtracts himself from the count: "only I / am not there, am not there, am a mistake, turn off my eyes, quickly, erase my shadow [*tseli*]."²² Suggested is either his mental flight from a painful memory—after the poet has failed to transfigure it—or a still deeper evasion, one from existence into nothingness.

Pagis conveys a complex mental state through a minimum of words. (The difference in this regard between his and Feldman's more expansive poetry is striking.) His preference for laconism and riddle matches his attempt at self-elision. One might have expected a greater emphasis on realistic eyewitness detail (some of Charlotte Delbo's cruelest depictions of camp life center on the *Appell*), yet Pagis focuses solely on the victim's self-disparaging state of mind. To call the officer in charge of the roll call a "diligent angel" is a peculiar euphemism for that *malakh ha-mavet*, while the narrator's "I am a mistake," *ani ta'ut* in Hebrew (playing on the banal telephone reply "wrong number," apt also because the camp inmate has been reduced to a number), normalizes the scene against all odds through this colloquialism and points to a disturbing self-erasure, reinforced by the word *tsel*.

In Pagis's "Testimony," which is specifically about the victim's mental state in the camps, *tsel* echoes *tselem*, image, used in Genesis where mankind is created "in the image of God." The victim allows himself a macabre joke: He apologizes for smoking, as he sees himself ascending "smoke to omnipotent smoke." The magnificently booted SS officers are made "in the image"; as for him, "A different creator made me." The speaker expresses once more a subversive current of abjection, *then* (in the camp) or *now* (having survived the camp). Does this survivor still wish to survive?

"Roll Call" ends on a mood indeterminate between abjection and acceptance: "I shall not want. The sum will be all right / without me: here forever."²³ "I shall not want," a phrase that seems to say "I shall not be missed," is taken from Psalm 23, "The Lord is my shepherd, I shall not want," a hymn of absolute trust and faith. Pagis's reversal of the phrase's meaning is not ordinary poetic irony, since his continued metaphor of counting and accountability is anchored in a Hebrew whose everyday use is still so recent that its sacred ancestry cannot be voided. While a relatively young vernacular Hebrew poetry grows strong in its very admixture of sacred and colloquial, the poet himself comes close to abnegating his own existence. An impersonality principle common to the poetics of the prewar modernists combines with an abnegation whose motive stems from the entirely different realm of racial persecution. The one who speaks the poem almost disappears into the final ambiguity of "here forever."

"Here"? "Forever"? Does this mean the speaker is still in the camp, doomed by memory to remain there, forever unliberated? Is the "diligent angel" (a phrase that transfigures the perpetrator and almost defeats irony) the executor of a divine judgment? Or does the survivor already dwell somewhere else, in the kind of peace and security that Psalm 23 ("The Lord is my shepherd ... he leadeth me to green pastures") evokes? In view of that indeterminacy, the "here" may suggest that poetry's heterocosm is the survivor's only world: his *olam*, his sole refuge. Whereas Feldman mobilizes the Song of Songs to inspire and bear him up, to save a poetry that hovers in dejection over the deep facelessness of a collective loss, Pagis guards his tongue, shepherds every word: not cursing but not blessing either, nor even seeking a blessing.

———+———

In a postwar culture where testimony, memoir, and biography play an increasingly major role, why is modernist impersonality still so influential? It is essential to note, in this respect, that the poetics of impersonality is not the same after as before the Holocaust. Paul Celan and Dan Pagis, while accepting the necessity to speak as witnesses, are more deeply affected than any prewar modernist could have been by the Shoah's depersonalizing and shaming events—shaming both with respect to their individual fate and their general regard for humanity. Indeed, these poets were so deeply affected that speech is inhibited at its source.[24] They nevertheless do not give it up but struggle to open the way to "un langage autre" (Maurice Blanchot), one that resists falling into what Adorno denounced as "verruchte Affirmation," a shameful attraction to the contaminating event.

To the writers already singled out I should add Ilse Aichinger, the most radical stylist of them all, except for Celan. Her prose is often a tissue of "widerständige[n] Texturen" (resistant and resistance textures).[25] In Aichinger's "The Angel" (1963) the writer actually mentions a Sophie who can only be the Sophie Scholl of the "White Rose" resistance, also calling her "Bianca" and introducing a Fate-like figure who weaves an uncooptable lifestyle.

After the Shoah, then, the eyewitnesses, whether victims or bystanders, had to respect their own survival, avoid overidentifying with their past, and so they create a distance between themselves and their experience. Fiction is not fabulation for them: Its discipline helped, if at all, the founding of a persona, the recovery of a precarious faith in communication, in a "Thou," or what Maurice Halbwachs called an "affective community." The poetics of impersonality are adapted to that end.

Today, however, we perceive the growing prevalence of a different problematic distancing. Now "Distance itself is at stake."[26] While that distance was previously achieved through psychological diversion and formalistic techniques, now the issue of authenticity becomes acute. A double or even triple distance must be respected—and overcome. Adding to the distance felt by the secondary witness, there is the sentiment shared by many writers of having abandoned or even betrayed the world of their fathers and mothers: After one or two generations that distance already feels "historical." For among many of these writers orthodox Jewishness itself becomes secondary. The Holocaust, however haunting, only deepens an unbridgeable distance. Study and awareness of the catastrophe cannot fill that void—especially when history, moving on, modifies the *hurban*'s aura of uniqueness. For the after-generations, Auschwitz is not necessarily the black sun at the center of the baleful and barely comprehensible universe it revealed. (This despite the fact that a realism rivalrous with Holocaust reality continues, even intensifies, especially in the cinema: Consider such films as Spielberg's *Schindler's List* and Polanski's *The Pianist*.)[27] Often that center is partially displaced or else accompanied by different trauma, so that the Shoah is only one of two foci in an elliptical structure. "Hatikvah" too, the hope for hope, has to be rehabilitated once the state of Israel reenters Jewish history as a complex fate rather than the place of a happy homecoming.[28]

―――+―――

I read, recently, a translation of Igal Sarna's *Makom shel Osher* (translated into English as *The Man Who Fell Into a Puddle*). Sarna is a hunter of memories, and some of his short stories are about Shoah survivors. He comes close to Sebald in the care with which delayed consequences are depicted, but he is also more forthright, a left-wing Israeli journalist surrounded by influxes of disaster. "The Itzbiskys," he writes, naming a family of survivors and their descendants, "were exterminated after the war, by a bomb on a fifty-year timer."[29] That bomb is memory's delayed action.

I turn, however, to the final story in Sarna's book. It concerns Ezra Angel, who spent nine years in Syrian captivity. When repatriated, this tortured prisoner, a shell of his former self, is confined in psychiatric hospitals, shuttled from one to the other, subjected to drugs, doomed by being labeled a madman. His official as well as personal identity has been all but erased when a niece finally gains his discharge.

Sarna's first reaction to Ezra adverts to the present: Interviewing this broken man the investigative journalist "felt positively ensnared, because here is stark evidence of a dark chamber that exists even in a democratic country where everything is ostensibly well-lit and open."[30] In democracies too people disappear, "bearing erroneous labels, erased from life, and their cries were not—were never—heard." Then the Holocaust analogy shows itself. Ezra is under the care of a psychiatrist in Beersheba named Bastiaans.

He turns out to be the son of the famous Dutch psychiatrist Jan Bastiaans, who, from the 1960s on, experimented controversially with psychotropic drugs that treated Holocaust and Japanese camp survivors by inducing them to relive the scene of their trauma. When Bastiaans the younger learns about Ezra, he thought, we are told, "that the long and cruel imprisonment and the endless period of hospitalization were similar to cases of Holocaust survivors" and "that to save him was like saving a Holocaust survivor."[31] Bastiaans and his assistant had seen many with similar symptoms who returned from the dead, from Nazi camps and prisons, humiliated, terrified, made into zombies, basically unable to show any emotion.

Pedagogical Coda. There has been an outpouring of fictional works on the Holocaust, in addition to essays, memoirs, and meditations. They should not be ignored; they are not ignored. The argument for teaching such literature comes from the very fact that it exists. What we must not do, however, is abandon our usual standards, our critical questioning of the value of particular texts because of a regard for their sensitive and highly charged content. Some doubtless think that studying Shoah literature is part of a dutiful imperative to perpetuate the memory of the victims. But the challenge to our discipline is separate from that imperative. It is to understand how literature and art have engaged through the ages with the extreme, with what is traumatic, scarcely bearable, and this source of a dejection is difficult to lift when we remember that mankind in aspect and action is supposed to express the "human form divine," *imago dei*. To maintain in our studies a principle of hope, to understand the seventh candle or a white rose placed alongside the six memorial candles at a Yom Hashoah ceremony, is an ever-present obligation.

12. Defining a Living Genre: The Survivor Testimony

Distinctions

In the past, I have often talked of survivor testimony as a new genre, especially when in videotape. But a genre of what? Of autobiography? Of memorialization? Of communication more generally?

The classification game, while thought-provoking, cannot as yet be clarifying. The reason is that the survivor testimony, as part of oral documentation, is quite recent. In its written form, of course, it goes back to slave narratives and other accounts of bare survival. In the era of audio and videotape, and amid large-scale genocidal persecution, survivor testimonies were first gathered systematically by David Boder. He used wire-recorded interviews in displaced person camps shortly after World War II. So we still need both a better ear-on knowledge of such interviews and a more thorough understanding of their frame conditions.[1] A careful definition of testimony in this developing context bears on our mode of study itself, on how we receive and value these records, made more immediate and affecting by technological magic.[2] I will discuss the work of Yale's Fortunoff Archive for Holocaust Testimonies, but my remarks should be applicable to any oral documentation effort in this era of genocides.

Frame Conditions

While Holocaust testimonies have an unusually direct emotional impact, their relation to the realities they describe is mediated by an array of factors. Boder recorded survivors in their native tongue; later, many witnesses speak in the acquired language of new, postwar homelands. Their speech is often that of exiles caught up by an involuntary displacement. At moments, the survivors may even feel exiled from language itself. There is also a displacement in time—the recording of testimonies is often delayed; a regard for cultural differences must enter significantly. Experience of the aftermath, of the period between liberation and taping the testimony, becomes part of the testimonial event. These displacements—from home, in time, and often into a different language—create a variable memory milieu, even if, as cognitive psychologists like Robert Kraft have shown, it is very probable that a core of original memories subsists unmodified. The variability of the memory milieu, in any case, is significant enough to create a humanistic field of study independent of physiologic research into the operations of memory, especially memory under stress.

History and Testimony, Poetics and Testimony

Until quite recently, Holocaust witness accounts were treated mainly as death stories and mined for perpetrator data. But they are also life stories with their own expressive integrity. Before the wave of these recordings, moreover, and despite the important Federal Writers Project of the late '30s and early '40s (which produced a populist oral history focusing on memories of the Great Depression), historians were slow to appreciate "history from below," wary of evidence offered by people who were not highly educated or did not belong to an influential elite.

The expansion of the historian's perspective, leading to accreditation of the orally recorded experience of individuals whatever their status or station in life, may have made more progress over the last half century than poetics has. Poetics too should become, in this matter, more than a selectively applied scholarly resource. It should foreground rather than neglect the colloquial and often spontaneous diction of the testimonies, even their sometimes semi-inarticulate character. Especially in the context of the Holocaust, witnesses go beyond reportage and transmit not only factual but also intensely burdened autobiographical stories, whose natural metaphors or imaginative condensations capture our attention.

Consider the resonance of the word *coupure* in the following testimony. "A woman tells of her experiences arriving at Auschwitz. The scene is notorious: bloodcurdling shouts, nightmare, the pajamas, the elegance of the SS, dogs. After a journey already fatal for a part of the mass packed into the wagons, she tells us that at a certain moment she passed into 'another state' (*un second état*) marked by dissociation and numbness. But when, exactly, did this happen? In the wagons, on arrival at the camp, at some point afterwards? She hesitates, then decides that it happened when her long and beautiful hair was brutally cut off. It was then, she says, that she experienced a 'cut' (*une coupure nette*) between the person she had been and the camp prisoner."[3]

A simplification occurs if too much emphasis is placed on narrative continuity, even when that is necessary to establish a chronology of the genocide or provide evidence that a survivor's core self still subsists, having integrated traumatic memories. Both of these interests are perfectly legitimate, but should the desire for coherence result in an exclusive emphasis on the narrative and quasi-cinematic element, it runs the risk not only of dulling the testimonies' texture and flash but also of eliding the relation between language patterns and psychology, an interest that motivated Boder, as well as Victor Klemperer's voluminous diaries.

A further issue arises because the rectification of distortions and other memory lapses is intrinsic to history as a discipline. When that hygiene becomes predominant in the analysis of witness accounts, as if their sole value were historical veracity, other dimensions are lost.

Narrative medicine too, as a recent and important addition to medical school curricula, is not exempt from the tendency to essentialize the narrative function. The latter does broaden the perspective of physicians who elicit, for both humane and diagnostic reasons, the life story of the patient. It may even, by making the patient more participatory, have a beneficial effect on both patient and physician. Yet the experimental evidence we have, in the case of Holocaust witnesses, does not definitively support the hope that telling about their experience (the "social sharing of emotional events") will provide a significant benefit.[4] The hope, nevertheless, it will do so draws attention to the fact that oral testimony about extreme events is not just another informative medium. It is a courageous effort to overcome silence. What is effective, as I will stress later on, is a sense *in* the witnesses that they are being listened to, that there is at least a *possibility* of "social sharing."

In this area, then, the appearance of communication is never free from crucial questions about the actual communicability of traumatic suffering and the need of the survivors *to converse with themselves as well as others*.[5] With themselves, because, very often, there had been no adequate recipient, or because something still all too present, all too oppressive, has to be relegated to the past, separated off, shunted to a crypt. "When one cannot turn to a 'you,'" Dori Laub remarks justly, "one cannot say 'Thou' even to oneself. The Holocaust created in this way a world in which one *could not bear witness even to oneself.*"[6]

Testimony and Trauma

Despite the inconclusive evidence already mentioned, does testimonial remembering contribute to recovery from a traumatized self; could it be considered, at least, as Dori Laub also suggests, a step toward resocialization?

Aleida Assmann makes a challenging remark, in defining the video testimony as a new genre. She points out that while in autobiography "memories are collected and selected in such a way that they can be integrated to construct and support a biography, in the case of these Video Testimonies, memories do the very opposite: they shatter the biographical frame."[7]

I agree with that, yet we should not deny that the testimony process can be enabling. It encourages the survivors to recover, by telling their story, a sense of being persons again, a sense of inner control, of coping with their memories after their death-immersion. A good interview frees them to speak in their own voice rather than through the proxy of impersonal narrators, and they address, via such self-representation, a maieutic listener rather than a phantom audience. Hence, while the interface of poetics and trauma studies needs to be explored beyond any easy assumption of a personal narrative's healing effect, there is hope for that healing insofar as the testimony interview stimulates the possibility of dialogue, of sharing even a traumatic experience with others and (however paradoxical this sounds) with oneself.

This dialogue does not always occur on the spot, during the interview. Sometimes there is silence, and sometimes the release felt by witnesses is such that they will talk much more openly than they have done before, so that many testimonies become a barely interrupted series of monologues. At the same time, the very presence of interlocutors who represent the contrary of a world that was indifferent or silent during the Holocaust conveys a sense of civic responsibility. It allows interviewer and interviewee to form a testimonial alliance aimed at making public awareness of the genocide a reality.

De-delimiting Subjectivity

Holocaust testimony remains personal and "subjective" even when a great number of converging accounts have been recorded. Objectivity is not an exclusive aim. There is a performative as well as informative dimension to the testimonies. Despite well-known types of error, such as the conflation of incidents or the retroactive blending-in of what was revealed in print or movie afterward, each witness account places us in the presence of an individual, communicates something of the original impact of what was experienced, retrieves in the spontaneous flow of the interview forgotten episodes, and is generally unafraid of the emotional aura.

The spirit in which the testimony interview is conducted plays a crucial role in achieving this result. It should respect the witnesses by not taking away their initiative, by resorting, for example, to a questionnaire for the sake of pursuing a research agenda. Ideally, the open-ended interview used at Yale is supposed never to interrupt ongoing trains of thought in order to follow set questions. (It does make sure, though, that, in addition to the persecution, the time before and after is covered.) The aim of the interview is to release all memories, including those latent or dissociated.

To this end the interview's support structure fosters an atmosphere that is the contrary of an interrogation. It includes a sympathetic questioner who is not an on-screen presence, so that the testimony-giver remains at the center. (This is very different from the not always admirable example of Lanzmann's highly visible, domineering presence in his film *Shoah*.) Moreover, as has already been suggested, each testimony addresses itself to a double recipient. Directly to the interviewer but also—by a reflexiveness that usually remains implicit—to themselves, those who are testifying, to survivor-narrators whose sense of identity has been shaken, sometimes so radically that corroboration and self-acceptance are still needed.

An urgent and related motive for testifying often mentioned by the persecuted is their concern for the disappearance of the eyewitness generation and, consequently, it is feared, an attrition of the collective memory of the Holocaust. Every survivor becomes, at some level of consciousness, the last—the only remaining—witness. Each is, as in Job, the "I alone have escaped to tell thee." Sporadic moments of despair arise, expressed by admonitory variants of "Has the world learned anything?" I surmise, then, like Dori Laub, that the testimonies extend the hands of speech beyond the interviewer toward a less defined but necessary other, akin to Paul Celan's intimate yet ghostly "Du" ("Thou") that evokes a listener who might remove the solitariness of those not-listened-to.

The Task of the Interpreter

I have suggested that the victim's wounded or isolated self reenters, through the interviewing process, albeit provisionally, a social as well as personal bonding. This effect is necessary for both the retrieval and transmission of memories. It is a process that continues with the historian exploring rather than dismissing undocumented or scarce evidence; it also benefits from the attentiveness of interpreters trained in the nuance of literary and psychological interpretation. Such contextualizing, of course, should be presentational rather than preemptive, ready to field questions about the universal implications of this genocide and the danger of further outbreaks.

When the persecution has been vast and vicious enough, a single voice may have to break the silence. As Jan Gross has written: The "fate of several hundred Jews murdered in the Belzec extermination camp must be unpacked from the one and only line that its victims have left."[8] "I am my town's archive," the survivor of a different Holocaust massacre told us in a Yale interview. Even in less radical instances, there is much unpacking to be done.

Because of the victim's trauma and the perpetrators' attempt to erase all traces, the concept of a "testimonial pact" is more adequate to what we are given to hear and see than Phillipe Lejeune's "autobiographical" pact.[9] For the testimonial pact does not involve an abstract promise to tell the truth, a promise addressed to a phantom audience. Instead, it enlists the interviewer as a helpmeet on a difficult journey toward truths that seem improbable. I have applied the adjective "maieutic" to the task of the interviewer, but the interview may also have a reverse effect of teller on listener, who is made to think actively about the inhuman facts.

The Archive as Collective Autobiography

The archive of Holocaust witnesses is not a Geniza of sanctified remnants or a storehouse preserving bureaucratic documents. It is a proactive ingathering designed to create a living monument of retrieved voices. It establishes a collective autobiography with a plural identity. Perhaps, as James Young suggests, we should talk of a collected rather than collective memory.[10] Its polyphony is essential, and it makes no sense to wall off and homogenize the testimonies by sacralization.

Without a proactive archive most of the oral testimonies would never have been retrieved, and certainly not written down. They give the word to more than an elite (the "Prominenz" or "Nomenklatura"); they represent, as has been mentioned, people from all trades and sectors of society—including many whose formal education was interrupted by persecution, war, and economic necessity. Since genocidal outbreaks have not ceased, the Yale project can be exemplary beyond what happened to the Jewish people.

Memory Action: "Here" and "Back There"

I have emphasized several dimensions of video testimony. Not all, by any means: not, for example, how its reliance on talking heads counters a more glossy type of videography. Nor has its nonjuridical character been discussed. But I have suggested that it fills a need of the witnesses by allowing them to speak despite inner obstacles. However difficult the subjection endured, the "memory of offense," as Primo Levi called it, or the "choiceless choices," as Lawrence Langer names them (depicted for example, in Ida Fink's "Spring Morning" or William Styron's *Sophie's Choice*), these are faced once more in the stories recounted by the survivors. By recalling these experiences publicly, the testimony givers become more than passive victims.[11]

Also mentioned has been the difference testimony projects have made or could make in the humanities, including the medical humanities. I should now add something about their effectiveness for education at all levels.

The videotaped witness accounts are bearable as well as poignant because the individuals who address us can be observed remembering as they slip into a "back there." The emphasis is shifted by this from the perpetrators' inhuman behavior to the humanity of the victim. Jolly Z., asked what she sees when she is "back there," struggles for words, and still feeling not entirely present, answers: "I'm not here. I don't even know about myself now. I'm *there*. Somebody else talks out of me. You see it's not me. It's that person who experienced it who is talking about those experiences."[12] An entire phenomenology of traumatic memory is encapsulated in statements like these. Let me add a further example, culled from a testimony in Lanzmann's *Shoah*, where the sweet singer of Chelmno, Simon Srebnik, says: "No one can recreate what happened here. Impossible. And no one can understand it. Even I, here, now. I can't believe I'm here. Always."[13]

Note that "here" accrues two meanings, refers to identical places separated in time: the fields outside Chelmno, where Srebnik saw thousands of exhumed bodies being burned, and "here, now," standing in the same place some forty years later, talking with Lanzmann. The added "Always" has its own grammatical disjunction and overtones. Does Srebnik mean that a doubt about being "here" is always present, indeed has spread over his entire existence? How come he is not dead but "here"? "Even I, here, now. I can't believe I'm here. Always." Since he goes on to describe how quiet the scene remained even at the time this atrocity was going on, the "always" also refers to that awful and grateful fact: Then as now, the natural setting was, is, peaceful, unchanged.

Memory Transmission and the Secondary Witness

I keep for last a discussion of how traumatic experiences can be approached in pedagogical contexts that include public education as well as what is transmitted to youngsters in the privacy of family life.

Ernst van Alphen joins the debate about the intergenerational and pathological transmission of trauma. He argues that memory is indexical (it has a direct, not indirect reality referent), so that what is transmitted cannot be the specific trauma of the survivor's own historical experience.[14] If what passes from the persecuted generation to their children has a traumatizing effect, it is precisely because of an underspecified communication, at once emotionally charged yet ominously full of gaps. A concept such as the later generation's "absent" or "post" memory not only acknowledges this but evokes the pathos of a suffering that includes a sense of guilt for not having suffered enough.[15] What is passed to the next generation can be described as a melancholy that must still be converted (if that can ever happen) into an appropriate work of mourning.

Let me also broach the issue of what should be, rather than what can be, transmitted. The testimonial imperative "Speak, Memory!" suggests an ethical consideration or, at the very least, since ethics involves choice, sufficient mental and emotional room for a decision to take place about what should be said. I believe the testimony interview itself helps provide that space. For it is unworthy to prescribe to the witnesses how forthright or how reticent they should be. Which does not mean they are not aware of the dilemma. Robert Antelme, close to death when liberated from Dachau, could not stop talking for several weeks yet felt deeply ashamed at his lack of reticence.

The balance has gradually shifted, after the camps were opened, from compulsive outpourings to a latency period of relative silence, then to public testimony, with recent oral documentation projects providing a safer, more intimate setting than the public trials and a less emotional and demanding context than the witness's family. But an ethical charge also touches us, the secondary witnesses.

Our response is bound to be problematic as well as painful. For the Holocaust experience transmitted via firsthand accounts and vast historical research tends to induce the sense of a bitter sort of nonmemory. It can also be described as a memory that seeks a memory, because it has recognized in itself a personal core that feels empty. Especially marked by that feeling of emptiness are those close to survivor parents struggling with the burden of a great and catastrophic event. The blessing of having been born after that event, or having escaped it for some other reason, does not of itself bring relief.

For something so horrific that it cannot be known, even by the secondary witness, without trauma induces the quasi-gothic image of a crime that may never be revealed fully, because it would damage the newly born, those who should be free of the past. The persistence of a nightmare memory in one generation becomes the "poisoned fruit," as Thane Rosenbaum puts it, of the next.[16] The psychic pain of the successor generation has also been compared to what is felt in a phantom limb: an anguish related to the very fact that there is no limb, or no frame of reference, at least none during childhood, that could explain the words and behavior of parents different from other parents.

Some cognitive dissonance, of course, between the world of adults and children is normal enough, and parents usually take it into account. But in this extreme case the symbol-making capacity is at once roused and immensely troubled. A frame of reference unintelligible or else injurious to the children excludes them, their life, their normalcy, and the youngster's imagination is haunted by a need to resolve the parents' silent or incongruous hints.

Part of the dilemma of the generation(s) after is, in fact, that the demand they feel is difficult to translate into a literary mode like tragedy. They tend rather to express this demand in a comic or grotesque form. Consider the young Momik of David Grossman's *See Under: Love*, who fantasizes over a leader called Sonder Kommando, or the puzzlement of the children in Carl Friedman's *Nightfather*, who cannot figure out their parents' allusions. What kind of place or disease is "camp"? "We've never had camp." "Camp is somewhere where no one fries eggs."[17] An authentic testimonial and tragic art seems out of the reach of all except the survivors.

At this juncture, then, aesthetic and ethical concerns join once more. Perhaps they were never all that separate. Testimony's contribution to the art of memory does not exact a distinctive level of artifice seeking to turn reality into art. Memory is always more than retentive-mimetic: An imaginative supplement enters at any point. Ethical concerns also enter at any point, sometimes even via their suspension in moments marked by cold candor and hyperclarity. "I wasn't afraid. I stripped the dead. Everyday I saw the dead, death for me was like smoking a cigarette" ("Je n'ai pas eu peur. J'ai déshabillé des morts. J'ai vu tous les jours des morts, la mort c'était pour moi comme fumer une cigarette").[18] This realistic, surrealistic, glimpse of the death-in-life of the concentration camp affects us beyond its specific context as if it were a visionary scene.

A concluding remark. I have not talked directly about political justice. But through testimony projects, historical research, and Truth Commissions or related organizations like Nunca Más, memory action has a chance of alleviating helpless grief and allowing hope to emerge in a nascent intellectual, in addition to emotional, form as probing questions that confront a past terror, never entirely past.

13. The Ethics of Witness: An Interview with Ian Balfour and Rebecca Comay

BALFOUR/COMAY: *As you know we are preparing a volume about archives, and we are hoping to get you to talk about the specificity of the Yale's Fortunoff Video Archive for Holocaust Testimonies, but also possibly in relation to or within a thinking about the archive in general, or what might now be a new culture of archives. Perhaps we could start with the complicated notion of witnessing. Contemporary thinkers such as Levinas have elaborated the issue of witnessing, which might be called a theological imperative in the Jewish tradition, as a core ethical event. How might you relate the testimonial activities in the Yale archives to this way of theorizing or understanding the scene of witnessing? It is interesting that Levinas stresses the asymmetrical and not the dialogical nature of witnessing, a certain fundamental distance that informs the ethical encounter. Is there tension between his way of thinking about this witnessing in general and the dialogical setup of the face-to-face of the interview scenario?*[1]

HARTMAN: When Moses proclaims: "Give ear, o earth, and listen, o heavens," or what would become the central prayer of Judaism, "Shema Israel," "Hear o Israel," he not only calls upon those addressed to bear witness but affirms the ear as a visionary organ (Deuteronomy 32:1, 6:4). The act of witnessing, moreover, requires the continuance of witness, its perpetuation. The instance from Deuteronomy, in particular, contains both an imploration and an implicit admonitory threat. The earth and heavens invoked are created by God and therefore—that is the implicit threat—can be made to pass away by the Creator who has made them. Such invocations are a complex speech act, bordering here on an adjuration, even an apotropaic conjuration.

Witnessing begins by being a physical fact involving eye and ear, but a moral dimension—the issue of responsibility for attestation, for continuing to make known what was (is) seen and heard—immediately appears. If we ask what exactly is being witnessed and attested, it cannot be only one theophany in the past or even a series of them. It is their continuing presence that witnessing as a performative reanimates. In brief, the object of witnessing is the covenant itself, its virtual presence and binding power.

Now Levinas accepts the fact that philosophy speaks in Greek, so that the concept of witness is not at the center of his thinking (insofar as that has a center). But his ethics do imply a covenant, one between unequals, a fundamental relationship between self and other that is not symmetrical or dialogical. Since that covenant seems threatened by the Holocaust, it is not wrong to insist, as Susan Handelman does, that with Levinas the witness of the Holocaust now enters the "reason" of philosophy. His recurring picture, moreover, of the face-to-face necessary for all acknowledgment of the otherness of the other brings us close to the scene of Holocaust testimony and the courage it takes to confront the memory of an irreversible disaster. The ethical psyche in Levinas is never stable: It was and continues to be subject to spiritual and other experiences close to traumatism.

We find, I think, something of that same stabilized precariousness in the testimonial interview. One senses the immediacy of a memory dangerous to recall. There is, especially when sight is added to voice, a directness of speech and of the person, a self-presentation that is not or does not appear to be mediated in any way. Despite the fact, then, that Levinas's understanding of moral action is not dialogic in the sense of aiming at a balanced mutuality, a potential space is opened for the immediacy, the directness of the witness to others, or to the other in the self.

The testimonial interview is also—how shall I put it?—proactive, indeed a situation for which the interviewers have to be trained, and in which there is equipment. Theoretical exploration of what the interview structure implies means providing a thicker description of the act of testifying. And you can't say that Levinas gives us a thick description. *He develops all the implications of post-Hegelian, rather than post-Holocaust, witnessing.* To explore Levinas further, we would have to go back to Hegel's understanding of the bondsman and liege-lord relationship.

BALFOUR/COMAY: *As you say, the general notion of witnessing is as much post-Hegelian as post-Holocaust. But is the specific sense of witnessing in the post-Holocaust world informed by this prior tradition of witnessing, and if so, what happens then to the character of this witnessing?*

HARTMAN: There probably is a retroactive informing of it. So that as soon as one thinks about the testimony project, one begins to wonder: "Ah! Maybe it has to do with Jewish witnessing." I don't think it started up that way, at least not consciously. It is true that witnessing and memorialization merge in the Jewish tradition. Still, I'm not happy with the cliché of claiming that their coupling is specifically Jewish. Because of the biblical emphasis on remembrance, one often hears statements of the kind, "The Jews invented history," etc.

Such statements can be true enough from the point of view of a memory that respects and records events—as they bear on the covenant between God and an emerging people. Yet, as Yerushalmi has shown, Jewish historiography, *the formal* discipline of historiography, comes in very late. While collective memory and its cultivation do play a part in the creation of this kind of archive (there is a long Jewish tradition of remembering catastrophe and exile in a collective manner, collective remembering being a way to affirm that the relationship of the covenant still exists), the massive descriptive detail of modern history writing points in a different direction. In short, our archival project, while it concentrates on a decisive segment of recent history, does not seek to turn the witnesses into historians. It has values in addition to those of recording what happened in terms of positive fact.

BALFOUR / COMAY: *Could we ask you to talk about the perhaps new element of the visual in this sort of testimony, an element that, by and large, was not so much part of the long-established Jewish tradition? You have said elsewhere something to the effect of: "Why not take advantage of this new technology, the addition of the visual content?" Can you say what is at stake or new here?*

HARTMAN: The addition of visuality (let's call it, more precisely, the video/visual) to the voice record is striking. However, we have actually tried to limit it in the sense that we are not afraid of, indeed we restrict ourselves to, "talking heads"—for we are not in the business of making films. There are some projects that have a different relation to the scene of taping than we do. Some organizers tape in the subject's home with the idea of producing films in addition to establishing an archival record. As such, they introduce a stronger visual interest: You see the survivor surrounded by familiar and colorful objects. At Yale we are resolutely ascetic; we may have a plant or a curtain but we have just two or three chairs and basically, that's it! And we found, almost by accident, that this bareness helps the survivors to go into themselves. Moreover, concerning the visual dimension, while an argument can be made for the importance of gesture and its expressive content, I myself would not overemphasize that. It can enter but can also distract: Not all gestures are meaningful.

Video is important because the voice as such, without a visible source, remains ghostly. That is, when you take away the visual, when you just hear the voice, the effect is that of disembodied sound, as if from the dead, from an absence. Voice has its own affective quality, but we feel it essential to add a face to voice, to reduce the ghostliness, even to reembody the voice.

Embodiment is essential because it was precisely the body—this is one way of putting it—that was denied, the full presence of the survivor that was denied in the time of persecution. Of course, in still photos from and of the past—as against the cinematic or the video/visual—you still experience something of that ghostliness. The survivors, to counteract that, can also be placed back into an actual milieu, a town or the countryside.

BALFOUR/COMAY: *As in Lanzmann's* Shoah?

HARTMAN: As in Lanzmann, right. He too eliminates ghostliness. In some respects, Lanzmann's work performs a kind of resurrection. A difference from Lanzmann's kind of interview is that, in the Yale project, the survivor doesn't face an interlocutor who appears on screen and can be a demanding presence. Our interviews are conducted in a reflective space that is nonconfrontational, noninterrogatory. We could explore that, then: what is involved in the noninterrogatory interview. In the relation of interviewer and interviewee.

BALFOUR/COMAY: *Just thinking about the spectrum of visual possibilities, it seems as if the Yale project in its pared-down way seems to be quite different from what we might call the "Spielberg Aesthetic."*

HARTMAN: Yes, they are quite different, also through our abstinence from closure, or Spielberg's tendency to stress, whenever possible, a happy ending, the nonfinal solution. At the end, the Spielberg interviewers, generally, ask whatever members of the family are present to come forward and kind of take a bow to the cameras, as if to say: "See! We have survived! Here is the family" (It's not always the original family, of course, but creating a new family is also a kind of victory). We recognize that something is gained by that gesture, yet at the same time, we feel that the interviews should not conclude that way, with a sense that the past has been overcome. You also had *Schindler's List* in mind, perhaps . . .

BALFOUR/COMAY: *Yes, trying to think about the spectrum of ways of presenting or representing the Holocaust. In one of your essays you talk about the difference of the video testimony from photos, for example, or one could think of, at some other extreme, the Riefenstahl aesthetic. It seems that the Yale project, while video/visual, is mainly in the aid of a story.*

HARTMAN: Yes, it is purely in aid of the "story." We should put "story" in scare quotes because the term is inexact; "narrative" is not much better, it's too cold. So what exactly to call it? Witness account? Testimonial narrative? I have said we are not interested in the staging, the technical mise-en-scène, such as arranging things in the survivor's home, putting more color into the picture. We are not into technical innovation at all. This is possibly why you mentioned Riefenstahl. There is no aesthetic in the Yale interview. There is an optic, there has to be an optic. But the optic on the whole is minimal. One of our affiliates in Israel insisted on no movement of the camera at all, on a totally fixed focus. The human eye needs some movement, however. So the organizers acceded, although at first they resisted: They were in danger of creating an artificial situation without knowing it. You have to move and refocus the camera, not to make the scene more dynamic, simply to respect what the human eye minimally needs.

BALFOUR/COMAY: *Perhaps we can examine a scenario that is at least superficially somewhat similar to the Yale project, namely, the scene of psychoanalysis or . . .*

HARTMAN: Let me interrupt you, and anticipate a possible misimpression. The Yale protocol, the interviewing protocol, was devised in good part by Dori Laub, who is a psychiatrist. But we do not, on the whole, use psychiatrists. It stands to reason that those who are psychiatrically trained, or whose interviewing experience comes from the social service and mental health professions, would already be familiar with interviewing techniques, so we welcome that. But we have been somewhat careful in asking psychiatrists to help because, perhaps even more than lay people, they have their agenda. So we actually avoid, on the whole, psychiatric questioning . . .

BALFOUR/COMAY: *And yet the scene itself, no matter who is asking the questions, seems to . . .*

HARTMAN: Instead of talking about a psychoanalytic dialogue it is better to talk about a testimonial alliance, modifying the notion of "therapeutic alliance." The term "therapeutic" would be ambitious to the point of arrogance, and it is mistaken to say we are engaged in therapy. But an alliance is necessary between interviewer and interviewee. Without that alliance there is no trust, and without trust you cannot have the testimony, the witness account. So we extract, as it were, something universal from the methodology of psychoanalytic dialogue.

BALFOUR/COMAY: *But could we explore a bit more the possible similarities with that psychoanalytic encounter, or the differences?*

HARTMAN: Part of the immediacy of the video-testimony interview is that, usually, it's a one-time event. With audiotape, the interviewer can easily go back to the witness and continue the conversation another time, to stretch things out, as in the psychoanalytic interview, over a space of time. But the intrinsic pressure of the camera on the witnesses is, in effect, to make them tell the story, now at last, as fully as possible. There is no *entretien infini*, unless we triangulate with extensions like the present interview.

With audio also there is less pressure, and the studio environment may be less daunting initially. There is no need for a soundproof room; there is no need for heavy equipment. With video you have a more complicated setup. Especially when the survivor travels for some distance, it is hard to say, come back tomorrow or in a week. Sometimes we get calls: "But I forgot this and that." On the whole, however, it is not bad that the interviewees feel they are on the spot. It concentrates the mind. It may block occasionally too, but the idea of the interview, in terms of what should come out, what is too coldly called the product, is a release of memory concerning the past. Not to go totally into the past or to obliterate the present for the past, because part of the interesting tension is between present and past, and we structure the interview to include the time after persecution, the return to life or resocialization. But also to release memories that are very painful and may have suffered repression. The immediacy and the ascetic environment of the interview help that; however, unless trust is established, the interview cannot work.

The alliance of which I talk has to be established fairly quickly. The witnesses know that the interviewers trained at Yale will not abuse their confidence. We are also helped by the fact that we schedule a preinterview telephone call that doesn't go into the content of what might be said but acquaints each witness with the interviewer and records some basic data. We keep the preinterview to a minimum of questions, so when the witnesses come for the actual interview they do not know in advance everything they are going to say. Some rehearse mentally, I'm sure; some also bring documents. These they can hold up, especially the photos, though we discourage them from reading aloud what they may have written. For, basically, it's the moments of spontaneity that are so important, when the survivor says, "I had not remembered this till now . . . now I recall such and such."

BALFOUR/COMAY: *May we ask how silence sometimes functions in these sessions? Are there moments of pregnant or awkward silence? Do you tend to let the interviewee alone with his or her silence?*

HARTMAN: That is a good question. We try to train interviewers to allow the silences to be. The effort doesn't always succeed because the interviewers may feel a pressure to be overtly sympathetic. Hence a tendency to be embarrassed by silence and even during flows of speech to say "Aha, aha" to give signals of recognition or encouragement. So we really take that under advisement. Sometimes we succeed, sometimes we don't. But the principle is "respect their silences," unless you feel the silences mean that the survivors *want* you to restart the conversation.

I recall a dramatic moment in which there wasn't complete silence but an interruption akin to one, when a survivor tells of his grandmother being loaded onto a truck by a German officer. And, the grandmother asks—I may get the details or words in what follows slightly wrong, but I can capture the spirit of the episode—she says something to her grandson or maybe her son and the German officer asks, "What is she saying?" She's an old woman. She has difficulty getting on the truck, and the son replies, "She says that she needs help." And the German officer says: "OK, I will help her." He takes out his pistol and shoots her. At that point the narrator, the witness, breaks down. There follows a mixture of silence and audible crying, which lasts a rather long time. Should an interviewer intervene or not?

There is no clear answer. As it happens in this particular interview, after a while, having respected the crying, the interviewer does intervene to ask: "Why did you then cry?" You and I might find this too much of an intervention. Let him alone with his grief, already! But the survivor's answer is a beautiful answer. Beautiful in the sense of precise and affecting. He says (I paraphrase) he cries because, instead of a humane, helping act, this atrocity takes place. It may have been an awkward intervention; in this case, however, it produced an answer that is more eloquent in its awkward English than I am able to convey. So yes, in short, we face such problems and we ask ourselves such questions. Joanne Rudof and Dana Klein, who supervise the interviewer training program, don't attempt to formulate a doctrinaire answer to this problem simply because the matter depends on the dynamic of the interview: Not everything in the interview—we stress this—is controllable. In fact, the one dogmatic principle we have for the interviewer is: Never take the initiative away from the witness.

BALFOUR/COMAY: *You talked a bit already about the alliance or trust that has to be established between the witness and the interviewers; we would like to ask you more about the scene of interlocution and your sense of an addressee, perhaps beyond the specificity of the immediate scene. In one of your recent pieces, you say something to the effect of "This is not addressed to 'Whom it may concern.'"*

HARTMAN: I made that statement when I was thinking about whether some of the testimonies should be put on the internet. My reluctance to do so (except for a few illustrative excerpts) comes from a sense that the viewer should not occupy the position of visual tourist or voyeur. An effort should be made to come to the archive—at Yale, Washington, or elsewhere—so that the interested researcher understands the spirit of the enterprise and can be helped with whatever issues arise. The same principle holds for showing these videos, or excerpts combined into short features, in the classroom: There should always be a teacher present to answer questions or discuss matters that might upset the students.

This does not alter the fact that the testimonial interview is an act of public witness, one addressed to a wide audience. The interlocutor is only a medium—not however, an impersonal one. More, rather, part of an ad hoc community. The interlocutor, the interview partner—in German, *Gesprächspartner*—is often a member of that community. Nor are the extras really extras. In our case the main extra (except for the camera person) is very much "intra": It is Joanne Rudof, the archivist, who welcomes the witnesses and makes sure everything has been set up, including the presence of someone to take down the names that later have to be checked for spelling. We have other helpers too. Sometimes there are two interviewers. These are all part of that ad hoc community which represents, to my mind—and I hope I am not wrong—the larger community that wants to hear the survivor. So I would say that the addressee, through this provisionally assembled group, addresses a larger community to which very difficult, grim, but not only grim, stories are to be transmitted. In addition, let us not forget that many survivors tell their stories so that their families will have a formal record.

BALFOUR/COMAY: *Can you sense sometimes the appeal of the narrator to this audience beyond?*

HARTMAN: Yes.

BALFOUR/COMAY: *As we understand, some survivors agree to tell their story to the video archives—yours, Spielberg's, and others—even when they have refused to tell the stories to the immediate members of their family.*

HARTMAN: That is true. They find it easier to use the relay of this ad hoc community. They are also informed that they have a right to their video and the option to give it to their family. There are some who restrict the dissemination of their testimony, in part for family reasons, or perhaps because they name names. We agree to that limitation, if it is for a specified number of years. The restriction cannot be, however, "until I die," simply because we can't keep track of so many people. So we generally suggest a limit of ten or twenty years from the date of the interview. Some do insist on this, but relatively few, because we inform everyone clearly that they should come in only if they realize that theirs is a public act of witness. The addressee is their family, if they wish. But there is a larger community that wants to, that should hear their stories. We are a public institution as well as a private university. We appeal to them as witnesses with a public purpose in mind. Others should know what has happened, through personal stories with which most people can grapple somewhat better than with professional historical narratives, on the one hand, or photos of atrocity, on the other.

BALFOUR/COMAY: *Could we switch to the question of how we, who are perhaps addressees, might read these texts? Clearly, they are not overtly literary. Some of the witnesses are highly literate people, some not. You have said in a recent essay that we need to develop a hermeneutics for reading these texts.*

HARTMAN: I am not sure that the hermeneutics that must still be developed will be new, so I may have given the wrong impression—even to myself! [Laughter] I meant to suggest that the testimonies, possessing as they do such affecting power and such immediacy, tend to silence comment. We are still close to the event, or they make us come so close, that it seems almost wrong to apply analytic instruments already in place. For our literary instruments have become very sophisticated, and a special diction has developed—one that I on the whole respect, although it is necessary to learn to use it and to use it humanely. There is a disparity, then, between the immediacy of what you hear and this metalanguage. By a hermeneutic, I meant the matter of language decorum: How are we going to discuss this impressive corpus of witness accounts? It's a matter of not imposing a sophisticated analytic language. A similar scruple when we discuss poetry. There is the object language—again, too cold a term—the language of the poem, of the story, and then the language of description, the metalanguage. This is one issue.

The other may have to do more directly with interpretability. When you asked the question about silences, you were going in that direction. How are the silences to be interpreted? Also, is there a semiotics or iconography of gestures, given the specificity of the "embodiment" that marks the scene of the audiovisual testimony? What I can hope for is that, as the testimonies are absorbed (and they can be testimonies from other historical traumas too, or traumas of everyday life)—we will learn not only more about everyday life in the camps and other extreme situations but also something about literature's power to represent.

This project is new, even if everything new has its antecedents. There has never been such a wide audiovisual documentation of an original, rather large corpus of narrated experiences. Moreover, these audiovisual documents are about a specific event limited in time, although a lot happened during this "event"—really, "events." There is a corpus of stories about the Gulag, nothing of this magnitude, however, of this quantity, of this intensity, even, and not of this immediacy, because most of the reports about the Gulag, some very powerful, are mediated in literary ways. That's nothing against them, of course.

The people we have recorded, who speak to us through their testimonies, are in the main, ordinary people, ordinary in the sense that they are not the elite. We did not go out and say "let's interview only professors and doctors, or the camp *Prominenz*, or those with unusual experiences." The door is open, and if you have lived through that period, you have lived through that period. Even though some survivors say: "But we were only refugees," we still want to hear their stories. "But I don't have anything important to tell you, you should go to a real survivor." Some even say: "I know people who had *really* terrible experiences." But let's attend and listen. Why be in a hurry? I can express the hope that we will learn more about what literature arises from, especially its source in personal or historical trauma. I am better now at recognizing the traumatic content of literature when it is not overtly "symptomatic."

BALFOUR/COMAY: *If we could imagine a spectrum of interpretive possibilities from say, at the one end, attention to the surface of the text—you might remember what Auerbach says about Homer: "There is nothing to interpret"—and at the other end of the spectrum, there might be the psychoanalytic mode, at times a way of reading through the text to get at some meaning behind or beyond it . . . Can one generalize about the testimonies along these lines?*

HARTMAN: I think Auerbach is wrong about Homer. And so his assumption would be wrong in its application to these texts. [Laughter] In any act of interpretation there are variables and constants. The constants would apply to the video testimonies also. As to the variables, not enough thought has been spent on what kind of visual and verbal texts these are. But one issue that does arise is how to understand errors in testimonial narratives that are factographic—that make the claim of being true to fact. Let me give an example but also refer you to my article "Learning from Survivors," because of what I say there about factual errors.

There is a typology of errors that could be established; the errors, moreover, though not always, have an important imaginary element to them. Like the impression of a survivor that Dori Laub always quotes, a survivor who, as an eyewitness, recounts the blowing up of four of the Auschwitz crematoria when historical documentation confirms that only one was blown up . . . Metaphor and error are closely related. Consider also the woman who says in a very emotional interview (I approximate): "In Auschwitz we got up at 4 o'clock, the sun was barely rising, it was very dark and when the sun rose it was not the sun. I swear to you! It was not the sun. It was never beautiful. It was black!" And suddenly this archetypal image of the black sun surfaces, one that we recognize from literature. These are moving moments of metaphor and hyperbole. Also, the "I swear to you," that rings true not because it comes out so traumatically, so dramatically, but because it reminds us how speech generates natural hyperboles, natural metaphors. Moments like these lead back to the, let's call it, genuineness of literary study. Sure, rhetoric can just be artificial, just rhetoric, but when you meet it in this situation, there is something incredibly spontaneous about it, and you do seem to touch something elemental.

BALFOUR/COMAY: *It seems clear that there is a certain kind of historical truth to the testimonies regardless of their factual truth. Perhaps, this kind of truth leads to the question of the relation between memory and history: The two terms nowadays often seem to be conflated. Could we talk about how the category of memory is functioning now, possibly in relation to these archives, to these histories?*

HARTMAN: "Memory" is a charged word, like "witness" and "testimony." These are whirly, swirly terms. In the case of "memory," you have one term standing in for too much. That is part of the confusion. You need something to hold on to, just like period terms, which are, or should be, heuristic. You are right to ask for a more discriminating approach. One of the values of Lawrence Langer's pioneering *Holocaust Testimonies: The Ruins of Memory* is that, on the basis of the Yale collection, he can point to the persistence in the survivor of an "Unheroic Memory."

Even the resonance, the basic resonance of the term "collective memory" is deceptive. Is that memory related to a collective unconscious, or is it a synonym for social memory? Many prefer "social memory," because the term "collective" has accrued other connotations.

For distinctions to be made, a good starting point would be Halbwachs's work, with its basic thesis that all memory is dependent on a social context; it is collective in that sense. And collective memory has a *saeculum*, at least in the era in which the oral tradition still predominates, a line of transmission from grandparents to grandchild. It is in a family milieu that memories are formed or given their narrative nexus. There is a larger world too, political events that perhaps affect the family, but the family remains at the center, especially since Halbwachs is still talking about a largely rural society, one that was certainly changing but not quite as fast as ours. Is he, in fact, writing in a time when this kind of memory is endangered because of the accelerating speed of change? His thesis is quite convincing to me, that memory is always of, or formed within, a milieu—a fictional or mythical extension of his thesis might be the Platonic theory of reminiscence. Halbwachs, that is, does not have to be applied reductively, to exclude all creativity: Imagination may be a form of memory, while memorialization is a "collective" or public way of preserving events beyond the *saeculum* of the eyewitness generation or the diaspora of later descendants.

But when the topic is the memories that are preserved by way of the testimony project, we are dealing with a different sort of memory-milieu. Then what Halbwachs calls the "affective community" works differently; now the essential social element is, as I mentioned before, the survivors' confidence that they are addressing a supportive group ready to be a "witness to the witness."[2] Those who give testimony enter, in other words, a new memory-milieu. Theirs is not primarily a personal memory in formation (though some malleability of memory may still be active). What is being formed is principally the collective memory in the sense of a communal, public memory. The personal memory can only recover and transmit itself if there is a conviction that it will be respected, that there is a community to receive and hand it on.

The "collective memory," then, collected this way, involves a more deliberate form of transmission than its genesis as the memory of the individual. In both instances stories are a medium of transmission, but for Halbwachs the fact that the individual memory does not come into existence without a social context was the point. One should add, therefore, that memory can't be transmitted beyond Halbwachs's *saeculum* (or immediate family context) without creating a secondary social milieu, a post- or extended family. There must be a conviction in the witnesses that their story is being received, really listened to. The issue of reception is crucial. Immediately after the Holocaust the conditions for reception (what in French is called *l'écoute*) were not strong enough. In the case of France (Annette Wieviorka has written about this), there was at first a lively reception, but it was politically motivated, in the main, encouraged, and directed by a communist cadre whose organization survived the camps—it was social in that particular sense, sociopolitical . . .

BALFOUR/COMAY: . . . *with an agenda of sorts.*

HARTMAN: With an agenda. When that faded, the *récits de déportation* stopped. Wieviorka can show, even statistically, that the public flow of these stories and memoirs soon dried up. With the Eichmann trial, they started up again. In other countries, such as Italy, there was even less of a reception at the beginning. There was almost no *écoute*.

BALFOUR/COMAY: *Given your account of the odd sense of nonreception of these experiences in the immediate wake of the events, it seems important to think about the felt imperative now, when we are so close to the end, or the dying out of, I guess, the generation that has direct experience of the Holocaust. To link, perhaps too pointedly, memory with archive, it seems that when memory is functioning actively it presupposes its own archiving, if only because the memories are in some sense already there and yet they don't always take the forms of memory.*

HARTMAN: That's right. The witnesses do not think in terms of archives, though we do. Some are even shy of videography, more in Europe, by the way; in America, videotaping has gradually been accepted. Those national, cultural, differences can be overcome, or have been over time, so that playing

John the Baptist to Spielberg [Laughter] ... so that by the time our project had run for fourteen years and Spielberg had won his spurs as a Shoah filmmaker with *Schindler's List*, the survivors accepted him with enthusiasm, especially in the United States, judging him to be the best director to bring their experience to the public.

While archives have always existed, they have not always been so proactive. We are adding to documents that are contemporary with the events. This later rescuing of the untold story is an important function of oral history, an activity that matures after World War II. Let me also mention another difference from the conventional archive. There are historical collections, of legal documents for example, necessitated by bureaucratic rules, like that enabling Natalie Davis to write *Fiction in the Archives* on the basis of sixteenth-century royal pardon petitions, or the incredible amount of—now incriminating—Nazi documentation. Then there is at least one accidental archive, the Geniza in Cairo (a dumping ground for scraps of Jewish documents, especially contracts, with the consecrated word for God in them and therefore not allowed to be destroyed), a treasure house many centuries later for the chiffonier-historian who discovered these wonderful fragments. But ours is neither an accidental nor a bureaucratic or institutionally mandated archive. The Yale Testimony Archive is motivated by the intensity of the catastrophe and its vast extent. Because we now have the technical means of recording, we can go out, find, and invite people to testify. So there is a confluence of circumstances that allows the recording of testimonies without setting up a court or a legal testimonial framework.

Such an archive, moreover, looks more deliberately to the future than do the others I have described. Libraries do so as well, insofar as manuscripts and books are precious. The other types of archive had to be there for a number of years, for reference or for the record, but probably did not seek the perpetuation of a collective memory. Except for heroic and "historic" events: In the Hebrew Bible, and among the ancient kings, deeds of renown were recorded for the edification of the future. One might even envisage the Hebrew Bible itself as a form of archive in this regard, testifying to, and spreading the fame of, the King of kings.

In the present case, the video archive preserves memories of people from all ranks of society, who were reduced to basically the same state of suffering or abjection, with no fame attaching to survival as such. The testimonies are testimonies because, like oral history generally, but countering the oblivion implied by the greatest genocide ever attempted, they create an inextinguishable memory. Each of our testimonies is treated like a rare manuscript, an original audiovisual print.

BALFOUR/COMAY: *The Yale video archive is being engendered at a time when we are witnessing an explosion of archives in general with the vastly increased possibility for recording, especially digitally.*

HARTMAN: Right, I want to talk about this a bit . . .

BALFOUR: *So it seems important to think about the place of the Fortunoff archive in the proliferating culture of archives.*

HARTMAN: We are at the end of a generation, a generation of Holocaust survivors. When we started twenty-one years ago, we already had a sense of urgency; we thought that a "lien vivant" was disappearing. Even the survivors can't survive forever. Now we really are in the last few years. In 1980, survivors who were twenty years old at liberation had reached fifty-five, and many were over seventy, and we felt we could not count on the retrieval of memories beyond a certain age. As it turned out, and perhaps partly because of the interest generated by archival projects like ours, the memories have lasted.

Our sense of urgency also had other determinants, such as the rise of revisionism. The more you insist on the importance of the Holocaust, the more the revisionists (negationists) make their counterpropaganda. So there is an unholy, unhelpful relationship there.

Now archiving, as you know, is not only collecting; it also involves preservation and making available what has been accessed. First the retrieval of memories, then their physical preservation, and—what tends to be forgotten—the cataloging that allows research and intellectual access generally. From the beginning the Fortunoff Video Archive thought of itself as integrating those three functions. Cataloging and preservation are both made possible by the technological revolution. Our computerized catalog allows summaries of all the testimonies to be read online. Researchers and teachers can determine from wherever they live whether they should come to the archive to see certain testimonies; there our archivist Joanne Rudof helps guide them. Physical preservation of the tapes, which has moved into an electronic phase with digitizing, I will discuss a bit later. I want to stress at this point that archives, insofar as they aim to provide always accessible memories, pose a problem beyond the hope they advance that future generations can learn from the past and minimize forgetfulness.

Three problem areas have opened. The first is often broached by quoting Nietzsche on the necessity of forgetfulness, given the excess or abuse of historical knowledge. Let me immediately say about this, that while the retrieval of memories through oral history has a positivistic aspect and seeks to augment, clarify, or amend what is factually known, it also has other values. I cannot discuss these here. One value, though, is forthrightly restitutive:

to restore, partially, belatedly, the speech and embodiment of which the persecuted were deprived.

A second problem area is related to precisely these values. Oral documentation, in the future, because of its powerful effect, its audiovisual immediacy, could be abused for propagandistic or ideological purposes. Just as witnesses in a courtroom often "see" things differently, so testimonies could be studied for minor discrepancies in order to be discredited, or deliberately created by slanted questions that draw them into a battle for the hearts and minds of viewers.

A third problem area comes from the new medium itself, both from its very strength as a form of communication and from the technologically advanced mode of material preservation. Concerning the former, we have not yet developed a critical visual culture or a sufficiently homeopathic remedy for the powerful, repetitive, everyday—and so potentially trivializing—effect of TV. Concerning the latter, digital modes of recording are easier to alter than analogue modes, so that the testimonies that have to be "migrated" from analogue tape to a digital-optical format must also be preserved in their original analogue version for proof of authenticity. This raises the cost of archival preservation enormously. Moreover, the shadow side of technology as it advances, and accelerates, is that it leaves the older technology behind. Not only does it make the tapes or diskettes in the older format obsolete, but by not maintaining the machines needed to play them it renders what was recorded inaccessible.

BALFOUR: *So that what you are trying to preserve remains fragile . . .*

HARTMAN: Yes. Videotape has a limited shelf life, much shorter than film. Every fifteen to twenty years there may have to be a technological renewal. Yale started taping early and, being pioneers, we are "penalized," historically penalized, as pioneers. For at the moment it is many times more expensive to preserve the analogue tapes than it was to record with them in the first place. And no one wants to pay for it. That's fragility! We knew we had to face this eventuality, we knew we had to face it sometime. But we also had to start the project—it was urgent. We couldn't say to the survivors: Come back in twenty years when the technology is perfected, and then we will take your testimony. But to add a positive note: Philanthropic donors have helped us in the past, and there is no reason to think they will not understand this new urgency.

BALFOUR/COMAY: *And you don't want to be in a position of economizing, of curtailing the project by choosing one survivor's story to record/preserve and not another.*

HARTMAN: Absolutely not. We can't do that. Everyone who wants to be heard should be heard. When Spielberg arrived on the scene, he immediately used the more advanced Betacam tape and digitized at the same time. But—I say this quite simply, without resentment—he has the funds, or can get them. For us, it's quite a different matter. Technological transfer is absolutely necessary, and we are only at the beginning of it. We've already spent $600,000 and require another million for preservation. Nor is digitizing as yet a perfect medium of preservation.

BALFOUR/COMAY: *How do you see or imagine the Yale video archive functioning within the context of the proliferation of archives in general? It seems for almost every project of this sort one runs the risk of being one among others and so becoming lost in the multitude.*

HARTMAN: Yes, that is the unfortunate part as it always is with pioneers. They start something that overtakes them. If we had the resources, the financial resources equivalent to our dedication, the problem would not be as great. The fact that there is a proliferation of archives doing similar work . . .

BALFOUR: *. . . broadly understood . . .*

HARTMAN: . . . broadly understood, is and is not a big worry. Consider Spielberg's Visual History of the Shoah Foundation. Compared to this gigantic effort, we are like the local grocery store when the supermarket moves in. Yet no one can claim that Spielberg's venture was superfluous. We too tried to find the maximum number of survivors to testify, not only in America but elsewhere. Fewer, however, were willing to tell their stories when we started in 1979/1980. We initiated affiliates throughout the United States and in many parts of the world, projects that adhered to our standards. Yale's total collection amounts to about 12,000 hours, gathered in over twenty years; Spielberg gathered over 100,000 hours in less than six years. As well, Israel's Yad Vashem, the US Holocaust Memorial Museum, and various other, smaller ventures came into being after we began. We say to ourselves that we set an example and that we helped, initially, both Spielberg and the Washington museum.

Was it necessary to record as many survivors (and bystanders, etc.) as in Spielberg's project? Is what happened excessive? Who can tell. It is possible that the numbers in this case were too great or that the Shoah Foundation proceeded at too great a speed. The issue of quality, of standards, can only be determined when the Spielberg tapes can be viewed. But they must be a very valuable deposit, because even if only 25 percent of them are worthwhile, that's 25,000 hours, while our total—and I'm not saying all our tapes are worthwhile—is 12,000 hours.

Eventually, in any case, all these archives will be electronically joined. Then, whatever territorial imperative remains will weaken. Personally, I would like to see the Shoah Foundation cooperating more closely with other video archives and to see it using more people from university circles to advise it in making educational films or curricula. I am hoping that an international consortium of video archives can be formed in the near future. Yale's policy, at the moment, is to give drawing rights (a kind of long-term library loan) to other educational institutions or museums that have curatorial integrity.

BALFOUR/COMAY: *Could we ask what you make of the philosophical or theoretical questions about the archive, which have lately become a topic, say in Derrida or Agamben? On the one hand, an impetus to theory seems to be given by this new possibility for archives. On the other hand, in both cases, Derrida and Agamben, the interest seems partly related to the Holocaust, though not exclusively. That is, there's an attempt to respect the absolute and compelling singularity of that "event" which seems, in Derrida and Agamben, to change the way we think about archives, about history and memory, even about lifespan.*

HARTMAN: At the moment, I don't think the implications of this "archive fever" are very clear, even in Derrida and Agamben, who are among its most active thinkers. Partly because both are theoretical thinkers and therefore have a powerful way of projecting from the singular instance to the general. I am somewhat suspicious or wary not of the power of their minds and the stimulus of their thought but of certain generalizations made without a hands-on (that kind of *main-tenant*) experience. I find the reflections of a social scientist like Yannis Thanasseikos of the Auschwitz Foundation in Brussels more cogent.

I am not a total empiricist, but many haven't seen enough of this corpus of materials. They would surely never generalize this way on a new philosophical or literary cache. Imagine a Derrida or Agamben at the beginning of something called literature. Well, maybe Plato did generalize, but one sees the risk of generalization when he talks about poetry. Aristotle's *Poetics*, in contrast, yields its theory on the basis of a distinctive corpus. There you feel the hands-on, eyes-on, quality. This impetus to try to use the energy of one's mind to externalize, exfoliate, make explicit everything that's implicit, is intellectually necessary, but the voracious proliferation of theoretical discourses is also a fever. It is part of a general acceleration. We are "poisoned by speed," Valéry wrote some time ago.

BALFOUR: *In Derrida's analysis of Freud, the impetus to archive arises in the face of death, with the looming prospect of death. Perhaps we could even say that of Derrida's own mentality . . .*

HARTMAN: If archiving is viewed as an extension of inscription (storing the written record, or one made visible by other graphic means), then, it seems to me, there are two related, if apparently contrary, drives at work. One is to record as much of the living person as possible, because of a vital quality that prompts our delight and imitation. We want to mark that delight, to inscribe it, perhaps also to record it in order to be able to go back to it. Death is barely a consideration here, or the sheer force of the inscription keeps that proleptic thought at bay. The other drive to inscribe is death related, however. Inscription and memorial writing may converge. In the midst of the delight—or other intense feelings—an echo intrudes of a death that has not happened, a melancholy adieu to a fullness not realized. In the Greek *Anthology*, you have epitaphic inscriptions, a very important section of that very ancient collection. But there are other epitaphs, which are memorializing before death. These are artificial obituaries, and some are playful, of course.

BALFOUR/COMAY: *Right, like poets writing their own epitaphs.*

HARTMAN: Exactly. Then it becomes a literary game but also a genre, a serious literary genre. You could say that this extension of *écriture* or writing looks beyond lifespan, looks beyond as well as toward the end of a life. But, in this respect, I can't read Derrida's thinking well enough, though he is famous for his concept of dissemination. It answers Plato's devaluation of writing (as against hearing through the living voice). It is the very virtue rather than defect of the written word, Derrida claims, that it does not gain its value by being referred back to an origin, however prestigious: that it is orphaned, as Plato saw, and must gain its authority independently of a parent-source that is no longer there to provide clarification. This poses a problem with regard to witnessing. Testimonies may collectively accrue a certain impersonality or independence from the authority of their origin, yet *individually* their authority cannot be separated from the eyewitness status of the person testifying.

BALFOUR/COMAY: *In Derrida and Agamben and others, there is the suggestion that—somewhat along the lines in which, in Adorno's terms, Auschwitz imposes a before and after, that is, epochal differentiation—the Holocaust forces us to change the way we remember, the way we archive.*

HARTMAN: Surely we live in the aftermath of an extraordinary and dispiriting event. Even those who do not explicitly assert that the Holocaust brought about the equivalent of a geological disruption of consciousness struggle to determine whether what happened can be integrated or not into our image of the human species. The question of the epochal, as I suggest in "Language and Culture After the Holocaust," is at least as important as the differential emphasis often placed on post-Holocaust generations.[3]

Yet the concept of epoch also enters intellectual history via the debate defining modernism and postmodernism. One intriguing and puzzling instance is Blanchot's *L'écriture du désastre*, where you cannot avoid identifying the disaster with the Holocaust and yet he is clearly not referring to the Holocaust alone. There is a dark light thrown by the Shoah on the way we view historical causes and epochs. Can we move away from the simple arithmetic, the relatively simple arithmetic, of period-term thinking? "Post-Holocaust" is a perfectly intelligible and useful category at the moment, even if it begins to conflate with post-traumatic, postmodern, poststructural …

The way I tend to approach the need to face and even draw something creative out of the destruction is through the idea of intellectual witnessing, which recognizes that we are gradually moving away from a generational trauma. One needs a witnessing concept that is not dependent exclusively on the eyewitnesses. Otherwise you will have a collective memory kept alive artificially by being ideologized and instrumentalized, and some object to a "Holocaust industry" precisely on that basis. Another concept, such as intellectual witnessing, is needed; it has always existed but is even more necessary when the subject position changes according to each generation and culture.

Now to get back to the philosophers. In Agamben's *Remnants of Auschwitz*, it's a characteristic strength but also weakness of his thought that, wishing to explain the modern force of testimony, he latches onto Primo Levi's strange, moving, self-critical, almost self-inculpating statements in *The Drowned and the Saved*: that those who were saved are not the true witnesses. Those who "went under," "the drowned," or who in the camps were named *Muselmänner* are—would have been—those exceptional witnesses. Along comes Agamben and spins a powerful symbolic construct out of that, based on no testimony at all except at the end of his book. There he excerpts the (supposedly nonexistent) testimony of some *Muselmänner* but totally neglects the thousands of survivor and bystander accounts that have been collected. In my opinion, Agamben's powerful symbolic construct is a quasi-theological response to questions raised about authenticity in a media age, an era of simulacra.

BALFOUR / COMAY: *Let's circle back to the category of memory, which, as you said, is such a swirly or slippery term. The term "memory" is applied both to memory as a phenomenological experience, the experience of a subject or subjects, as well as to the quite different process of remembrance or memorialization on the part of people who have absolutely no direct experience of the Holocaust. Yet there is a widespread injunction to "remember," which seems to attempt to bridge these two distinct states. Perhaps now we are supposed to remember memory or remember remembrance. Is that what helps engender what you call "memory envy"?*

HARTMAN: Yes, the prevalence of those strong, even traumatic memories (where "traumatic" is an adjective that contradicts the noun) on the basis of a group has a twofold effect. It raises the question, we have already discussed, of how those who come later and have no direct experience of such extreme events can engage with them, and it prompts other groups to affirm a history of their own that should have been transmitted through a collective and identity-forming memory. Needless to say, to found personal or group identity on trauma or catastrophe has questionable consequences. While it doesn't delegitimate the recent emphasis on memory, it is certainly a factor in the explosion of memoirs and autobiographies, including academic ones, and raises the issue of how to value them and even, at times, to evaluate their authenticity.

BALFOUR/COMAY: *That's a whole other topic!*

HARTMAN: Yes, I know, yet I would link even the problematic phenomenon of "recovered memory" to that issue. The foresight of the archive, the activity of listening to survivors, to their stories, as well as the films, novels, and critical discourse about them—the whole emergence of these memories in the last thirty or so years, even perhaps starting with broadcasts of the Eichmann trial in 1961–1962—has percolated into our culture, certainly into American culture. And what I find fascinating and disturbing is my suspicion that people want memories even if they are painful, rather than having no memories, or no significant memories. Now, you might object: Can't they recapture good memories? Yes, but we're talking about a level of intensity that's traumatic. Traumatic memories, however, are either so painful that they weary themselves out of the memory or they are ecstatic and again only leave traces. So that the choice is between defined public memories and a methodical purging of all memories, an induced oblivion, for which a different religion, such as Buddhism, is necessary, but which goes against the ethos of this-worldly engagement fostered by the very concept of the archive.

BALFOUR/COMAY: *Concerning memory-envy, it's almost as if some people, well, let us suppose, people of our generation and later, want to have the burden of memory. Remember the line in* Hamlet *where he says: "Heaven and earth, must I remember?"*

HARTMAN: Precisely. That "heaven and earth" is like the witnesses to whom Moses appeals in Deuteronomy, "Give ear, o earth, and listen, o heavens."

14. Terror and Art: A Meditation

We have entered an age in which terror is an increasingly familiar experience. By terror I do not mean primarily what may result from the usual mayhem of criminal acts but something driven by larger and often ideological ambitions. We now confront a deliberate "terrorism," state or group sponsored, targeted or purposefully random, involving single atrocities or massacres. Warfare, whether conventional or asymmetric, is not its only breeding ground. Whereas war, in the past, was not necessarily total but intended to resolve a conflict that could not be settled by other means (see Johan Huizinga's *Homo Ludens*), terror suggests a sempiternal enemy (not unlike the devil in theology) who must be eradicated, not just deterred, to assure the community's survival or presumed destined greatness.

In its absolute form, terror becomes less the means to an end than a foundational, self-justifying "divine violence." It seems to mirror—and is even flashed back at—a God whose world in its worldliness compels at times brutal solutions. These are anticipated by the votaries of the French Revolution, Maximilien de Robespierre and Louis Antoine de Saint-Just, who insist, as is well known, on the necessity of a "virtuous" use of terror.

The basis of government in revolutionary times, Robespierre declared, "is both virtue and terror: virtue without which terror is murderous, terror without which virtue is powerless. Terror is nothing else than swift, severe, indomitable justice; it flows, then, from virtue."[1]

Yet terror is bound to strike fear into more than the faction specifically under attack. It induces a trauma of the body politic; its sequelae threaten to occlude the future of all who learn of it. All the more so today, where its contagion works not only locally but also from a distance—brought to us by the new media.

Linking two radical beginnings, Rome at its founding and England after the regicide of 1649, the poet Andrew Marvell recalls in his "Horatian Ode Upon Cromwell's Return from Ireland" that Rome is said to have foreseen its "happy fate" in a bleeding head, excavated, according to legend, by architects when they were building the new Capitol. This auspicious omen seemed to justify a "capital" event. Implied is that an important change in government, tantamount to a new foundation, cannot take place without a severe wounding of the previous body politic.

The philosopher Jacques Derrida too broods on such mystifications, but in the context of a "credit" accorded to "faith" and irreducible to rational explanation. He describes that credit or faith-based credence as resulting from a "messianity without messianism"—an expectation not fostered by a particular religion but "a general structure of experience," a universal desire for a more visible, present justice.[2] Indeed, Derrida's formulation has an affinity with what is so often portrayed in Franz Kafka's fiction: the quest for a definitive moment of enlightenment or justification. Yet when that moment comes, it always does so too late, as in "Before the Law" and "In the Penal Colony."

Such failed expectations, moreover, intensify the terror that seeks to impose or enforce them in the name of justice. This can be seen from the many times in which a fierce version of Islamic Sharia law is immediately installed without respect for other versions of the same religion or a general principle of peaceful conversion. How thoughtful, in contrast, Karl Barth's demands are, despite his being the sternest philosopher of modern Protestantism. He writes in his commentary on Paul's *Epistle to the Romans*:

> We must recover that clarity of sight by which there is discovered in the COSMOS the invisibility of God; we must recover that sacred terror in the presence of the creature, not by the mere createdness of the things which attract us, but as well of the things which frighten us, until we see in their relatedness the mirror of our own.[3]

—|—

Jean-Lambert Tallien, the propagandist for the French Revolution's "September Massacres" and organizer of the Reign of Terror associated with a phrase of the Revolution that sacrificed tens of thousands to "Saint Guillotine," describes terror's effect as "a habitually generalized trembling."[4] Terror, or, more exactly, The Terror, does not affect only those targeted; it sensitizes the entire social fabric. Even those who only hear about it feel it like a chill that cannot be shaken off: You shudder, both body and mind shudder.

162   Terror and Art: A Meditation

The future too is subject to this trembling, since the act establishing a New Order brooks no delay. Time must not become merely history once more—the era of a God who failed. In a fanatical portion of Islam this hope is scandalously repackaged to motivate the suicide bomber with the promise of an immediate and richly rewarded life after his sacrificial death.

—┼—

William Wordsworth, in Paris, shortly after the French Revolution's first internecine butchery, the massacres of September 1792, describes how he experienced the Terror as a haunting "spot of time." A passage of unusual eloquence in *The Prelude* reveals how Terror propagates itself even when there are no media of diffusion. A poetic mind especially, which describes so sensitively in *The Prelude* how certain early experiences of Nature by the youngster, or more precisely of the youngster alone with Nature, keep resonating in later years (I shall soon quote another instance of that), here once more set his imagination working:

> With unextinguished taper I kept watch,
> Reading at intervals; the fear gone by
> Pressed on me almost like a fear to come.
> I thought of those September massacres,
> Divided from me by one little month.
> Saw them and touched: the rest was conjured up
> From tragic fictions or true history,
> Remembrances and dim admonishments.
> The horse is taught his manage, and no star
> Of wildest course but treads back his own steps;
> For the spent hurricane the air provides
> As fierce a successor; the tide retreats
> But to return out of its hiding-place
> In the great deep; all things have second birth;
> The earthquake is not satisfied at once;
> And in this way I wrought upon myself
> Until I seemed to hear a voice that cried,
> To the whole city, "Sleep no more."[5]

Terror here is like a cosmic repetition-compulsion; its rhythmic fatality reaches beyond the severe original point of occurrence. Though the poet still sees a Law of Nature at work even in nature's wildest manifestations, today's era of manmade disasters makes us suspect an unstoppable momentum. The argument, moreover, introduced by seventeenth-century thinkers who acknowledged, yet hoped to limit, the divine right of kings—the argument that Nature itself (i.e., "natural law") would autocorrect any royal abuse of power (they pointed for confirmation to the English regicide), as well as thinkers in the Enlightenment, who held that history displays more political stability and moral resurgence as it progresses in time—all these optimistic beliefs are made more questionable by the advent of Terror.

Without faith in progress, then, or a stabilizing natural law, can the pervasive anxiety, the chill or tremor in the wake of manmade terror, be endured?

As the shock takes hold and keeps resonating, as clips, for instance, of the destruction of the Twin Towers are obsessively played over and again and re-creations of the horror of genocide, films of the quality of Claude Lanzmann's *Shoah* or Steven Spielberg's *Schindler's List*, are produced, the enigma of how it could have happened and the fear of a recurrence do not lessen. The very sensationalism of the extreme event, reconstructed via the spectacular medium of motion pictures or other visual representations, exerts a hypnotic spell, as if something in us wanted to render such images intimate and neutralize ("integrate" is too optimistic a world) their impact.

The thought of art's mimetic skill enters at this point. Could art-mediated representations defuse the fatalism or sense of impotence produced by extreme events, at least events ascribed to human agency, and declared to be "facts on the ground"? Think it over, we say about less critical situations; turn it over in your mind. To regain control we adapt or create a narrative, change a storyline.

Political terrorism's effect, however, even if one considers it as differing only in degree from other fearful experiences, may not allow us, I have suggested, enough time—*enough future*—to be "worked through." For it has also a long-distance psychic effect. So Wordsworth talks of a fear heightened by "remembrances," "tragic fictions," "dim admonishments." Even when only heard about, and not directly experienced, the extreme enters by way of the imagination (the poet slips from "I thought of" to "Saw . . . and touched").[6] We too seek to escape insomnia and nightmare by acts of reading and writing that extricate both present and future from the past.

I wish to suggest that art's very grounding in myth can help fortify us (at least somewhat) against the effects of terror. Our hope in the future might not succumb to a sense of dread, or loss of faith, if we would look more closely at how poetry deals with "spectre shape[s] of terror," rescuing for us, even creating, amalgams of terror and beauty that mitigate deadly fear and obsessive anxiety.[7]

So Wordsworth describes in *The Prelude* how a corpse, fished from Esthwaite Lake near his birthplace, did not terrify him as a child, because it seemed familiar, swathed in a fairy-tale aura:

> At last, the dead man, 'mid that beauteous scene
> Of trees and hills and water, bolt upright
> Rose, with his ghastly face, a spectre shape
> Of terror; yet no soul-debasing fear,
> Young as I was, a child not nine years old,
> Possessed me, for my inner eye had seen
> Such sights before, among the shining streams
> Of faëry land, the forests of romance.
> Their spirit hallowed the sad spectacle.[8]

Are we not, in effect, charmed by a traditional fantasy element and even given courage by the very power of the presenting imagination? In Shakespeare's *Macbeth*, the "fear to come," that troubles Nature's life as well as the human conscience, is keynoted by a catchy nursery rhyme, the witches' "Fair is foul, and foul is fair / Hover through the fog and filthy air."[9] Fairy tales forebode.

Museum exhibits, memorializing atrocity by showcasing gruesome relics, reveal a further problem, not resolved by the aesthetic kind of immunization just described. Such exhibits tend to produce a helpless astonishment or abhorrence. Immanuel Kant already tried to value this curious mixed emotion arising from him in a very different context—namely, as a result of the mathematical sublime (when the observer is confronted by an immeasurable magnitude).[10] To transpose this into the present: Who could "add up" (mentally, emotionally, imaginatively) masses of hair shorn from murdered Holocaust victims or neat rows of skulls in a Cambodian museum? (One skull at a time, please, an incongruous inner voice tells me, as I recall memento mori portraits showing Philosopher or Divine meditating in a famous skull.) Is the whole world becoming Golgotha?

Despite all our difficult looking, what remains of such reality shows us a macabre riddle. If there is, nevertheless, the possibility of an imaginative or cognitive modification of the haunting sight—its resetting in a tolerable frame narrative—then we glimpse a diffusion that may lead back to the founding and valuing of art as an artful, therapeutic, socially necessary institution.

Hope revives that we could benefit from freely undertaken reenactments, within a concentrated and consecrated time-limited space that would provide just enough aesthetic distance. A *legomenon*, as James Frazer, Jane Harrison, Gilbert Murray, and other anthropologists of the Cambridge school name such reenactments, gives voice to, but also draws a containing circle around, a primal scene. They describe this in religious rather than psychoanalytic terms as a *dromenon*, a ritual mystery scene (perhaps a pantomimic trauma-spectacle) believed by these scholars to have been the forerunner of festive Greek tragedies. A parody of such a *dromenon* somehow finds its way into *Hamlet*'s "play-within-a-play," its "Mouse-trap," as Hamlet calls it, which not only points to the king as murderer and usurper but as a poisoner of the ear, and so, one might say, of language itself. The royal usurper's florid manner of speech is set off and undermined by the exaggerated, bumpkin-like style introduced into literary English by Edmund Spenser's eclogues with the Colin Clout pastoral speech.

These Shakespearean links are passing strange, of course. They issue from a mind whose creative uptake of things verbal and visual is incomparably sensitive. In this mind, self- and stage-consciousness compete. Shakespeare is fully aware in the skull scene of *Hamlet*'s last act—where all the world's a grave—that art must expand our sensitivity by employing enigmatic sights or situations, since many visuals and verbals, given acculturation, lose their immediate capacity to puzzle or shock.

Thus art often defamiliarizes by inventing moments of (quasi-unresolvable) strangeness. In certain moods everything human becomes alien to us. Literature, certainly, offers us episodes that portray startling changes of character, disastrous reversals of fortune, inexplicable coincidences, motiveless killings, mysterious corpses, gothic gore, and chilling sounds. These "grabbers" often launch the action and an inquest.

So from *Oedipus Rex* to the modern detective novel, the basic plotline is akin to that of the *surnaturel expliqué* (the supernatural explained) of the gothic story, which became popular in the latter part of the eighteenth century. An intrusive, ghostly/ghastly event, after complications and misapprehensions, resolves into its natural causes and (barely) satisfies the criterion of "probability" demanded by Aristotle's *Poetics*, while the protagonist's settled mental state ("purpose"), suddenly unsettled, goes, via a crisis phase of radical doubt, turmoil, and suffering ("passion"), to a deepened and wiser state ("perception").

I borrow this formulation of tragic drama's basic structure from Francis Fergusson's *The Idea of a Theater*, but the pattern of shock and eventual resolution also recalls Tzvetan Todorov's *The Fantastic*. There must be, in any case, a moment of wonder or woe (mostly both) that takes us out of ourselves.

———+———

A further plot device might stress the hero's initial passivity, delay, or failure to engage. Not only *Hamlet* but the story of Parsifal comes to mind, where there is a lapse in time before inquest turns into quest. Medieval stories about Parsifal have many variants, but usually he encounters an extraordinary spectacle-tableau, most famously that of the wounded, eternally bleeding Fisher King. Parsifal must then decide between asking and not asking its meaning. The mythographer Jessie Weston tells us that "the hero [Parsifal] fails to enquire the meaning of what he sees in the Castle of Wonders, and is told in consequence: 'Hadst thou done so, the King would have been restored to health, and his dominions [the Waste Land] to peace.'"[11]

Parsifal's failure is eventually redeemed. No guarantee exists, however, that the questions *we* ask will be redemptive—questions after standing before the sheer dead presence, the physicality of skull and hair, synecdoches of horror no longer economized but simply, endlessly, heaped up.

What can give closure to such brooding or transmute it into actionable knowledge? I recall Primo Levi's anecdote of how his "Why?" was met by the curt and brutal reply of the death camp guard: "Here there is no Why."[12] This is even more crass than the mocking "Arbeit Macht Frei" ("Labor makes you free"), the slogan over the entrance to Levi's camp, the Auschwitz-Inferno he describes and that brings together two of the greatest lies of Nazi propaganda: that, racially, the Jews were parasites, who everywhere undermine instead of support nation and culture, and that, after their reeducation, provided by Auschwitz and other concentration camps, they would be set free—whereas, in reality, "free" meant having been worked to death.

———+———

My own brooding, I admit, shares a visual desire that has become a public malady. Today the relation of knowledge to the means of representation has changed. There is an overload of information, for example, a plethora of detail about the "Final Solution," thanks to the techniques of modern historiography, the testimonial courage of the survivors, and the punctilious, overconfident recordkeeping of the perpetrators themselves. Powerful audiovisual media stand by to convert this information, also of more recent genocides, into simulacra of the original event. Inevitably, therefore, questions arise about the limits of representation: questions not just about whether extreme events can be represented but about whether truth is served by a "realism" that, wishing to stay as true to fact as possible, becomes reluctant to moderate the horror of manmade catastrophes.

The escalation of mimetic devices, then, has its negative side. When episodes from the repression and violence of our time, and our efforts to cope in their wake, are made into action movies whose competitive context is other action movies, do we not blur the distinction between history, docudrama, and fiction, without wishing to do so? Realism, in any case, does not always reinforce reality. Movie realism, especially, is closer to the surreal: to a self-imposed trial by nightmare and illusion in the way it speeds up incidents, heaps up coincidences, and, by zooming, booming, and montage, destabilizes perspective.

Some devices, of course, such as condensing the passage of time or montaging and fusing locations, are inevitable. They express the economy of a besieged, precariously filtering mind and hit the emotions hard. The aesthetic distance achieved by an opening reflective textual approach, as in Art Spiegelman's graphic novel *Maus*, is less coercive and didactically more effective. Holocaust video testimonies, too, viewed as a new oral history genre, are on the nonfictional side, however grim, of what is being remembered.

Critical commentary is not helpless in this situation. It indicates the limits of media that give the appearance of having no limit—yet, in fact, limit themselves by what theology characterized as the path of excess (the *via eminentia*). It is futile, for example, to advocate an anti-iconic "Second Commandment" prohibition that forbids the imaging of a particular subject matter because of its sacred or obscene character. Just consider today the cultic proliferation of horror movies or freak shows of various kinds, including over-the-top comic caricatures—the equivalents of satyr plays. They have become our TV diet (except for the news and the cooking shows). We afflict ourselves with an obscene rictus, hoping in vain for a desensitization or (at best) purgative laughter. The result hastens the twilight of all taboos.

A related issue is how exposure to terror, even at TV or movie remove, might be counteracted. I have already suggested that ways must be found to avoid the foreclosure of hope caused by actual or televised shocks, by what the French sociologist Luc Boltanski has called our *souffrance à distance*—our suffering at a distance.[13] So it is again useful to recall the role of the arts, of forms and rules of decorum. While these are often transgressed, our very consciousness of transgressing recalls them, and they are employed throughout history to strengthen reader or beholder.

Eighteenth-century aesthetics (founded initially as the study of "subjective" value judgments based on feelings arising from sense-perception) formulates theories of the Sublime, preeminently those of Edmund Burke and Kant. Such theories, going beyond the analysis of what is felt to be pleasurable or beautiful, stress the psychological impact of cosmic nature's "terrific" phenomena (the Lisbon earthquake devastation, the Alps, the sudden burying and calcification of Pompeii and Herculaneum). But they go on to describe a dialectic not found in religion, one in which the phase of awe and abjection is followed by a self-conscious rebound that reaffirms the competitive strength of our rational and spiritual powers as they strive to equal what is great, vast, mysterious, and frightening in the external world.

Art's engagement with realities, then, is not realized by constantly trying to shock or to transmit an actual moment of terror. However adverse or overwhelming the circumstances depicted may be, we look for a response named by Longinus "magnanimity": greatness of mind. Through art or other means, we must also deal increasingly with the fallout from *human* sources of terror and trauma that dim our perception of a peaceful nonhuman world, of Nature in its idyllic aspect, and contribute to a special type of despair, described by the poet John Keats as "the feel of not to feel it."[14]

It is also Keats whose *The Fall of Hyperion: A Dream* yields what is surely one of the most intriguing dream-image sequences of terror in literature, although it refuses to give up romance furnishings and conventions. So the testing of the poet begins conventionally with "white, fragrant curtains" from behind which the goddess Moneta, one of an older and mysteriously disempowered race of gods, admonishes the poet: "If thou can'st not ascend / These steps, die on that marble where thou art." In Keats's *Dream*, these steps lead back to Hyperion's temple and the deities displaced by Apollo, the new Sun God. Because the poet, despite his belief in progress—even poetry's progress—does not write off the older gods but devotes to them his (also unfinished) *Hyperion: A Fragment*, there is a second, more complete unveiling, again accompanied by the poet's "terror." For as Moneta finally parts her veils, the poets sees "a wan face / Not pin'd by human sorrows, but bright blanch'd / By an immortal sickness, which kills not; / It works a constant change which happy death / Can put no end to; deathward progressing / To no death was that visage...."[15]

Keats, a strong believer in the Enlightenment, is embedding the schema of what the eighteenth century called a "progress poem" into a Dream Vision narrative. For some readers, Keats's use of marble / marvel and other romance elements may not resolve sufficiently into a humanistic quest poem, yet they do express directly both the "giant agony"—i.e., the agony of the giants or older gods, as they lose their power without knowing why to a mysterious progress—and that of the modern poets, who must find a way of expressing the "giant agony" of ordinary men and women—like Keats himself, who eventually lost brother, mother, and himself to the "wasting disease" of tuberculosis.

Do we, then, still have the possibility to change the insomnia—the "Sleep no more!" heard in *Macbeth* and haunting Wordsworth in Paris two centuries later—to change it into a wakefulness sustained by art's education of sense and thought? Or does a suggestion of this kind overestimate the possibility of being guided by the arts, as the anxiety about terrorism grows and even fosters a secret attraction? In Luis Buñuel's 1977 film, *That Obscure Object of Desire*, fear and desire mingle as the explosions from an insurgency come near and nearer, foreshadowing an end to bourgeois complacency.

Keats's two large epic fragments mean to be no less than revolutionary: It comes as a surprise, but they explicitly condemn the only other original poetic current of his time, that of Wordsworthian subjectivity. So when Moneta makes her famous distinction between dreamer and poet and suggests Keats is merely of the "dreamer tribe" ("The dreamer and the poet are distinct, / Diverse, sheer opposite, antipodes. / The one pours out a balm upon the world, / The other vexes it"), Keats explodes, calling upon Apollo to bring the pestilence to "all mock lyrists, large self worshipers, / And careless Hectorers in proud bad verse."[16] Aiming that phrase clearly at Wordsworth, we understand how seriously Keats takes his Apollonian theme of wishing to renew the powers once ascribed to epic poetry. Despite his extraordinary attempt, already mentioned, to create a progress poem, he cannot deny Moneta her lament that the era of the "large utterance of the early Gods" has passed. Indeed, despite all these complexities, Keats will not give up "uttering" the gods: His romance revivalism maintains the "Sleep no more," is a revival of or answers Thomas Gray's "Awake Aeolean Lyre!"—which already called upon eighteenth-century English poetry to waken from its drowsiness. So Moneta, in *The Fall of Hyperion*, still laments the passing of Hyperion's power:

> I cannot cry, *Wherefore thus sleepest thou?*
> For heaven is parted from thee, and the earth
> Knows thee not.[17]

Passing to our own time, the status of literature as judged by a novelist like Philip Roth is not encouraging. In Roth's *Exit Ghost* (2007), the ghost is not only the ill and aging writer Nathan Zuckerman, brought back from Roth's earlier fiction for a final gamble testing his powers of candor, rage, and seduction. Foreseen is the end, the ghosting and exit, of an entire literary ethos. Roth's cultural pessimism, his sense of the subversion of an ethos by "ideological simplification and biographical reductionism" (to which one could add hyperbolic visual media), makes the question of what guidance literature can offer difficult to answer. We would have to come to terms with testamentary words attributed by Roth's Amy Bellette (a.k.a. Anne Frank, who has mysteriously survived the Holocaust) to the self-sequestered literary idol E. I. Lonoff, a character migrating, like Bellette herself, from *The Ghost Writer* of 1979, in which Zuckerman first appeared: "Reading/writing people, we are finished, we are ghosts witnessing the end of a literary era."[18] The thirty years between the first Zuckerman novel and, presumably, the last mark for Roth an epoch.

Yet when I recall that terrorism has not prevented the witness of so many great writers of the present age, how strongly and justly they have made us understand its impact, I remain convinced that even if the ethos surrounding the appreciation of literature has deteriorated (as Roth suggests), it has not touched the core of literature itself.

There are, on the other hand, scrupulously difficult authors like Maurice Blanchot. In such extended essays as *The Writing of the Disaster* and *The Instant of My Death* he seeks a secular, countertheological mode of meditative prose and creates a distinctive literary space in the very shadow of terror's *tremendum*. On the other hand, we can also turn to a more traditional kind of literary writing. Even if, as Roth fears, a parasitic, gossipy, commercially driven celebrity journalism (to be distinguished from courageous frontline reporting) has weakened literary appreciation, we cannot but close-read Primo Levi, recognizing clause by clause the writerly as well as moral integrity of his description of the aftermath of torture, a practice all too common in the epoch of Terror: "It extends through time; and the Furies, in whose existence we are forced to believe, not only rack the tormentor ... but perpetuate the tormentor's work by denying peace to the tormented."[19]

Coda

It may strike the reader as naive to argue that art can restrain or influence the ideology of terror in any way. But what I bring into consideration holds that art creates a mentality of its own, in the absence of which terror as a political temptation moves more freely and damages the shaky humanism we have left.

I can cite as a present danger Alain Badiou, a French "post-Communist" philosopher, who also identifies an epoch, although a much more alarming one. He singles out most of the twentieth century as a distinctive slice of history, a "siècle" primarily marked by state terror, which he interprets (favorably) as the product of a "Passion for the Real" that could not attain the Real. It became increasingly violent, therefore, and staged, from Lenin and Stalin, to Mao Zedong, from Hitler's persecutions to the Cambodian genocide, deadly theatrical trials and other forms of a persistently unreal *Realpolitik*. The quest for what is real, and being part of it, even has Badiou bring back "Terror" formally as a necessary political goad, if History and even life itself are to accomplish their positive destiny.[20]

Living in the aftermath, however, even those who were once seduced no longer have such a worshipful attitude toward a "Passion for the Real" that was to have ultimately created, through an annihilative "Final Solution," a purified New-Man Nation. Today, sixty-five years after World War II, we are still learning about a slaughter of the Innocents, with Father Patrick Desbois uncovering hundreds of previously unknown mass graves of Jews in the Ukraine, in which, the local population recalls, infants, not worth a bullet, were thrown alive.

15. Future Memory: Reflections on Holocaust Testimony and Yale's Fortunoff Video Archive

I wish to discuss crucial issues confronting those living in the present as well as at present, those who do not evade the past yet seek to sustain the energizing hope that is their very birthright. The passing of the eyewitnesses to the Holocaust, the eruption of new genocides, and the role of technology—in particular its contribution to audiovisual witnessing—are the background to what I will have to say.

Because of its scale—political, psychological, territorial—the immense genocidal ambition of the Shoah needed a long time to be exposed fully. It will take even longer for its implications to be fully absorbed. As more recent attempts at genocide accumulate and as extermination is used openly as a political threat, horrors of the present compete with horrors of the past. There is progress in the juridical realm of human rights, but each such success is like the beam of a flashlight in an ever-encroaching darkness. "The darkness," Paul Celan wrote in "Backlight" (*Gegenlicht*), "has gone into and deepened itself."[1]

Witnessing: Concept and Development

As a mode of witnessing, testimony differs from reportage. The reporter, today, can come very close to on-the-spot, real-time delivery of information. In the testimony interview, however, memory enters affected by a sensitive temporal component. What is recalled may be psychologically distanced as well as chronologically distant.

For most survivors of the Shoah there was a significant hiatus, sometimes of several decades, between their experience and its delayed testimonial recall, and the aftereffects of the genocide during this interval become an integral part of their testimony. Traumatizing memories will have caused some of the delay. But there were also difficult social factors involving the survivors' reception, or "écoute," and the rebuilding of lives in their homeland or foreign country of resettlement.[2]

In 1981 Yale University agreed to care for and develop a local New Haven video testimony project launched two years before. Using an open, less restrictive interviewing protocol instead of a set questionnaire, this effort soon expanded. Yale established affiliates throughout the United States and in South America, Canada, Europe, and Israel. By affirming the expressive dimension of video and training interviewers to leave the initiative and flow of speech as much as possible to the witness, the project strengthened the "testimonial alliance" of survivor and interviewer in order to release repressed memories and obtain a fuller picture of daily life and death in the camps, ghettos, and hiding places.

The motivation for Yale's delayed project included a mounting anxiety. Was there a future for Holocaust memory? What would happen after the passing of the eyewitnesses? Could their experiences be conveyed to the public at large without the simplifications of network television's 1978 miniseries *Holocaust*? Holocaust denial too was causing serious concern.

Today, more than thirty years after the opening of the Yale Video Archive, we see that the question of who would preserve the memory of the Holocaust is being answered. Not only do we find an ever-greater sense of that obligation among the children, and now the grandchildren, of the survivors; we find it also among witnesses by adoption, men and women of conscience without any direct—ethnic, religious, family—links to the victims.

Moreover, as the testimonies increasingly stand in for the survivors and as post-Shoah genocides reveal a danger that has not ended, a new type of witness appears, a secondary witness, as it were, dedicated to studying the era's genocidal outbreaks and the pursuit of remedies through a continuation of testimony projects, the archiving and safeguarding of documents from Truth and Reconciliation Commissions, and a continued striving for the universal propagation of human rights.

The result is that the memory of the Holocaust has retained an unexpected focalizing power. The enormity of the fact sinks in that, after initial, limited phases, and often not deterred even by the labor needs of the Nazi war effort, the persecution of the Jews turned into a planned total extermination. Had Hitler's war succeeded, what could have stopped him postwar from targeting Jews wherever they lived or singling out any other community for extermination or slavery?[3] The testimonies support an admonitory consciousness necessary for the very survival of humanity as a humane species.

The Survivor as Witness

With some exceptions, such as David Pablo Boder's audiorecordings in the displaced persons camps shortly after the war, most Holocaust research centered at first on the perpetrators, in order to identify and prosecute them. The survivors and other eyewitnesses were chiefly debriefed to that end. Gradually, though, by the very force of the personal testimony offered in the Eichmann trial, the Fortunoff Archive's video testimonies, and Claude Lanzmann's *Shoah*, the survivors' voices and bearing, as well as their words, broke through. They became individuals again, rescued, as Haim Gouri remarked when reporting on their testimonies at the Eichmann trial, "from the danger of ... being perceived as all alike, all shrouded in the same immense anonymity."[4]

Although the testimonies as victim stories are similar, and what Jewish prisoners, in particular, could observe was severely restricted by their abject status in the camp hierarchy and all-absorbing struggle against death, the survivors convey, through oral interview and storytelling impulse, the humanity and individuality denied them during their many years of persecution. Oral testimony, moreover, showing the populist strength of an emerging communicative genre, proved to be an alternative medium for many who might never have testified except in this impromptu way.

The Testimonial Challenge

However important court-solicited testimonies have been, a new genre of extrajuridical acts of witnessing has come into being. It is this freely communicated genre I wish to emphasize. For some time now, every other kind of memoir has moved to the center of attention. A distinctive testimonial literature, preserved and shared in the form of oral history, should not get lost amid this mass eruption of memoirs in our culture. One result, moreover, of today's "memory boom" is that questions arise about the genre. There always has been some wariness, of course; many years ago, one scholar called biography, and by implication autobiography, fiction under the conditions of remaining true to fact. Yet survivor testimonies in the bad news era we have entered (if we ever left it) create a special case and challenge.

It is a challenge—for both witness and receiver. Given the content of the testimonies, our willingness to listen is, first of all, a moral engagement. Little in the testimonies is comforting; mainly, the courage of the victims in telling, and so to an extent reliving, their story. Arthur Frank, author of *The*

Wounded Storyteller, writes: "One of our most difficult duties as human beings is to listen to the voices of those that suffer."[5] That suffering persists, since terrifying memories never entirely subside.

Moreover, if "to listen to the witness is to become a witness," the empathic powers of those who were not there come under pressure.[6] We feel our inadequacy. "Not ours, this death, to take into our bones," the poet May Sarton writes.[7] In the omnipresence of trauma stories, though not everything is dark, but interspersed with episodes of resistance, extraordinary bravery, organizational cunning, even resilient humor, where do we invest limited resources of compassion?

This leads to a central aspect of the testimonial challenge. Those who try to learn from what others have endured must trust the authenticity of such narratives. Authenticity in this context implies more than an absence of fakery, or self-deception of the Binjamin Wilkomirski kind.[8] The worry about who could talk for the witnesses resolved when they began to talk for themselves, to go beyond proxy representation and convey their own stories—that worry shades into a more troubling concern. For, given the extremity of genocidal suffering, can the survivor witnesses speak for themselves, let alone for companions who did not survive?

Interviewing the Dead

Primo Levi's sad conclusion, in *The Drowned and the Saved*, that none but the dead could be the authentic or (his word) "integral" witnesses, renews a concern we are obliged to acknowledge. *I Did Not Interview the Dead* was Boder's title for his book containing a sample of the oral histories he gathered in the displaced persons camps.[9]

Survivor testimony, however direct and affecting, is not immune to questions, whether of a malicious kind, those of Holocaust deniers, or deeply honest, that of Primo Levi, who understood the psychological aftermath of extreme suffering. In such testimony not truth alone is at stake but also justification. I have in mind the working through of a special type of self-doubt afflicting concentration camp prisoners and others forced to exist in "the gray zone," as defined by Levi in *The Drowned and the Saved*. The camps were a constricted world of "choiceless choice" (Lawrence L. Langer), and this can haunt survivors who feel in need of being justified—to themselves, as well as in the eyes of those who think, naively, that such words as "hunger," "cold," "thirst," etc. denoted the same thing in the camps as at home.

Factual or historical accuracy is rarely the heart of the matter when the issue of trusting a testimony arises. Most errors or distortions are corrected easily enough by historians with access to a deluge of documents. At the heart of the matter is our quality as listeners, the patience and stamina of listening to unbelievable atrocities, of summoning a necessary suspension of disbelief, and this can come about only if we are not distracted by insignificant and correctable mistakes.

The small number of fake accounts, like that of Wilkomirski, are probably motivated by a peculiar memory-envy, by a wish to share vicariously major events—a wish indulged more commonly and innocently through literary fictions. The very increase, however, of Holocaust narratives, and their dissemination by the media, may encourage memory thieves. Sigrid Weigel has aptly characterized deceptive psychogenic memories: They provide, she says "a free pass [*Entréebillet*] by means of which everyone irrespective of their particular position in history can become part of a historical drama."

Even more sad and crucial is that, despite the mostly successful postwar recovery and resocialization of the survivors, trauma keeps taking its toll. The passage of time cannot quite extinguish a feeling that the death camp is still in them or they in the death camp. While rituals of mourning and commemoration are how we normally delimit staying in contact with the dead, the survivors' situations, especially vis-à-vis murdered family, friends, and companions, remain psychologically hazardous. "And so they are ever returning to us, the dead," Sebald writes in his first novel.[10]

A deeper analysis of what it means to live with the dead, if only in imagination, could develop this theme of Holocaust trauma. Primo Levi's poem "Survivor" tells of being haunted by his dead companions: "'Stand back, leave me alone, submerged people.'" When Charlotte Delbo has one of her narrators say, "I died in Auschwitz but no one knows it," she refers to a permanent paradox that besets Holocaust memory.[11] The survivor person harbors a dead person as well as a radically changed one: She is two, one who remains "over there," trapped in the eternal misery of the camp, and one who has separated from the living dead and shed—is still shedding, even in the act of writing and remembering—her death-camp skin.

Toward an Authentic Reception of the Testimonies

As secondary witnesses, we struggle to gain an authenticity of our own. Can we come close enough to extremity to take in what the witnesses are saying? Lawrence L. Langer, the first to study the Yale testimonies in depth, resists the need to find meaning of the uplifting kind in grim and comfortless stories. He doubts that words, other than the victims' own, can be found, given their "death immersion." "The innocent language of Eden," Langer writes, "survived the expulsion, and must now die another death."[12]

Reception, of course, has meaning in itself. It honors the testimonial act and the singularity of each act of this kind. Radically speaking, every testimony says "I was there" and negates the obscene Nazi jargon that reduced prisoners to a number, a disposable "Stück Jude." While the historical information in many witness accounts is certainly not negligible and often supplements other sources, there is a necessity for acknowledging this "I was there" as well as satisfying the quest for definitive information, or aiming to make the genocide intelligible—not fatally damaging, that is, to our species image, our concept of the human.

Media Witnessing 1: Trauma

The change from audio to video in order to record the witnesses might seem like a minor adjustment in sync with the trend from radio to TV and internet as our main sources of information. Yet surely it is the act of witnessing that matters, rather than the medium. The change to video consolidates three interdependent elements of Holocaust witnessing. First, it is part of a distinctive move by the survivors into the public consciousness. At the same time, we become more aware of the role of the interviewers, whose main function is no longer a standard debriefing, as was the norm via questionnaire in the immediate postwar years, but who now assist witnesses in the release of both ordinary and traumatic memories. This in turn creates an intensified relation between witness and interviewer, often described as a "testimonial alliance," with the interviewer becoming more of a partner. Finally, in an essay collection, *Media Witnessing: Testimony in the Age of Mass Communication*, the editors, Paul Frosh and Amit Pinchevski, formulate a third essential element that they call "audiencing." They suggest that "the function of media technology in [Fortunoff's] project was more than the establishment of an audiovisual archive: video cameras effectively constituted a technological surrogate for an audience of the witnessing process."[13] This "audiencing," as they call it, adds a third important element: "bearing witness" as a hopeful community-building or rebuilding process.

Much depends on "building a discourse with an interlocutor."[14] For while in ordinary media interviews the failure to engage does not always matter, in testimonies, the interviewers' role is not ancillary but fundamental. The interviewers come before the witness as more than a questioner: He or she is, at the same time, a supportive addressee. Dori Laub develops the thought concisely: "It is only through the testimonial process in the company of an intimate, total listener that the lost internal 'Thou' can begin to be reestablished, and the process of internal dialog, symbolization, and narrative formation can resume."[15]

"Building a discourse with the interlocutor": This seems to contradict Yale's principle not to take the initiative from the survivor. Actually, it strengthens both parties. For in ordinary interviews, when the stakes are not particularly high, it does not much matter what is resolved. But in testimonies that seek to emerge beyond trauma, the interviewer's role, as Pinchevski notes, is "not merely ancillary but ... fundamental to the process, serving an interpellative function."[16]

This is a crucial insight, one valid for other instances of genocidal trauma. For Laub traces the dyadic structure of the interview back to the parent-child relationship and its protected "holding space."[17] Replicating a mature version of that space, the ideal interview enables (if anything can) the recovery of a "Thou." Laub designates by means of this personal pronoun a trusted respondent who tolerated the infant's stress and distress during its original struggle for an articulate communication and a distinctive sense of self. It follows that bearing witness in a situation marked by massive trauma involves bearing up the witness by turning the interviewer into something of a medium—one who recalls from the unconscious of the survivor a sense of the unlimited intimacy and trust Holocaust trauma had disabled. The interviewer becomes for the witness the surrogate for an audience ready after several decades to be fully informed. The interviewer, as part of the scene in which the interview takes place, blends functionally with the internal figure or imago that originally, though not even then without pain or struggle, guaranteed the infant what might be called, ironically, its "living space" (*Lebensraum*). The survivors who go on this intrasubjective, not only intersubjective, journey will be able to restore to memory incidents that deterred their will to communicate.

Media Witnessing 2: Reembodiment

Video technology, moreover, allows us to penetrate, as if physically present, the testimonial scene itself. We observe not only how a repressed memory sometimes surprises the witness but also how, in general, the testimonies make us more aware—even than audiotape—of silences, pauses, and other non-narrative aspects. That kind of attention can also focus on the idiosyncratic yet often lively texture of the displaced person's way of speaking in a newly adopted language. The confluence of all these traits in what may be named the videotext can then be elucidated by the literary-critical mode scholars call "close reading."[18]

Consider this reembodiment also from the perspective of the victims. In captivity they were not allowed to face their oppressors. There was never the possibility of a face-to-face. They could not even raise their eyes to them. The systematic attempt to shame them was heightened by the guards' domineering stance, which intended to implant a feeling in the prisoners of absolute nothingness. Compared to the guards, "I was a shade," Dan Pagis writes in his near-Manichean poem "Testimony." "A different creator made me."[19]

The Nazi pseudoscience of race (*Rassenwissenschaft*) contributed to this dehumanization: a vicious ideology that denied Jews the very ability to feel shame. It claimed that however assimilated they seemed to be, they remained, by blood, "treacherous Asiatics," non-Aryans without a true identity, who tried to look like true Germans, and had to be unmasked. This unmasking was crudely reinforced by a widely disseminated caricaturing of "the Jew": in books for children, in newspapers, and on posters of the notorious *Der Stürmer* that (dis)graced many street corners with an advertising pillar.

But now, via their testimonies, the survivors are seen and listened to, all the more human for having the courage to recall their former abjection. Video testimony gives them their face back.

If video testimony focuses, moreover, on the individual in the act of remembering, there is an effect of real and restored presence. I have mentioned that during the interview we sometimes glimpse the actual emergence of a lost memory. Should the traumatic moment, as trauma theory claims, embed itself like a flash, becoming an *instantané* without adequate temporal and reflective extension (because too terrible, too threatening), that moment, in the interview's safe atmosphere, has a chance not only of emerging but of taking hold—that is, allowing the survivor to survive it, to accept the reality of having had such an experience and come out human, alive. Trauma at that point becomes productive, and we too, alerted by great writers like Levi, Semprún, Antelme, Améry, Wiesel, and Blanchot, are made aware of a rebirth to life out of the "death life" (Langer) experience of the witness. In contrast, movies that try to recreate the camps and killing places and turn the past into a specious present often remain strangely unreal despite realistic shock effects.

Media Witnessing 3: Derealizing Tendencies

This brings up an issue not sufficiently examined: the derealization effect of modern media. While improved technologies of emission and reception guarantee an audience, they cannot guarantee an increase in the audience's receptiveness.

Tragically, moreover, the only advantage of the speed with which news is disseminated is that we now learn of genocides as they are happening, so that the immediacies of television or other media reportage make everyone into an involuntary bystander.[20] None of us can plead: "I did not know." Christiane Amanpour has called the role of Serbia in the systematic killing and inhumane imprisonment of the Muslim population during the Bosnian conflict between 1992 and 1995 a genocidal atrocity committed in prime time. Our talk is about action, but the reality remains the pain of passivity, of an intervention that has always arrived too late.

Video and film, therefore, even as they reach out to an extended public, heighten at the same time an anxiety that is the byproduct of *our cancerously enlarged ability to create semblances of the real*. "To space conspiracy theorists," I read in the *New York Times* (January 11, 2004), after photos from Mars were relayed back to Earth, "there was no moon landing and there is no mission to Mars, just a lot of special effects."[21] The ability to produce simulacra, called up repeatedly, instills a certain caution, however urgent the matter demanding action.

Media Witnessing 4: Grief and Globalization

Transmitting images of human suffering and victimization occurring anywhere on the globe has brought about an era of what Luc Boltanski names "souffrance à distance" (exposure to the suffering, however far away, of others).[22] Such global extension also involves the world of scholarship. The field of Holocaust and genocide studies is established to encompass numerous deadly episodes and severe violations of human rights since the Holocaust. Each collective ordeal, of course, retains its own specific character. Its entire historical and memory-milieu can differ. It is important, however, to note the leveling or universalizing impact of information technology. We have not examined carefully enough the fallout from the electronic media's ability instantly to record and disseminate.

Today the flood of information relayed from anywhere is so great that TV and internet images can become *electric phantoms* derealizing the real. When that happens, telecommunications disturb the work of mourning. Confronted constantly by so much death and trauma, is there still a way to grieve close to the actual grave or designated memorial place—without a universalizing shadow on consciousness?

One reaction is to dig in all the more, to insist on the uniqueness of each loss, to mark and consecrate the site and date of the traumatic event. It may also have influenced the disjunctive, elliptical phrasing of Celan's later poetic style, which seems to aspire to the inscriptive conciseness of dates, as if the poet wanted all his words to have an epitaphic resonance and consolidate around a missing "Thou." Lyric fluency gives way to a cursive, hammering beat.

Testimony and Subjectivity

Testimony's informative aspect cannot be dissociated from the individuating performance. It is precisely during acts of witnessing, in the unpressured, extrajuridical context of the testimony interview, that subjectivity comes forth in a more significant manner than the quirks, memory lapses, and other idiosyncrasies that often characterize personal behavior. Jean Améry says simply that the act of remembering is what keeps memory alive, and he asks that his autobiographic *Unmeisterliche Lehrjahre*—with a title that points to the perversion in Nazi Germany of Goethe's ideal of *Bildung*—should be understood as a work of "unverschleierte Subjektivität" (a subjectivity without veils).[23] Others, like Robert Antelme, a prisoner in Buchenwald and Dachau and author of *L'espèce humaine*, hope that a new postwar ideal of both formal and informal discourse will emerge, a "parole désarmée," words born of a "sovereign weakness."[24] Without giving up a vision of human fraternity, courageous affirmations like these are unafraid of the subjectivity intrinsic to witnessing and rethink language and literature after the enormous manmade suffering characterizing the period from 1914 to the present.

Conclusion

Thousands of edited and unedited video testimonies are now available to schools and museums. Encouraging their study is the immediate practical task we face. The Shoah Foundation has digitized all its interviews, and the Fortunoff Video Archive has completed the digital migration and development of a remote access system. There is no reason why the testimonies could not enter curricula dealing with modern European history, political science, trauma studies, memory studies, media studies, ethics, or oral history. Eventually their classroom and museum presence should create the climate needed in order to achieve a more effective pursuit of human rights.

While this pursuit, no doubt, requires a long-term intergenerational commitment, and although our present capacity to invoke legal remedies is limited, we already have the means to foster a more comprehensive cultural memory in order to counteract racial and nationalistic prejudice.[25] Oral histories of the Holocaust are not a closed canon. Nor do they seek to provoke a competition among those who suffered from the Nazis. But in addition to describing the time of persecution, they yield glimpses of the new life animating a defamed, desecrated, and victimized people whose peaceful institutions and learning centers amounted, without exaggeration, to a pillar supporting Europe's culture, one as important as the classics or Christianity.

The testimonies expect the survivors to engage with an interlocutor, to reach deep into the past, but also to share memories of life after repatriation or resettlement. They contribute to the depiction not only of a macro-historical event but also of states of mind ranging from severe to lesser forms of post-traumatic stress. It is important to understand that by taking a narrative form, and avoiding atrocity photos or similar footage, the testimonies do not retraumatize but grip rather than freeze the emotions and may have the strength to convey into the future what we can bear to remember. Their educative and humanizing value includes allowing the witnesses their image, their voice, their emotions.

Walter Benjamin, in his last thoughts on "The Concept of History," regrets how often historians have failed to stay with affective and disturbing memories. Too often, he charged, they transmit a false sense of closure or progress, and, turning away from defeated but still accessible energies, purge lament from history.[26]

Let us, however, respect the voice of lament. What we grieve for is never the dead alone but their unconsummated life: the ghosts of so many vital communities and a lost wisdom that might have strengthened rather than undermined our species image. Let us continue to build an audience for those who have had the courage to testify and who must represent the many who did not survive.

Acknowledgments

As editors, we wish first and foremost to thank Geoffrey Hartman for many years of friendship and inspiration. In life and in work, his example continues to guide us, and we are honored to help him realize a late wish in publishing this last collection of his essays. The final preparation of this volume was sobered by the death of Renée Hartman less than two weeks before the book entered production at Fordham University Press. A survivor of Bergen-Belsen and early contributor to the Fortunoff Video Archive for Holocaust Testimonies, as well as an author and poet, her example animated much of Hartman's work in *Holocaust and Hope* and elsewhere. We dedicate this book to her.

We benefited tremendously from the expert editorial assistance of Natalie Ruby, who helped us collect the missing documentation that Hartman left out, as well as from earlier help from Aidan Coley and Elena Durant in transcribing the manuscripts. We thank Jan Mieszkowski for help finding a late reference and Ulrich Baer for his early interest in the project. We are most grateful to Leslie Brisman and Joanne Rudof for their roles in making these chapters available for publication and to Rebecca Comay and Ian Balfour for supporting the inclusion of their important interview with Geoffrey Hartman (Chapter 13). We thank Sara Guyer for supporting the book in the Lit Z series. Finally, great thanks go to everyone at Fordham University Press, including Tom Lay, Robert Fellman, Kem Crimmins, and the anonymous reviewers.

Chapter 11, "Shoah Literature: The Universal Aspect," and **Chapter 12**, "Defining a Living Genre," were both left in draft by Hartman at the time of his death and have not appeared previously. They appear here by permission of the Literary Estate of Geoffrey Hartman.

Chapter 2, "Holocaust and Hope," originally appeared in *Catastrophe and Meaning* (2003), ed. Moishe Postone and Eric Santner, and is printed here with permission of the University of Chicago Press. **Chapter 6**, "Afterword to *Lodz Ghetto*," appeared in *Lodz Ghetto: A Community History Told in Diaries, Journals, and Documents*, compiled and edited by Alan Adelson and

Robert Lapides, copyright © 1989 by The Jewish Heritage Writing Project; it is used by permission of Viking Books, an imprint of Penguin Publishing Group, a division of Penguin Random House LLC. **Chapter 8**, "Breaking with Every Star: On Literary Knowledge," originally appeared in *Comparative Criticism* 18 (1996) and is reproduced here with permission of Edinburgh University Press through PLSclear. **Chapters 9 and 10**, "Learning from Survivors" and "Public Memory and Its Discontents," previously appeared in *The Longest Shadow: In the Aftermath of the Holocaust* (Palgrave MacMillan, 2002) and appear here by permission of Springer Nature (SNCSC). **Chapter 14**, "Terror and Art," originally appeared in *The Hedgehog Review*, Fall 2013, volume 15, number 3; it appears here by permission.

We also acknowledge the publishers who printed earlier versions of the following chapters, which also appear here thanks to the Literary Estate of Geoffrey Hartman. **Chapter 1**, "Shoah and Intellectual Witness," originally appeared in *The Partisan Review* 65, no. 1 (1998). **Chapter 3**, "Words Not from on High," originally appeared in *Nowhere Without No: In Memory of Maurice Blanchot*, ed. Kevin Hart (Vagabond Press, 2003). **Chapter 4**, "Wounded Time: The Holocaust, Jedwabne, and Disaster Writing," originally appeared in *The Partisan Review* 69, no. 3 (2002). **Chapter 5**, "Elie Wiesel and the Morality of Fiction," originally appeared in *Obliged by Memory: Literature, Religion, Ethics*, ed. Steven Katz and Alan Rosen (Syracuse University Press, 2006). **Chapter 7**, "Unbearable Truths," originally appeared in *The Partisan Review* 63, no. 4 (1996). **Chapter 13**, "The Ethics of Witness: An Interview with Geoffrey Hartman," was previously published in *Lost in the Archives*, ed. Rebecca Comay (Alphabet City Media, 2002). **Chapter 15**, "Future Memory: Reflections on Holocaust Testimony and Yale Fortunoff Video Archive," appeared in the published conference proceedings, *Preserving Survivors' Memories: Digital Testimony Collections About Nazi Persecution: History, Education, and Media*, ed. Nicolas Apostolopulos, Michelle Barricelli, and Gertrud Koch (Stiftung Erinnerung, Verantwortung und Zukunft, Berlin 2016).

In all cases, we have provided new notes for those omitted in the earlier publications, while also supplementing those that were there. We have also provided English translations for Hartman's quotations from German, French, and texts when we thought they would be helpful to readers.

Notes

Introduction: The Limits of Realism and the Future of Witness

1. Geoffrey H. Hartman, *The Third Pillar: Essays in Judaic Studies* (University of Pennsylvania Press, 2011), 14.

2. Geoffrey H. Hartman, "Public Memory and Its Discontents" and "Learning from Survivors," in *The Longest Shadow: In the Aftermath of the Holocaust* (Indiana University Press, 1996).

3. Geoffrey H. Hartman, ed., *Holocaust Remembrance: The Shapes of Memory* (Blackwell, 1993); *Bitburg in Moral and Political Perspective* (1986; Indiana University Press, 2000).

4. Marianne Hirsch, *The Generation of Postmemory: Writing and Visual Culture After the Holocaust* (Columbia University Press, 2012), 4. This generation includes both the children of survivors and those who belong to their generation: Hirsch distinguishes between "familial and 'affiliative' postmemory" in order "to account for the difference between an intergenerational vertical identification of child and parent occurring within the family, and the intragenerational horizontal identification that make that child's position more broadly available to other contemporaries" (36).

5. Examples include "Beyond Formalism," in *Beyond Formalism: Literary Essays, 1958–1970* (Yale University Press, 1970); "The Fate of Reading," in *The Fate of Reading and Other Essays* (University of Chicago Press, 1975); and "The Unremarkable Wordsworth," in *The Unremarkable Wordsworth* (University of Minnesota Press, 1987).

6. Accordingly, Hartman chooses as one of two epigraphs to "Holocaust and Hope" Yosef Yerushalmi's comment: "One cannot write the history of Jewish hope without a parallel history of Jewish despair."

7. Geoffrey H. Hartman, *The Unmediated Vision: An Interpretation of Wordsworth, Hopkins, Rilke, and Valéry* (Yale University Press, 1954).

8. For an important historical account of the difference between and the different historical trajectories of "media" and "mediation," see John Guillory, "Genesis of the Media Concept," *Critical Inquiry* 36, no. 2 (2010): 321–62.

9. Geoffrey H. Hartman, *Wordsworth's Poetry, 1787–1814* (1964; Yale University Press, 1971).

10. Geoffrey H. Hartman, "I. A. Richards and the Dream of Communication," in *The Fate of Reading*, 29.

11. Geoffrey H. Hartman, *Saving the Text: Literature, Derrida, Philosophy* (Johns Hopkins University Press, 1981); *Criticism in the Wilderness: The Study of Literature Today* (Yale University Press, 1980); *Easy Pieces* (Columbia University Press, 1985); *Minor Prophecies:*

The Literary Essay in the Culture Wars (Harvard University Press, 1991); *The Fateful Question of Culture* (Columbia University Press, 1997); *Scars of the Spirit: The Struggle Against Inauthenticity* (St. Martin's, 2002).

12. Adam Phillips, "Where Did the Hatred Go?," *London Review of Books* 30, no. 5 (March 6, 2008), https://www.lrb.co.uk/the-paper/v30/n05/adam-phillips/where-did-the-hatred-go.

13. The co-founders were, in addition to Hartman, Laurel Fox Vlock, Dori Laub, and William Rosenberg. See https://fortunoff.library.yale.edu/about-us/founders/. On the archives' history and interview methodology, see https://fortunoff.library.yale.edu/about-us/our-story/.

14. Geoffrey H. Hartman, *A Critic's Journey: Literary Reflections 1958–1998* (Yale University Press, 1999), xxvii. For a fuller outline of these issues, see xxvii–xxix.

15. Hartman, *A Critic's Journey*, xxviii. Compare, in "Breaking with Every Star" (in this volume), Hartman's appreciation of Peter Szondi for understanding "art as aesthetic education in the broadest sense. No illusory hope or sympathetic magic is suggested, but a gradual temporal process implanting the conviction that human freedom from personal compulsion and arbitrary authority is a *possibility*." Emphasis added.

16. Hartman, *A Critic's Journey*, xxix.

17. In an unpublished draft of a late article on Christopher Smart ("Trauma and Literature: The Case of Christopher Smart," whose revised and edited version was very recently published posthumously in *Eighteenth-Century Studies* 57, no. 4 [2024]: 531–46), Hartman distinguishes between the study of trauma as a "specifically literary endeavor" and its study in other fields, notably medicine and psychology but also history, which might seek to "pinpoint its determinants." "Neither a pathology nor a therapy is the subject of trauma study in literature," Hartman's draft began; instead, "the subject is speech under conditions that induce speechlessness, a nevertheless speech formed into expressive writing." For an account of the draft, see Kevis Goodman, "Introduction to 'Trauma and Literature,'" *Eighteenth-Century Studies* 57, no. 4 (2024): 527–29. For Hartman's own detailed and extended treatment of the relevance of trauma studies to literature, see his influential article "On Traumatic Knowledge and Literary Studies," *New Literary History* 26, no. 3 (1995): 537–63.

18. Hartman, "Words and Wounds," in *Saving the Text*, 123.

19. Hartman, "Christopher Smart's *Magnificat:* Toward a Theory of Representation," in *The Fate of Reading*, 74.

20. Dori Laub, MD, "An Event Without a Witness: Truth, Testimony, and Survival," in *Testimony: Crises of Listening in Literature, Psychoanalysis, and History*, ed. Shoshana Felman and Dori Laub, MD (Routledge, 1991), 81.

21. In addition to Laub, others who have addressed the question of why survivors did not or did not want to speak have included Jean-François Lyotard, in the searching first section of *The Differend: Phrases in Dispute,* trans. George Van Den Abbeele (University of Minneapolis Press, 1988). Here, Lyotard takes on the claim or pretense of the Holocaust denier Robert Faurisson that the silence of the survivors about the gas chambers meant that the chambers did not exist. Not so, argued Lyotard: Such silence "can just as well testify against the addressee's authority . . . against the authority of the

witness him- or herself (we, the rescued, do not have authority to speak about it)" or "against language's ability to signify gas chambers (an inexpressible absurdity)" (14).

22. Hirsch, *The Generation of Postmemory*, 3, 5. On "absent memory," see Ellen Fine, "The Absent Memory: The Act of Writing in Post-Holocaust French Literature," in *Writing and the Holocaust*, ed. Berel Lang (Holmes & Meier, 1988), 41–57. On "vicarious witnessing," see Froma Zeitlin, "The Vicarious Witness: Belated Memory and Authorial Presence in Recent Holocaust Literature," *History & Memory* 10, no. 2 (Fall 1998): 5–52. On "received history," see James Young, "Toward a Received History of the Holocaust," *History and Theory* 36, no. 2 (1997): 21–43. On "haunting legacy," see Gabriele Schwab, *Haunting Legacies: Violent Histories and Transgenerational Trauma* (Columbia University Press, 2010).

23. For Halbwachs's formulation of "collective memory," see Maurice Halbwachs, *On Collective Memory*, ed. Lewis A. Coser (University of Chicago Press, 1992). "Collected Memory" is the variation on Halbwachs's "collective memory" proposed by James E. Young in *The Texture of Memory: Holocaust Memorials and Meanings* (Yale University Press, 1993). Young's aim was to break down any unified notion implied by the word "collective" in order to emphasize "the many discrete memories that are gathered into common memorial spaces and assigned common meaning" but that are often diverse and even competing (xi).

24. Hartman, *The Fateful Question of Culture*, 141–64.

25. Hartman, *The Fateful Question of Culture*, 144. On "telesuffering," see "Telesuffering and Testimony," in *Scars of the Spirit*, 66–99.

26. The quote is from line 21 of the poem "In Drear Nighted December." See John Keats, *The Major Works*, ed. Elizabeth Cook (Oxford University Press, 2008), 165.

27. Hartman, *The Fateful Question of Culture*, 144.

28. Hartman, "Holocaust Testimony, Art, and Trauma," in *The Longest Shadow*, 151. As he continues: "It should not be assumed, in other words, that questions about representing the extreme are only technical in nature (how can we find *means* strong enough to depict what happened?) rather than scruples about the *end*" (151). Compare "Terror and Art."

29. Hartman, "The Cinema Animal: On Spielberg's *Schindler's List*," in *The Longest Shadow*, 82–98.

30. Hartman, "Holocaust Testimony, Art, and Trauma," in *The Longest Shadow*, 152–53.

31. Hartman, *The Longest Shadow*, 157. As Hartman's comment about the *unreality* effect suggests, not only does realism fail to reinforce reality; it also has the opposite effect: "While there is more realism, there is also the liability that goes along with that: a gnawing distrust of public policy"—or what we, in the decade of the 2020s, know well as conspiracy theories ("Public Memory and Its Discontents").

32. Hartman, *The Longest Shadow*, 159.

33. In "Shoah and Intellectual Witness," Hartman calls this active but reflective reception, which is forward looking and public facing, "intellectual." An alternative might be the better-known phrase "secondary witness," a term used by Terrence Des Pres and Lawrence Langer. Hartman does occasionally use "secondary witness," but it seems

not to have satisfied him because of its suggestion of passivity, or at least diminution of quality or quantity within witnessing. Yet "intellectual," as a term, is also problematic, as he knows, on several fronts—not only because of its apparent selectivity but also because many of the well-educated and professional thinkers in the Nazi era ("Hitler's professors," as Max Weinreich called them) stood by, did nothing, and in some cases became active accomplices during the Holocaust. Moreover, "intellectual witness" is also difficult because it can be easily misunderstood, especially if one takes Hartman to be denoting some exclusive group of select individuals defined by education or other cultural acquisitions. While he is obviously interested in certain figures who fall into such a category (Blanchot, Celan, and other literary authors), "intellectual" is not primarily something earned by education or sophistication, and it is a quality that Hartman hopes public projects like the video testimony archives will disseminate widely at all levels of education. As he uses it, the term is more adverbial, denoting a *way* of witnessing, a stance. In this volume and elsewhere, it involves a constitutive distance, which Hartman considers intrinsic but not limited to intellectual inquiry but which we may have difficulty achieving when discussing radically shocking events. For Hartman, while it may seem like coldness, it is not just indifference. "Without a struggle for and against that distance," he writes, "our reception of what happened is impoverished."

34. Hartman, *The Longest Shadow*, 155. The quoted words are from Aaron Appelfeld, whose work Hartman is commenting on at this point.

35. Compare Hartman's comment in "Wounded Time": "The cry [Why?] surfaces again, as much as an irrepressible cry as a call for historical explanation. The historian can turn that cry into a rational narrative of Nazism's mobilization of irrationality as it escalates from persecution to genocide. Yet making the exterminating process intelligible by dividing it up into functional solutions at the local level, solutions motivated by ideology, or ethnic and religious hatred, or a perceived military necessity, explains neither the face-to-face murderousness nor the rare acts of goodness."

36. Maurice Blanchot, *The Writing of the Disaster*, trans. Ann Smock (University of Nebraska Press, 1995), 42.

37. Jean-François Lyotard makes this case powerfully in *The Differend*: "The silence that surrounds the phrase 'Auschwitz was the extermination camp' ... is a sign that something remains to be phrased which is not, which is not determined" (57). It is worth remembering that Lyotard is also interested in cases of witnessing in the courtroom sense of the word: He defines the "differend" as the case in which "the plaintiff becomes a victim when no presentation is possible of the wrong he or she has suffered" (8).

38. Theodor W. Adorno, *Prisms*, trans. Samuel and Shierry Weber (MIT Press, 1983), 34. Adorno offered the dictum first in 1951. Not as often remembered or quoted is Adorno's later qualification: "The abundance of suffering tolerates no forgetting," *yet* such suffering "also demands the continued existence of art while it prohibits it; it is now virtually in art alone that suffering can still find its own voice, consolations, without immediately being betrayed by it." "Commitment," in *Aesthetics and Politics*, ed. Fredric Jameson (Verso, 1980), 188.

39. Readers familiar with Hartman's *Wordsworth's Poetry, 1797–1814* (1964) may find in this comment a version, in a more explicitly traumatic context, of what his literary

criticism called "surmise," which resists "the purely determinate" and instead "points to liberty and expansiveness of spirit" (9).

40. Geoffrey H. Hartman, *A Scholar's Tale: Intellectual Journey of a Displaced Child of Europe* (Fordham University Press, 2007), 164. Compare, in *Scars of the Spirit*, Hartman's worry that "a fallacious sense, arises, quite routinely, and despite an underlying awareness of the complexity of computer codes, that the media are not mediations but 'transparent' in the sense that nothing intervenes between sender and receiver, or that something has been transmitted in direct, undistorted fashion" (26–27).

41. Noah Shenker, *Reframing Holocaust Testimony* (Indiana University Press, 2015), 3. Shenker quotes from Geoffrey Hartman, "The Humanities of Testimony: An Introduction," *Poetics Today* 27, no. 2 (Summer 2006): 250. On the importance of such frame conditions, see also Hannah Pollin-Galay's work on how distinct social ecologies of witnessing shape the emphases that emerge in testimonial dialogues, in *Ecologies of Witnessing: Language, Place, and Holocaust Testimony* (Yale University Press, 2018).

42. For a detailed discussion of the Visual History Archive of the USC Shoah Foundation and its importance to future ethnographic work, and in general a defense of their filmic practices, see Jeffrey Shandler, *Holocaust Memory in the Digital Age: Survivor's Stories and New Media Practices* (Stanford University Press, 2017).

43. The quotation is from Hartman, *A Scholar's Tale*, 171, where Hartman is discussing Eric Auerbach. In "Breaking with Every Star" in this volume, talking about Peter Szondi, Hartman again refers to *Wirklichkeit*, defining it as "effective reality."

44. Hannah Pollin-Galay, "When the Index Is Wrong: Exploring Black Holes in Victim Memory," in *Lessons and Legacies*, vol. 14: *The Holocaust in the Twenty-First Century: Relevance and Challenges in the Digital Age*, eds. Tim Cole and Simone Gigliotti (Northwestern University Press, 2021), 245–46.

45. A strikingly resonant version of this problem faced Paul Celan upon the publication of his famous poem *Todesfuge* ("Death Fugue"), in Germany, as controversy developed around its famous opening line: "Black milk of daybreak we drink it at evening." Celan was impugned for the use of the metaphor in "black milk": Its force was undermined not only by the implicit accusation that it lacked veracity but also on the (false) grounds that it was not original enough—because it was not originally his. The widow of the poet Ivan Goll accused Celan of plagiarism from her husband, and the German press seized the story and prolonged it. For a fine discussion of this episode and Celan's poem itself, see John Felstiner, "Translating Paul Celan's *Todesfuge*: Rhythm and Repetition as Metaphor," in *Probing the Limits of Representation: Nazism and the "Final Solution,"* ed. Saul Friedländer (Harvard University Press, 1992), 240–58. We follow Felstiner's translation of the title and first line.

46. The often-quoted phrase originates in Paul Celan's poem "Ashglory" ("Aschenglorie"), whose last lines are: "No one / bears witness for the / witness." In Paul Celan, *Selections*, ed. Pierre Joris (University of California Press, 2005), 105.

47. Paul Frosh and Amit Pinchevski, eds., *Media Witnessing: Testimony in the Age of Mass Communication* (Palgrave Macmillan, 2009), 4.

48. Vivek Shankar, "Netanyahu Asserts Israel's Right to Fight Its Enemies in Defiant Speech," *New York Times*, May 6, 2024, https://www.nytimes.com/2024/05/06/world/middleeast/netanyahu-holocaust-gaza-yad-vashem.html.

1. Shoah and Intellectual Witness

1. William Shakespeare, *The Tempest*, in *The Norton Shakespeare*, ed. Stephen Greenblatt et al. (Norton, 2016), 1.2.50.
2. Wyndham Lewis, *Blasting and Bombarding: An Autobiography* (University of California Press, 1967), 342.
3. Amos Elon, "The Antagonist as Liberator," *New York Times Magazine*, January 26, 1997.
4. See Alexander and Margarete Mitscherlich, *The Inability to Mourn: Principles of Collective Behavior* (Grove, 1975).
5. Henri Raczymow, "Memory Shot Through with Holes," trans. Alan Astro, *Yale French Studies* 85 (1994): 104.
6. Dominick LaCapra, *Representing the Holocaust: History, Theory, Trauma* (Cornell University Press, 1994), 198.
7. See Jorge Semprún, *Literature or Life*, trans. Linda Coverdale (Penguin, 1997), 200. Translation modified. For the original French, see Jorge Semprún, *L'écriture ou la vie* (Éditions Gallimard, 1994), 261.
8. The term has been widely influential. See Marianne Hirsch, *Family Frames: Photography, Narrative, and Postmemory* (Harvard University Press, 1997); and *The Generation of Postmemory: Writing and Visual Culture After the Holocaust* (Columbia University Press, 2012).
9. Charlotte Delbo writes: "Je ne suis pas vivante, Je suis morte à Auschwitz et personne ne le voit." *Le convoi du 24 janvier* (Minuit, 1965), 66. See also Charlotte Delbo, *Auschwitz and After*, trans. Rosette C. Lamont (Yale University Press, 1995), 267. See Semprún, *Literature or Life*, 248.
10. Semprun, *Literature or Life*, 200–1. Translation modified.
11. Jürgen Habermas, *Eine Art Schadensabwicklung* (Suhrkamp, 1987), 163.
12. Ida Fink, *A Scrap of Time and Other Stories*, trans. Madeline Levine and Francine Prose (Northwestern University Press, 1995), 4.
13. See Maurice Blanchot, *The Infinite Conversation*, trans. Susan Hanson (University of Minnesota Press, 1993), 41.
14. Irving Howe, "High Mandarin. *In Bluebeard's Castle: Some Notes Towards the Redefinition of Culture*, by George Steiner," *Commentary* 53, no. 2 (February 1972): 99.
15. Daniel Jonah Goldhagen, *Hitler's Willing Executioners: Ordinary Germans and the Holocaust* (Knopf, 1996).
16. Tadeusz Borowski, *This Way for the Gas, Ladies and Gentlemen* (Penguin, 1992), 132.
17. Jürgen Habermas, "Concerning the Public Use of History," *New German Critique* 44 (Spring/Summer 1988): 44.
18. Walter Benjamin, "Theses on the Philosophy of History" (1968), in *Illuminations: Essays and Reflections*, ed. Hannah Arendt, trans. Harry Zohn (Mariner, 2019), 196–209.
19. Paul Celan's poem "Singbarer Rest," in *Gesammelte Werke*, 5 vols., eds. Beda Allemann and Stefan Reichert (Suhrkamp, 1983), 2:36.
20. Louis D. Brandeis, *Other People's Money and How the Bankers Use It* (Frederick A. Stokes Co., 1914), 92.

21. Nicholas Boileau, *Satires, épîtres, art poétique*, ed. Jean-Pierre Collinet (Gallimard, 1985).

22. Primo Levi's memoir *Se questo è un uomo* [*If This Be a Man*] was published in English as *Survival in Auschwitz*. See Dan Pagis's poem "Testimony" in *The Selected Poetry of Dan Pagis*, trans. Stephen Mitchell (Carcenet, 1972), 24. See Paul Celan's poem "Sprich auch du," in *Gesammelte Werke*, 1:135.

23. Celan was born Paul Antschel, with "Celan," his pen name, an anagram of the Romanian spelling, Ancel. *Amsel* is German for blackbird. The quoted line is from Percy Bysshe Shelley's "Hymn to Intellectual Beauty," in *The Major Works*, ed. Zachary Leader and Michael O'Neill (Oxford University Press, 2003), 114–20.

24. Maurice Halbwachs, *The Collective Memory*, trans. Francis J. Ditter (Harper Colophon, 1980); Michael Pollak, *L'expérience concentrationnaire: Essai sur le maintien de l'identité sociale* (Métailié, 1990).

2. Holocaust and Hope

Epigraphs: Arthur A. Cohen, "Thinking the Tremendum: Some Theological Implications of the Death Camps," *Leo Baeck Memorial Lecture* 18 (Leo Baeck Institute, 1974): 3; Yosef Hayim Yerushalmi, "Vers une histoire de l'espoir juif," *Esprit* 104/105, no. 8/9 (1985): 27.

1. Issued in English translation as *Literature or Life*.

2. Jorge Semprún, *Literature or Life*, trans. Linda Coverdale (Viking, 1997). See for the French edition *L'écriture ou la vie* (Gallimard, 1994): "La certitude qu'il n'y avait pas vraiment eu de retour, que je n'en etais pas vraiment revenue" (126) and "Je n'etais rien d'autre, pour l'essentiel, qu'un residu conscient de toute cette mort" (131).

3. See Albert Friedlander, in Friedrich-Wilhelm Marquardt and Albert Friedlander, *Das Schweigen der Christen und die Menschlichkeit Gottes: Gläubige Existenz nach Auschwitz* (Kaiser Tractate, 1980), 46–49. The most compelling remarks on Jewish-Christian relations after the Holocaust remain for me those of Emil Fackenheim in *The Jewish Return into History: Reflections in the Age of Auschwitz and a New Jerusalem* (Schocken, 1978), 32–40.

4. Marquardt and Friedlander, *Das Schweigen der Christen und die Menschlichkeit Gottes*, 12. In this there is a double meaning, intended or not: Christians cannot learn this lesson unless they identify with what happened to the Jews, their "shunning." Dostoyevsky's Ivan Karamazov tries to sustain his faith despite the "tears of humanity with which the earth is soaked from its crust to the center." But it is impossible for Jews to accept his vision of reconciliation, even if it echoes the Book of Job and other biblical sources. "I want to see with my own eyes the hind lie down with the lion and the victim rise up and embrace his murderer." Fyodor Dostoyevsky, *The Brothers Karamazov*, trans. Constance Garnett (Dover, 2005), 558–59.

5. Robert Antelme, "Témoignage du camp et poésie," in *Le Patriote Résistant* 53 (May 15, 1948); reprinted in *Robert Antelme: Textes inédits, Sur l'espèce humaine, Essais et témoignages* (Gallimard, 1966), 44–48. Fifty years later Lawrence Langer, in *Preempting the Holocaust* (Yale University Press, 1998), xv, will strongly acknowledge what he calls "the legacy of permanent disruption" caused by the survivors' experience.

6. On this, consult Annette Wieviorka, *L'ère du témoin* (Plon, 1998), 172–75. Primo Levi's influence, in this respect, began to be felt in America and Europe somewhat later.

7. See Arthur W. Frank, *The Wounded Storyteller: Body, Illness, and Ethics* (University of Chicago Press, 1995), chap. 5. Lawrence Langer coins the striking phrase the "legacy of unheroic memory" in *Holocaust Testimonies: The Ruins of Memory* (Yale University Press, 1992), 205.

8. David Halivni, *The Book and the Sword: A Life of Learning in the Shadow of Destruction* (Farrar, Straus & Giroux, 1996).

9. In this respect, *Life Is Beautiful* is one of many films in which "the survival of a child, even a single one, signifies a resistance to the brutal facts, a ray of hope for the future." Froma I. Zeitlin, "The Vicarious Witness," *History & Memory* 10 (1998): 32. It has not been noted, however, that there is an affinity between the father-child relationship in *Life Is Beautiful* and an entirely different film that is a classic of postwar Italian cinema: Vittorio De Sico's *Bicycle Thieves*.

10. Heinrich Mann, "Das weiss eigentlich jeder," reprinted in *Heinrich Mann Das Führer Prinzip/Arnold Zweig Der Typus Hitler: Texte zur Kritik der NS-Diktatur* (Aufbau Taschenbuch Verlag, 1993), 19.

11. Now partly available in translation. Victor Klemperer, *I Will Bear Witness: A Diary of the Nazi Years, 1933–1941*, trans. Martin Chalmers (Random House, 1998).

12. "Das Leiden, das eine fortwährende Selbstreinigung mit sich hätte bringen müssen, wäre ja so stark gewesen, daß Sie hätten den Verstand verlieren müssen." He adds: "Das ist es ja gerade, was uns Emigranten so unverständlich ist! Wie die Menschen in Deutschland nicht den Verstand verloren haben" (That is what is so incomprehensible to us emigrants! How the people in Germany have not lost their minds). The letter is addressed to Hugo Friedrich. Cited by O. G. Oexle, "Zweierlei Kultur. Zur Erinnerungskultur Deutscher Geisteswissenschaftler nach 1945," *Rechtshistorisches Journal* 16 (1997): 383. See also Elisabeth Langgässer, "Schriftsteller unter der Hitler-Diktatur," in *Erster Deutscher Schriftsteller-kongress 4.–8, Oktober 1947*, ed. Ursula Reinhold, Dieter Schlenstedt, and Horst Tannenberger (Aufbau-Verlag, 1997), 136–41. I should add the following thought. That an ambitious and ruthless regime should conspire with the aggressive side of human nature and idealize war and the removal of the shame of a prior defeat is not surprising: Imperialism and militarism, which coexisted with a high degree of personal and artistic culture in Rome, continued to appeal to a later European elite. Nazi ideology, often under the auspices of the SS, resurrected the *völkisch* myth of a Nordic race whose ancient Aryan rites and *Herrenvolk* character had supposedly been suppressed by the Romans. (It became, thus, a perverse kind of high culture.) Added to this myth was a biological *Rassenlehre* that made the extrusion and killing of the so-called antirace of Jews appear not only legal but normal. Citizen was alienated from citizen; years before the Final Solution murderous acts took place with immunity in the camps, which sprung up immediately after the transfer of power in 1933, and the fear of Jewish contamination—based on an insidious form of blood libel—was deliberately propagated.

13. See, e.g., a book written beginning of 1946 by the theologian Martin Dibelius but only recently published: *Selbstbesinnung des Deutschen*, ed. Friedrich Wilhelm Graf (Mohr Siebeck, 1997), 2–4.

14. Cf. D. Bar-On, *Legacy of Silence: Encounters with Children of the Third Reich* (Harvard University Press, 1989). The "black box" of unopened memory also contained many personal disasters suffered by the German populace: see, e.g., Elisabeth Domansky, "A Lost War: World War II in Postwar German Memory," in *Thinking About the Holocaust: After Half a Century*, ed. Alvin H. Rosenfeld (Indiana University Press, 1997), 233–71. The Mitscherlichs, well-known German psychiatrists, diagnosed an incapacity to mourn; that incapacity involved verbal as well as psychic impotence.

15. Langgässer, "Schriftsteller unter der Hitler-Diktatur," 137. One must acknowledge, at the same time, the fact to which Karl Kraus is the most outspoken witness, of a more general debasement of language, not only in Germany but in the West before (and after) Hitler. George Steiner's admonitions are well known; see also Cohen, "Thinking the Tremendum," and my remarks in what follows on the language-consciousness of modernism.

16. George Orwell, *Shooting an Elephant* (Harcourt, Brace, and Company, 1950), 92.

17. On the role of academics, in addition to Max Weinrich's classic *Hitler's Professors*, see Oexle, "Zweierlei Kultur," 359–91.

18. After the war, Blanchot emerged as a political activist principally during the Algerian crisis (when he joined the famous Declaration of the 121) and the student turmoil of 1968. An "essai biographique" of Blanchot has finally been published: see Christophe Bident, *Maurice Blanchot: Partenaire invisible* (Champs Vallon, 1998). Philippe Mesnard has focused on Blanchot's complicated incursion into and withdrawals from politics in *Maurice Blanchot: Le sujet de l'engagement* (L'Harmattan, 1996). For a remarkable account of Antelme and his rescue—an account that takes as its point of departure from the *explication de texte* of a letter Antelme wrote to the author in June 1945 about his recuperation and dealings with speech—see Dionys Mascolo, *Autour d'un effort de mémoire: Sur une lettre de Robert Antelme* (Maurice Nadeau, 1987). Also, for Blanchot's most direct statements on Antelme, see *Robert Antelme: Textes inédits*, 72–87. Blanchot met Antelme through Mascolo circa 1958: see his "For Friendship," *Oxford Literary Review* 22 (2000): 28–29.

19. "Und der die Geige spielt, ist ganz weiß geworden und setzt einen Takt lang aus" (And he who plays the violin turns pale and misses the beat for a long time). The complexity vis-à-vis the Shoah of this description in Ingeborg Bachmann's "Was ich in Rom sah und hörte" (1955) is carefully demonstrated by Sigrid Weigel, who recovers for us Gershom Scholem's poem of 1967 referring to this scene in Bachmann's sketches, a poem that contests a messianic allusion—and the possibility of messianic hope after the Shoah—that is probably not there. See Weigel, "Gershom Scholem und Ingeborg Bachmann. Ein Dialog über Messianismus und Ghetto," *Zeitschrift für deutsche Philologie* 115 (1996): 608–16. The literary burden is that of the walker-tourist-flâneur, from Schiller's "Spaziergang" through Rilke's *Malte Laurids Brigge* to Walter Benjamin. The "Spiel weiter" may recall Celan's "Todesfuge."

20. Stéphane Mallarmé, *Poésies* (Éditions de la Nouvelle Revue Française, 1914), 43.

21. Terrence Des Pres, *Writing Into the World: Essays: 1973–1987* (Viking, 1991), 27.

22. See Catherine Coquio, "L'extrême, le génocide, l'éxperience concentrationnaire," *Critique* 600 (1997): 339–64; Michael A. Bernstein, "Homage to the Extreme: The Shoah and the Rhetoric of Catastrophe," *Times Literary Supplement* (London),

March 6, 1998, 6–8; and Tzvetan Todorov, *Les abus de la mémoire* (Arléa, 1998). See also the report by Dominique Dhombres in *Le Monde* (Paris), July 11, 1998, 1, 12, on a conference in Lisbon organized by the Calouste Gulbenkian Foundation. Under the headline "Malaise dans la culture européenne," Dhombres quotes George Steiner on this crisis as a language crisis from the First World War on. René Girard, also participating, sees another crisis, one that actually unifies European and world culture: a troubling major focus on the victim.

23. Langer, *Preempting the Holocaust*, xix.

24. History yields not simply an explanatory cause but a justification, in the sense in which Yosef Yerushalmi writes (though of the *Wissenschaft des Judentums* rather than specifically of Hegel): "History becomes what it had never been before—the faith of fallen Jews. For the first time history, not a sacred text, becomes the arbiter of Judaism. Virtually all nineteenth-century Jewish ideologies, from Reform to Zionism, would feel a need to appeal to history for validation." *Zakhor: Jewish History and Jewish Memory* (University of Washington Press, 1982), 86.

25. Or, "without being able to" (*sans pouvoir*). See Sarah Kofman, *Paroles suffoquées* (Galilée, 1997), 16: "Parler—il le faut—*sans pouvoir*: sans que le langage trop puissant, souverain, ne vienne maîtriser la situation la plus aporétique, l'impouvoir absolu et la détresse même, ne vienne l'enfermer dans la claret bonheur du jour?"

26. Blanchot takes up the issue of the engagement of the intellectual in *Les intellectuels en question: Ebauche d'une réflexion* (Fourbis, 1996), with relevant remarks on Sartre on pages 57–58.

27. This echoes Mallarmé's famous "une fleur ... l'absente de tous bouquets." See Stéphane Mallarmé, *Oeuvres complètes* (Gallimard, 1945), 368. As Barbara Johnson translates: "I say: a flower! And, out of the oblivion where my voice casts every contour, insofar as it is something other than the known bloom, there arises, musically, the very idea in its mellowness; in other words, what is absent from every bouquet." Stéphane Mallarmé, *Divagations*, trans. Barbara Johnson (Harvard University Press, 2007), 210. The point at which this withdrawal touches words themselves points to the difference between Blanchot's spirituality and that of Judaism. In the latter, meanings may withdraw into the text, but the text (as Scripture) is always maintained. Yet his essay on Jabès conflates "cette écriture qui est la difficulté du poète," the one who wants to find the *mot juste*, and "la justice difficile, celle de la loi juive, la parole inscrite avec laquelle on ne joue pas, et qui est esprit parce qu'elle est le fardeau et la fatigue de la lettre." Maurice Blanchot, *L'amitié* (Gallimard, 1971), 252.

28. Maurice Blanchot, *La part du feu* (Gallimard, 1948), 328. My translation.

29. Blanchot, *Les intellectuels en question*, 56–59.

30. Blanchot, *La part du feu*, 45. Levinas's attitude toward this phenomenal exteriority is very intricate, however: Derrida has exposed its complexity or ambivalence in his essay on Levinas, "Violence and Metaphysics," in *Writing and Difference* (University of Chicago Press, 1978). Exteriority in the sense in which it is opposed to Hegel's phenomenological perspective owed something to Heidegger's concept of Existence as a standing-outside-of (ek-sistence) and endurance (punning on the German *ausstehen*) of this outsiderness.

31. The phrase comes from Baudelaire's description of Constantin Guys in his essay *Constantin Guys: Le peintre de la vie moderne* (Nilsson, 1925), 42. My translation.

32. Maurice Blanchot, *Thomas the Obscure: New Version*, trans. Robert Lamberton (David Lewis, 1973), 26.

33. Wallace Stevens, "Notes Toward a Supreme Fiction," in *The Collected Poems of Wallace Stevens* (Knopf, 1954), 381.

34. Maurice Blanchot, *L'entretien infini* (Gallimard, 1969), 189. My translation. I should add that Levinas does not seem to share Blanchot's view of art, which he says gratifies, like politics, "the essential violence of action." See Emmanuel Levinas, *Totality and Infinity: An Essay on Exteriority*, trans. Alphonso Lingis (Duquesne University Press, 1969), 298.

35. "La parole, celle qui invite l'homme à ne plus identifier avec son pouvoir." Blanchot, *L'amitié*, 253. My translation.

36. This is the context in which we should read Levinas's protest against Hegel, that moral knowledge is "other than being and beyond essence." See Levinas's book of that title and, for a summary, *Éthique et infini: Dialogues avec Philippe Nemo* (Fayard, 1982). Other Levinas quotations come from "Ethics as First Philosophy," in *The Levinas Reader*, ed. Sean Hand (Basil Blackwell, 1989), 75–87. In how far Levinas and Blanchot are influenced by Kojève's famous proposition that "history" in the Hegelian sense is complete, that we are "beyond essence" in that sense, cannot be discussed here.

37. Edith Wyschogrod, "Concentration Camps and the End of the Life-World," in *Echoes from the Holocaust: Philosophical Reflections on a Dark Time*, ed. Alan Rosenberg and Gerald E. Myers (Temple University Press, 1988), 335. Emphasis in the original.

38. Blanchot, *L'écriture du désastre*, 180: "L'holocauste, l'événement absolu de l'histoire, historiquement daté, cette toute-brûlure où toute l'histoire s'est embrasée, où le mouvement du sens s'est abîmé." My translation.

39. See also Michael Rothberg's development of this insight as it surfaces in both the fictional and discursive work of Maurice Blanchot, in *Traumatic Realism: The Demands of Holocaust Representation* (University of Minnesota Press, 2000), 85ff. Blanchot, as I have mentioned, hints at various times that with Auschwitz history has come to an end, in the sense that Kojève talked about Hegel's end of history. It is, to invert the Kantian formula, a "fin sans finalité." Negativity remains—part of the sequelae of the Holocaust—but cannot operate as a dialectical machine producing new meanings.

40. Blanchot, *L'écriture du désastre*, 104.

41. My summary is based mainly on *L'écriture du désastre*. "Veiller sur le sens absent" is on p. 72, and the remark on "imposture" on p. 79, in a discussion of the relation between Hegel, meaning, and system, pp. 79–80. *Veiller*, the French for "to watch over," is also the word for watching at the bedside of a dying person, looking for a sign of that person's salvation, of whether he makes a "good end." Blanchot's "wake" inverts this religious watching, without forgetting Pascal's "Il ne faut plus dormir."

42. Unlike many modernists between the wars, who were attracted to the idea of a "conservative revolution," Blanchot does not seek to "make it new" or break through to an antibourgeois or archaic stratum. Ezra Pound and Gottfried Benn are obvious examples, though the latter moved away from his *Schwärmerei* for the Nazi regime.

43. See Blanchot's "Postface," in *Vicious Circles: Two Fictions & "After the Fact"* (Station Hill, 1985), 68. Also on passivity, *L'écriture du désastre*, 28ff.

44. For Blanchot's phrase (applied to Bataille), see *The Writing of the Disaster*, trans. Ann Smock (University of Nebraska Press, 1995), 109. Smock translates as "the harshness of a restless language."

45. Blanchot comes very close, also, with his antisystematic bent, to Walter Benjamin's concept of the "expressionless," depicted in Benjamin's essay on Goethe's *Elective Affinities* as both an interruption and perpetuation of the semblance (*Schein*) of the harmonious and beautiful. "Das Ausdruckslose" (the expressionless) is at the base of a work's completion *as* fragments of the truth. It "zerschlägt was in allem schönen Schein als die Erbschaft des Chaos noch überdauert: die falsche, irrende Totalität—die absolute" (It shatters whatever still survives as the legacy of chaos in all beautiful semblance: the false, errant totality—the absolute totality). Further, "Dieses erst vollendet das Werk, welches es zum Stückwerk zerschlägt, zum Fragmente der wahren Welt, zum Torso eines Symbols" (Only the expressionless completes the work, by shattering it into a thing of shards, into a fragment of the true world, into the torso of a symbol). See Walter Benjamin, *Illuminationen: Ausgewählte Schriften* (Suhrkamp, 1961), 127. For the English, see *Selected Writings*, ed. Marcus Bullock and Michael W. Jennings, 4 vols. (Harvard University Press, 1996–2003), 1:340.

46. The smile of the Rheims angel in Antelme's description comes to mind. See *Robert Antelme: Textes inédits*, 15–16.

47. Maurice Blanchot, "From Dread to Language," trans. Lydia Davis, in *The Gaze of Orpheus*, ed. P. Adams Sitney (Station Hill, 1981), 4. Originally published in *Faux pas* (Gallimard, 1943).

48. Ernst Simon, "Der neue Midrash," *Aufbau im Untergang: Jüdische Erwachsenenbildung im nationalsozialistischen Deutschland als geistiger Widerstand* (C. B. Mohr, 1959), chap. 4.

49. Miklos Radnoti, "The Seventh Eclogue," trans. Clive Wilmer and George Gömöri, in *Poetry of the Second World War*, ed. Desmond Graham (Pimlico, 1998), 144.

50. Miklos Radnoti, "Fragments," trans. Clive Wilmer and George Gömöri, in *Poetry of the Second World War*, ed. Desmond Graham (Pimlico, 1998), 17.

51. See Primo Levi, "The Canto of Ulysses," in *Survival in Auschwitz* (Simon and Schuster, 1996), 109–15.

52. Theodor Adorno, "Die Verdunklung der Welt macht die Irrationalität der Kunst rational: die radikal verdunkelte," in *Aesthetische Theorie* (Suhrkamp, 1970), 35. When Paul Celan, in a famous pronouncement, says that, after the Holocaust, and "despite a thousand eclipses [*Finsternisse*] language remained," he is refusing, despite an increasingly radical poetic practice, to reject the culture, even if suborned, of the mother tongue. See Paul Celan, *Gesammelte Werke*, ed. Beda Allemann and Stefan Reichert (Suhrkamp, 1983), 3:186.

53. Johann Wolfgang von Goethe, *Iphigenie auf Tauris: Ein Schauspiel* (De Gruyter, 2019), 105.

54. In a conversation related by Johannes Falk. See Johannes Falk, *Goethe aus näherm persönlichen Umgange dargestellt. Ein nachgelassenes Werk* (Leipzig: Brockhaus, 1832), 121.

55. William Shakespeare, *Macbeth*, ed. Roma Gill (Oxford University Press, 2009), 5.5.13.
56. Anna Akhmatova, in *Poetry of the Second World War*, 62.
57. Goethe, *Iphigenie auf Tauris*, 105. My translation.
58. Goethe, *Iphigenie auf Tauris*, 104. My translation. Emil Fackenheim said the following about Goethe in 1976: "It is not certain how long the world will be inspired by the wisest German. But we must live with the grim certainty that the shadow of the most depraved German [Hitler] will never cease to haunt it." *The Jewish Return into History*, 261.

3. Words Not from on High

1. Paul Celan, *Poems of Paul Celan*, trans. Michael Hamburger (Persea, 2002), 31.
2. See Lawrence L. Langer's introduction to Charlotte Delbo, *Auschwitz and After*, trans. Rosette C. Lamont (Yale University Press, 1995), x.
3. Theodor W. Adorno, *Negative Dialektik* (Suhrkamp, 1966), 358.
4. Maurice Blanchot, *The Space of Literature*, trans. Ann Smock (University of Nebraska Press, 1982), 26. Translation modified.
5. Maurice Blanchot, *L'écriture du désastre* (Éditions Gallimard, 1980), 79. Ann Smock translates the phrase as the "travesty of completed Meaning." See *The Writing of the Disaster*, trans. Ann Smock (University of Nebraska Press, 1995), 47.
6. Blanchot, *The Writing of the Disaster*, 42.
7. Job 6:11. See *The Bible, Authorized King James Version*, with an introduction and notes by Robert Carroll and Stephen Prickett (Oxford University Press, 1997), 611.
8. All three quotations are from Wallace Stevens, "Notes Toward a Supreme Fiction," in *The Collected Poems* (Vintage, 1982), 381, 381, 380.
9. Søren Kierkegaard, *The Sickness Unto Death*, trans. Walter Lowrie (Princeton University Press, 1941), 26.
10. Maurice Blanchot, "The Essential Solitude," in *The Space of Literature*, trans. Ann Smock (University of Nebraska Press, 1982), 27.

4. Wounded Time: The Holocaust, Jedwabne, and Disaster Writing

1. Shoshana Felman and Dori Laub, *Testimony: Crises of Witnessing in Literature, Psychoanalysis, and History* (Routledge, 1992), xx.
2. Maurice Blanchot, *The Writing of the Disaster*, trans. Ann Smock (University of Nebraska Press, 1995), 47.
3. Maurice Blanchot, *The Infinite Conversation*, trans. Susan Hanson (University of Minnesota Press, 1993), 172.
4. Charlotte Delbo, *Auschwitz and After*, trans. Rosette C. Lamont (Yale University Press, 1995), 11.
5. Jan T. Gross, "Neighbors," *New Yorker*, March 12, 2001, 64. See also Jan T. Gross, *Neighbors: The Destruction of the Jewish Community in Jedwabne* (Princeton University Press, 2001).

6. Gross, "Neighbors," 64.
7. Claude Lanzmann, "The Obscenity of Understanding: An Evening with Claude Lanzmann," *American Imago* 48, no. 4 (Winter 1991): 473–95.
8. Gross, *Neighbors*, 167.
9. Gross, *Neighbors*, 169.
10. Czeslaw Milosz, "Child of Europe," in *The Collected Poems, 1931–1987* (Ecco, 1988), 88.
11. Czeslaw Milosz, "In Warsaw," in *The Collected Poems, 1931–1987* (Ecco, 1988), 76.

5. Elie Wiesel and the Morality of Fiction

1. Egil Aarvik, "Award Ceremony Speech," NobelPrize.org, https://www.nobelprize.org/prizes/peace/1986/ceremony-speech/.
2. Elie Wiesel, "The Nobel Peace Prize Acceptance Speech," in *Night* (Hill and Wang, 2006), 118.
3. Quoted by Egil Aarvik in his "Award Ceremony Speech."
4. Elie Wiesel, "The Nobel Acceptance Speech," in *Night*, 118.
5. My translation. Also translated as "Such a vengeance, the vengeance for a small child's blood/—Satan himself never dreamed—." Hayim Nahman Bialik, "On the Slaughter," in *Songs from Bialik: Selected Poems of Hayim Nahman Bialik*, ed. and trans. Atar Hadari (Syracuse University Press, 2000), 11.
6. Elie Wiesel, *Twilight*, trans. Marion Wiesel (Summit, 1987), 111.
7. Elie Wiesel, *The Fifth Son*, trans. Marion Wiesel (Summit, 1985).
8. Elie Wiesel, *Dawn*, trans. Frances Frenaye (Bantam, 1982).
9. Elie Wiesel, *A Beggar in Jerusalem*, trans. Lily Edelman and Elie Wiesel (Schocken, 1985), 201.
10. Wiesel, *Twilight*, 114–17.
11. Wiesel, *Twilight*, 115.
12. Wiesel, *Twilight*, 114.
13. Wiesel, *The Fifth Son*, 145. Even more haunting is Wiesel's portrait of Zelig, the sky-gazer, in *Twilight*, 172–73. "Like Zelig, Raphael sees a trail of glittering stars set like gravestones in a velvet sky. He sees dead men and women entranced by a mute speaker."
14. Quoted in Geoffrey Hartman, "Preface," in *Le passage du témoin: Portraits et témoignages de rescapés des camps de concentration et d'extermination nazis* (La Lettre Volée, 1995), 7.
15. Elie Wiesel, *One Generation After*, trans. Lily Edelman and Elie Wiesel (Random House, 1970), 38.
16. Elie Wiesel, *One Generation After*, 8.
17. Elie Wiesel, *The Trial of God*, trans. Marion Wiesel (Random House, 1979).
18. This and the following stories are found in Wiesel's *One Generation After*, 87–90. The second story is also found, with slight variations, in Elie Wiesel, *Four Hasidic Masters* (Notre Dame University Press, 1978).
19. Wiesel, *Twilight*, 115–16.
20. Elie Wiesel, *Le mal et l'exil: Rencontre avec Elie Wiesel, dialogue avec Philippe-Michaël de Saint-Cheron* (Nouvelle Cité, 1988), 103.

21. Elie Wiesel, *The Oath*, trans. Marion Wiesel (Random House, 1973).
22. Wiesel, *One Generation After*, 253.
23. Emmanuel Levinas, *Proper Names*, trans. Michael B. Smith (Stanford University Press, 1996), 130.

6. Afterword to *Lodz Ghetto*

1. This chapter was originally published as the afterword to *Lodz Ghetto: Inside a Community Under Siege*, ed. Alan Adelson and Robert Lapides (Viking, 1989). Page references will be to this edition and included parenthetically in the text.

7. Unbearable Truths

1. This chapter was originally published as a review of Gitta Sereny, *Albert Speer: His Battle with the Truth* (Knopf, 1995). Page numbers to this edition will be included parenthetically.
2. This principle is often summarized in Vico's dictum "Verum ipsum factum." Giambattista Vico, *The New Science of Giambattista Vico (1744 Edition)*, trans. Thomas Goddard Bergin and Max Harold Fisch (Cornell University Press, 1984).
3. Saul Friedländer, "The 'Final Solution': On the Unease in Historical Interpretation," *History and Memory* 1, no. 2 (Fall/Winter 1989): 68.

8. Breaking with Every Star: On Literary Knowledge

Epigraphs: "Auch die sternische Verbindung trügt. / Doch uns freue eine Weile nun / Der Figur zu glauben." Rainer Maria Rilke, *Duino Elegies and The Sonnets to Orpheus: A Dual-Language Edition*, trans. Stephen Mitchell (Vintage, 2009), 102–3; "So, da wären wir nun (wieder) per aspera—nicht Sternen—den Sternen sei gedankt!—, aber bei Worten, die von Händen herkommen und die man mit Händen greifen kann." Paul Celan, Letter to Gottfried Bermann Fischer, in *Paul Celan*, ed. Werner Hamacher and Winfried Menninghaus (Suhrkamp, 1988), 20.

1. "What use are academics in times of need?" See Friedrich Hölderlin's poem "Brot und Wein" (Bread and Wine), in which the speaker asks of poets: "Wozu Dichter in dürftiger Zeit?" See Friedrich Hölderlin, *Poems and Fragments*, trans. Michael Hamburger (University of Michigan Press, 1966), 250–51.
2. His interventions always aim to name the issues, however complex, with honesty. What he said in a radio talk about "Germans and Jews," on the occasion of a published symposium of that title, can stand for every political circumstance in which reconciliation must be considered, however painful or impossible that seems. "Die Sprache dieser künftigen Versöhnung dürfte nicht zuletzt die nüchterne Entschlossenheit vorbereiten helfen, allem Quid proquo abgewandt, Menschen und Dingen ihre Namen zu lassen" (The language of this future reconciliation should help to anticipate the sober determination to turn away from every quid pro quo and name things and people by their names). Peter Szondi, *Über eine "Freie (d.h. freie) Universität": Stellungsnahme eines Philologen* (Suhrkamp, 1973), 67. All translations, unless otherwise indicated, are mine.

3. Including information technology, a wonderful learning aid, but whose proponents pretend that information in this format can speak for itself—that it is self-interpreting and can elide fallible (and expensive) educational intermediaries.

4. Peter Szondi, *Einführung in die literarische Hermeneutik*, ed. Jean Bollack and Helen Stierlin (Suhrkamp, 1975), 425.

5. There is strictness, of course, but it is what Gershom Scholem called the "strict light of the canonical" ("das strenge Licht des Kanonischen"). This involves the literary object of study or literary consciousness of the artist as much as the reflective process of understanding the work of art. The title of Szondi's tractate may recall Hegel's "Vorrede" to the *Phaenomenologie des Geistes*, "Vom wissenschaftlichen Erkennen," or Benjamin's "Erkenntniskritische Vorrede" to *Ursprung des deutschen Trauerspiels*.

6. All the German quotations on this page are from the "tractate" on "Über philologische Erkenntnis," which introduces *Hölderlin-Studien* (Insel Verlag, 1967): 9–34. The essay is translated in *On Textual Understanding*, trans. Harvey Mendelsohn (University of Minnesota Press, 1986), 3–22.

7. More would have to be said about this bidirectionality of *intentio* (a medieval term of philosophic art adapted by Benjamin and Husserl), as well as about the dyadic structure of "work of art" and "work of criticism." See Szondi on Celan as a translator of Shakespeare's sonnets, "Poetry of Constancy—Poetik der Bestaendigkeit," in *Celan-Studien* (Suhrkamp, 1972), 18–19.

8. Szondi, *Hölderlin-Studien*, 11.

9. In his speech accepting the Prize for Literature given by the city of Bremen. Paul Celan, *Gesammelte Werke* (Suhrkamp, 1983), 3:186.

10. Szondi, *Hölderlin-Studien*, 11.

11. Szondi continues: "In diesem prägnanten Sinn beginnt das Gedicht mit dem Wort *Hyperbole*, es muß ihm keine Vorstellung, die unabhängig vom Wort existierte, vorausgegangen sein" (It is in this strong sense that the poem may be said to begin with the word *Hyperbole*; it cannot have been preceded by any image or notion independently of the word). Szondi, *Hölderlin-Studien*, 28.

12. Applied in his *Origins of German Tragic Drama* to "the genuine": see *On Textual Understanding*, 158. Szondi also cites Wittgenstein's remark on the difference between the natural sciences and philosophy as relevant for literary study: "Philosophy is not a theory but an activity. A philosophical work consists essentially of elucidations." *On Textual Understanding*, 6.

13. Psalm 19:1. [Ed.: Hartman offers his own translation of Psalm 19.]

14. If the language of the Hebrew Bible often presents a "reconciliation" of various sources or the accommodation of earlier ritual prayers and narratives, this might be another reason for asking for the acceptability of the words being spoken before God, of the "offering" or "sacrifice" of prayer. In addition to intratextual biblical references, there may be intertextual residues to displaced cultic texts that remain unknown.

15. Section epigraphs: John Donne, "The First Anniversary," in *The Anniversaries*, ed. Frank Manley, (Johns Hopkins University Press, 1963), 79. Paul Valéry, *La jeune parque* (Gallimard, 1998), 17. For an English translation, see Paul Valéry, *Selected Writings* (New Directions, 1950): "Great clusters glitter to my thirst for dangers" (15).

16. My translation for "ein Dasein, das unmittelbar selbstbewusste Existenz ist." See

G. W. F. Hegel, *The Phenomenology of Spirit*, trans. A. V. Miller (Oxford University Press, 1979), 430.

17. I realize that we are dealing here with a woman "star," and in a theatrical context, but the sense of theater, of that kind of focused *presence*, is part of the larger, cosmic story. Gérard de Nerval, "El Desdichado," in *Les filles du feu nouvelles* (Giraud, 1854), 329. See also Geoffrey Hartman, "Nerval's Peristyle," *Nineteenth Century French Studies* 5 (1976–1977): 71–78.

18. Paul Celan, *Zeitgehöft: Späte Gedichte aus dem Nachlass* (Suhrkamp, 1976), 29.

19. "Spoke, spoke. / Was, was." See Paul Celan, *The Poems of Paul Celan*, trans. Michael Hamburger (Persea, 2002), 120–21.

20. Maurice Blanchot, *The Writing of the Disaster*, trans. Ann Smock (Nebraska University Press, 1995), 56.

21. Blanchot, *The Writing of the Disaster*, 56.

22. Rainer Maria Rilke, *Duino Elegies and The Sonnets to Orpheus*, 56–57. The stars can also be made "säglich" by being given earthly names, as happens with the constellations, and in the Tenth Elegy's wonderful *Weltinnenraum* (world-inner-space) allegory of the "new" stars of the Country of Suffering ("Sterne des Leidlands"). See Rilke, *Duino Elegies*, 66–67.

23. See Blanchot, *The Writing of the Disaster*, 75.

24. "Was, wenn Verwandlung nicht, ist dein drängender Auftrag? / Erde, du liebe, ich will" ("What, if not transformation, is your urgent command? / Earth, my dearest, I will"). Rilke, *Duino Elegies*, 58–59.

25. Nelly Sachs, *Späte Gedichte* (Suhrkamp, 1965), 139. "Dreams from wounds." For an excellent account of Sachs's "symbolic biography" as well as the politics of her reception in Germany, see Erhard Bahr, *Nelly Sachs* (C. H. Beck, 1980).

26. Sachs, *Späte Gedichte*, 28. For the English, see Nelly Sachs, *Flight and Metamorphosis: A Bilingual Edition*, trans. Joshua Weiner (Farrar, Strauss and Giroux, 2023), 47. For an explicitly astrological poem, see "Mischung / dieser Mutter / dieses Vaters / unterm geschlossenen Augenlid / Aus Stern" in Sachs, *Späte Gedichte*, 32. "The mixing of / this mother / this father / beneath the closed / star-spun lid." Sachs, *Flight and Metamorphosis*, 51.

27. Blanchot, *The Writing of the Disaster*, 50.

28. Sachs, *Späte Gedichte*, 28. Sachs, *Flight and Metamorphosis*, 47.

29. Sachs, *Späte Gedichte*, 30. Sachs, *Flight and Metamorphosis*, 47.

30. The last stanza is an epilogue that signals, without crossing over to it, a realm beyond words ("Hier ist / Amen zu sagen / diese Krönung der Worte die / ins Verborgene zieht" ["Here is the time / to say Amen / this coronation of words / moving into hiding"]) and attempts to transform the idea of a closed destiny into an image of peaceful closure. To adopt her own quiet pun, the poem becomes an "Augenlid" ("Augenlied"). See Sachs, *Flight and Metamorphosis*, 48–49.

31. On that "Ungefähr," see his letter of January 29, 1959, to Gleb Struve, *Paul Celan*, ed. Hamacher and Menninghaus, 11.

32. Paul Celan, *Sprachgitter* (S. Fischer, 1961), 51. [Ed. English is the editor's translation.]

33. I am thinking of Rilke's "gedeutete Welt" (*Duino Elegies*) and the opening of

Stevens's "Notes Toward a Supreme Fiction." "Blau" as in "Der Blaue Reiter" concentrates in itself both a maximum semantic load and a resistance to that load. See also Georg Trakl's obsessive use of the word, and an intriguing reference to "blue" in Dennis J. Schmidt's "Black Milk and Blue," in *Word Traces: Readings of Paul Celan*, ed. Aris Fioretos (Johns Hopkins University Press, 1994), 129n42. In Celan's *Zeitgehöft*, "blau" is at once the color of hope and nothingness or dissolution. See 18, 26; also "Azur," 29. (I should remind the reader that Jews in the Nazi Generalgouvernement were, for a time, made to wear white armbands with a blue David's star. Frank ordered the blue star for Jews of over twelve years effective December 1, 1939; on September 1, 1941, Jews everywhere were ordered to wear the yellow star.)

34. These lines are a continuation of "Ein Holzstern, blau." Celan, *Sprachgitter*, 51.

35. See also Celan's "ein ansprechendes Du vielleicht, . . . eine ansprechbare Wirklichkeit" (an approachable you, perhaps, . . . an approachable reality), from his Bremen Speech. Celan, *Gesammelte Werke*, 3:186. I am uncertain how to read the "Du" in "während / Du Salz aus der Nacht fällst." Is the poet's wish to say "Du" to the word usurped by the notion of salt and gall, of "Abfall"? We sense an interrupted verbal motion. On "fallen," including its transitive (chemical) meaning, see my continuing analysis.

36. On poetry and "Handwerk," see the wonderful letter to Hans Bender, in Celan, *Gesammelte Werke*, 3:177–78. See also Rilke's concept of "Handwerk," from the time of his apprenticeship to Rodin, a very different, because mimetic, passion.

37. Celan, *Gesammelte Werke*, 3:186. The speech contains a reference to other "Lyriker der jüngeren Generation" ("poets of a younger generation"), which may link it to the "jüngsten Hände" of the "Holzstern" poem.

38. Celan, *Sprachgitter*, 51.

39. A late poem, "Es wird etwas sein, später" (*Zeitgehöft*, 47), brings together with unusual lyrical pathos this emphasis on hand, on writing, and a later reception or generation. It is also distinguished by a vein of imagery I have neglected, which might be called that of star-sound or inspiration (intoxication). See also my remarks on "Bei Wein und Verlorenheit" in what follows.

40. For the first quotation, see Celan, *Gesammelte Werke*, 3:186. For the second, see Szondi, *Celan-Studien*, 51.

41. I am thinking of Walter Abisch's image in his story "The English Garden," in *In the Future Perfect* (New Directions, 1977).

42. See Nelly Sachs, "Hängend am Strauss der Verzweiflung," in *Späte Gedichte*, 138.

43. There is no clear indication that the wood star is a hexagram or Magen David. That symbol, of course, blue against a white background, was adopted by Zionism and the flag of Israel after some debate. There is a wonderful essay by Gershom Scholem, "Das Davidschild: Geschichte eines Symbols," published in Hebrew in 1948 and expanded in German translation in *Judaica* (Suhrkamp, 1963).

44. Thus Celan concludes his speech on the occasion of receiving the Literature Prize of the Free Hanseatic City of Bremen. In Rosmarie Waldrop's translation: "racked by reality and in search of it." For the German, see Celan, *Gesammelte Werke*, 3:186. For the English, see Celan, *Collected Prose*, trans. Rosmarie Waldrop (Sheep Meadow, 1986), 35.

45. Szondi, *Celan-Studien*, 52.

46. I do not intend to evade the issue of mimesis but think it is misleading to simply reverse the dualism of "Text" and "Reality," so that what was secondary is now seen as first and foundational. The concept of mimesis, according to Celan, leads both poet and reader into a lie. They are lured into a dualism that envisages the poem as an imitation of a reality beyond/outside language. Seeking to represent that reality their speech becomes not only too "gebildet" but "bebildert"—idolatrous. "Bei Wein und Verlorenheit" ("Passing Through Wine and Abandonment") makes that clear, satirizing both the sublime poet, who is compelled into a rhetoric of supernatural inspiration (the folkloric source is Odin's rout in the Northern sky), and others (poets or critics) who hear his "Gewieher," his mad, transcendental whinnying. Though imposed on by the bard's pseudomimesis, they "duck" that forceful illusion by writing in a lying, overly picturesque language ("sie / schrieben, sie / logen unser Gewieher / um in eine / ihrer bebilderten Sprachen" ["they / wrote, they / lied our whinnying / into one / of their be-imagined languages"]). That the speaker's god-intoxicated pose should not be taken literally is suggested by at least two features. The opening "Bei ... bei ...," followed by a colon, suggests that his narrative (the next five lines) is a boast; this boast is also undercut by the interlingual pun of "Neige"/"Schnee." See Celan, *Poems*, 132–33. There is a connection, then, as Philippe Lacoue-Labarthe saw, between Celan's non-mimesis and his understanding of the Second Commandment's image prohibition (the *Bilderverbot*). See Lacoue-Labarthe, "Catastrophe," in *Word Traces*, ed. Fioretos, 130, 152–53.

47. The "er, es / fiel nicht ins Wort" ("it / did not cut in") of "Engführung" indicates a failure. See Celan, *Poems*, 120–21.

48. Genesis 15:5. *The Bible, Authorized King James Version* (Oxford University Press, 1997), 15. It must also be read with and against lines from "Engführung": "die Nacht / braucht keine Sterne, nirgends / fragt es nach dir" ("the night / needs no stars, nowhere / does anyone ask after you"). Celan, *Sprachgitter*, 57. Celan, *Poems*, 115. The structure of this verbal fugue, as many have pointed out, is a sequence of "Gegenwörter." For the "graphical stars" (asterisks) of "Engführung" and a critique of Adorno's comment on Celan's "language of dead matter, of stones and stars" (*Ästhetische Theorie*), see Aris Fioretos's "Nothing," in *Word Traces*, ed. Fioretos, 329–33.

49. Celan, "The Meridian," *in Gesammelte Werke*, 3:200.

50. Celan, "Engführung," in *Poems*, 118–19.

51. Celan, *Sprachgitter*, 51.

9. Learning from Survivors: The Yale Testimony Project

1. Just one example. A woman tells of her experiences arriving at Auschwitz. The scene is notorious: bloodcurdling shouts, nightmare, the pajamas, the elegance of the SS, dogs. After a journey already fatal for a part of the mass packed into the wagons, she tells us that at a certain moment she passed into "another state" (*un second état*) marked by dissociation and anesthesia. But when, exactly, did this happen? In the wagons, on arrival at the camp, at some point afterward? She hesitates, then decides that it happened when her long and beautiful hair was brutally cut off. It was then, she says, that

she experienced a "cut" (*une coupure nette*) between the person she had been and the camp prisoner. [Ed.: For searching the entire holdings of Yale's Fortunoff Video Archive, visit this site: https://fortunoff.library.yale.edu/research/search-the-archive/. For selected edited collections of testimony, see these educational resources prepared by the archive: https://fortunoff.library.yale.edu/education/edited-programs/].

2. The way the "recording imagination intersects with the will to interpretation," or "the memory of atrocity meets traditional moral authority, and they vie for the control of the narrative"—in the survivor but also in the interviewer—has been scrupulously analyzed by Lawrence Langer. See his "Interpreting Survivor Testimony," in *Writing and the Holocaust*, ed. Berel Lang (Holmes & Meier, 1988); and more comprehensively *Holocaust Testimony: The Ruins of Memory* (Yale University Press, 1991).

3. Hannah Arendt, *Eichmann in Jerusalem: A Report on the Banality of Evil* (Penguin, 2006), 53.

4. Cf. Paul Thompson, *The Voice of the Past: Oral History*, 2nd ed. (Oxford University Press, 1980), chap. 4, "Evidence." Marc Bloch, according to Bruce M. Ross in *Remembering the Personal Past: Descriptions of Autobiographical Memory* (Oxford University Press, 1991), 168–69, held that "faulty witnessing and the unreliability of memory testimony need not unduly worry historians, because ... the historians' task is to understand the meaning of events, not their concrete representations. Understanding meaning is abetted rather than hindered by the complications of multiple causation of events." Chapter 11 on Testimonies in *Les échos de la mémoire: Tabous et enseignement de la second guerre mondiale*, eds. Georges Kantin and Gilles Manceron (Le Monde, 1991), is a sensible discussion by teachers and witnesses of the "subjectivity" issue. One point made (on page 322) is that "Il serait important de rélier le témoignage et l'écrit et d'insister sur cette nécessité de concevoir aussi les témoignages comme amenant à une rectification de ce qui est écrit, et pas seulement de rectifier les témoignages par les écrits" (It would be important to connect oral and written testimony and to insist on that necessity, understanding also that the testimonies may lead to rectification of what is written, not only that the written be used to rectify them).

5. Paul Fussell describes in *The Great War and Modern Memory* (Oxford University Press, 1975) the struggle of war memoirists to find a perspective for experiences that are, as they occur on the battlefield, traumatic or senseless or both. At some distance from the Great War a kind of period style emerges, which Fussell characterizes as irony or "the abridgment of hope," which then affects writing generally. To answer what type of stylistic coherence is emerging from the oral testimonies or the literary memoirs of the Holocaust is too ambitious for this essay. But if some type of coherence is basic to the possibility of narration, then temporal distance is not necessarily a disadvantage. Fussell quotes Robert Kee, an RAF flyer in the Second War, on the relative unintelligibility of his diaries: "There's nothing you could really get hold of if you were trying to write a proper historical account of it all. No wonder the stuff slips away mercury-wise from proper historians. No wonder they have to erect rather artificial structures of one sort or another in its place. No wonder it is those artists who re-create life rather than try to recapture it who, in one way, prove the good historian in the end" (311).

6. See Clifford Geertz, *Local Knowledge: Further Essays in Interpretive Anthropology*

(Basic Books, 1983); and Michael Walzer, *Interpretation and Social Criticism* (Harvard University Press, 1987).

7. Primo Levi, moreover, emphasizes in *The Drowned and the Saved* (Summit, 1988) how few camp inmates were "privileged" enough to gain an overview of events. See this essay, section VI. The same caution is stated in *Les échos de la mémoire*, 313: "Il n'existe pas de témoin du fait concentrationnaire dans sa globalité. Il n'y a que des faits quotidiens et partiels" (There is no witness to the concentration camp event in its entirety. There are only daily and partial facts).

8. See Anna Ornstein, "The Holocaust: Reconstruction and the Establishment of Psychic Continuity," in *The Reconstruction of Trauma: Its Significance in Clinical Work*, ed. Arnold Rothenstein (International Universities Press, 1986), 177ff.

9. Judith L. Herman, *Trauma and Recovery* (Basic Books, 1992), 181. Herman refers to I. Agger and S. B. Jensen, "Testimony as Ritual and Evidence in Psychotherapy for Political Refugees," *Journal of Traumatic Stress* 3 (1990): 115–30.

10. Edith P., "Edited Testimony," posted August 27, 2009, Yale University, 30:58, https://www.youtube.com/watch?v=gbaSloeu-WQ&t=2s.

11. Jean Améry, "Preface to the Reissue, 1977," in *At the Mind's Limits: Contemplations by a Survivor on Auschwitz and Its Realities*, trans. Sidney Rosenfeld and Stella P. Rosenfeld (Indiana University Press, 1980), xi. Writing from the point of view of high school teachers, Annie Badower notes: "Il y a un problème de communication entre le monde de la déportation et le monde enseignant . . . . Il faut se donner les moyens, en rassemblant tous ces témoignages sur cassette vidéo, de sauvegarder cette possibilité d'un support émotionnel qui permet à l'intelligence des élèves de s'accroître." *Les échos de la mémoire*, 308.

12. Beyond the signal of this dedication, the novel is the powerful "rememory" of a story that is nearly impossible to pass on, both because of its painful and brutal contents and because there seems to be no central memory-place, only a "disremembered and unaccounted for" human subject, evoked by the ghostly and haunting figure of the "devil-child" Beloved. Toni Morrison, *Beloved* (Knopf, 1987), 274.

13. I follow the Israeli historian Yehuda Bauer in this careful definition.

14. This issue of how images, in a modern context especially, can be part of an emotional kind of education, one that does more than point in a cool and cognitive way (also important, of course) to a defining or traumatic event, is beginning to be more carefully considered. See James Young, *The Texture of Memory: Holocaust Memorials and Meaning* (Yale University Press, 1993); and Don Handelman and Lea Shamgar Handelman, "The Presence of the Dead: Memorials of National Death in Israel," *Suomen Antropologi* 4 (1991): 3–17.

15. Virgil, *Aeneid: Six Books*, trans. William R. Harper and Frank J. Miller (American Book Company, 1892), 6.128.

16. "Je ne suis pas vivante, Je suis morte à Auschwitz et personne ne le voit." Charlotte Delbo, *Le convoi du 24 janvier* (Minuit, 1965), 66. A survivor of the Pol Pot regime who has become blind without a clear physiological disorder expresses a similar feeling. "Now, in her small dark apartment, she sometimes wonders if she is really alive or if she died in the rice fields; that is, she feels that the beatings she received caused her soul

to be driven from her body, and she sometimes believes that it is back there." See Alec Wilkinson, "A Changed Vision of God," *New Yorker*, January 24, 1994, 53.

17. They also intervene, as a representational mode, in overobjectified historical accounts, such as the chilling documentation of the perpetrators, "a field dominated by political decisions and administrative decrees which neutralize the concreteness of despair and death" (Saul Friedländer) or other bureaucratic prose. Saul Friedländer, "Trauma, Memory, and Transference," in *Holocaust Remembrance: The Shapes of Memory*, ed. Geoffrey H. Hartman (Basil Blackwell, 1994), 254. Dan Pagis, an Israeli poet and a survivor himself (he died in 1988), has written "Draft of a Reparations Agreement," which parodies the at once commanding and falsely consoling tone of such documents: "Everything will be returned to its place, / paragraph after paragraph. / The scream back into the throat. / The gold teeth back to the gums / The terror." Dan Pagis, *Selected Poems*, trans. Stephen Mitchell (Carcanet, 1972), 25.

18. Narrator or anchor, that is, establishes an artificial and automatic mode of *address*. Whereas survivors of a traumatic experience often lose contact—cannot find a self in them to address, let alone one outside, while desperately and all the time hoping for a correspondent—the narrative that accompanies reportage simply assumes such a presence, the very thing that is absent or has been badly injured. There may be the "punctual agony" of flashbacks, of course, but these occur without—or with an arbitrary—addressee and usually lack the sustained consciousness of the person who suffers them. The remarkable fact is, however, that artists have the capacity to *invent* or *restore* an addressee, an "I-Thou" relationship. See Nanette C. Auerhahn and Dori Laub, "Holocaust Testimony," *Holocaust and Genocide Studies* 5 (1990): 447–62.

19. For the term, see Avital Ronell's interesting work on the ethics of technology, especially "Video/Television/Rodney King: Twelve Steps Beyond *The Pleasure Principle*," *Differences: A Journal of Feminist Cultural Studies* 4 (1992): 7–10. She views testimonial video installed as a "bug or parasite" in television itself and capable of producing the "ethical scream" that television "has massively interrupted."

20. Primo Levi, *The Reawakening* (Summit, 1985), 182–83.

21. See *Holocaust Testimony: The Ruins of Memory* (Yale University Press, 1991), 64. Also Charlotte Delbo, who observes in *Days and Memory*, trans. and with a preface by Rosette Lamont (Marlboro, 1985), 4, that "not only the world but the word was split in two."

22. Compare the overdetermination in Ezra 3.11–13, in which the writer describes a "great shout," first by doubling it as weeping and joy, then making that distinction indistinguishable because of the distance at which the shout, because it is so great, is still heard.

23. See chapter 5 in Michael Pollak, *L'expérience concentrationnaire: Essai sur le maintien de l'identité sociale* (Métailé, 1992).

24. Levi, *The Drowned and the Saved*, 17.

25. Levi, *The Drowned and the Saved*, 23, 34–35, 94.

26. For other pressures on memories, which makes them transmittable, see F. C. Bartlett, *Remembering* (Cambridge, 1932), on the "effort after meaning," and James Fentress and Chris Wickham, *Social Memory* (Blackwell, 1992). The testimonies as oral history might seem to fall under what Jan Assmann calls "das kommunikative

Gedächtniss" (communicative memory) marked by an interchangeability of roles ("Rollenreziprozität"), but as a potential legacy, with a strong commitment to maintaining this memory too, however painful—thus fulfilling the traditional commandment of *zakhor* in an unexpected and negative context—they also seek to enter "das kulturelle Gedächtniss" (cultural memory). There is an interesting tension, therefore, between the significant "small" (i.e., everyday) detail of the accounts, which suggests the specificity (rather than interchangeability) of each witness's experience, and the collective or assimilative aspects of their stories. See Jan Assmann and Tonio Holscher, ed., *Kultur und Gedächtniss* (Suhrkamp, 1988), 9ff.

27. Levi, *The Reawakening*, 182–83.

28. During this time, however, because of the insensitive way the German Indemnification Law (passed in 1953) was administered, many survivors were subjected to an "enforced remembering" that "brought on a distinct feeling of renewed persecution, renewed interrogation, disbelief and degradation." Martin S. Bergmann and Milton E. Jucovy, eds., *Generations of the Holocaust* (Columbia University Press, 1990), 60ff.

29. Financially it proved a difficult choice: What a single made-for-TV film costs is what the Yale Archive existed on during its first four years. In 1987 Alan Fortunoff's generous gift to an Endowment Fund established by many donors guaranteed the archive a curator and a permanent place in Yale's Sterling Memorial Library. Till then the Charles R. Revson Foundation had been the main funding source of operations, and it continues to support some projects.

30. On this "communal dimension of trauma" and the case that "the traumatized view of the world conveys a wisdom that ought to be heard in its own terms," see Kai Erikson's sensitive "Notes on Trauma and Community," *American Imago* 48 (1991): 455–72. On the "communité affective" (Maurice Halbwachs's phrase) that makes testimony possible despite the traumatization of the individual, Pollak's *L'experience concentrationnaire* is essential.

31. Because the life history details in the testimonies are neither impersonally microhistoric nor *fait divers*, they are difficult to categorize. We say too easily that they are comparable to the highly selective detail we find in literary constructs. For an important discussion of the testimonies' relation to a *histoire non-événementielle*, see Yannis Thanasseikos, "Positivisme historique et travail de mémoire. Les récits et les témoignages des survivants comme source historique," *Bulletin de la Fondation Auschwitz* 36/37 (1993): 19–39.

32. More interviewers have volunteered from the mental health professions than from history or sociology. Yet the way the interview is presented makes it a historical rather than therapeutic occasion. Martin Bergmann remarks: "The danger of breakdown in the videotaped interview is less than would have been expected from therapeutic consultations with survivors. This may be due to the fact that the survivor whose story is filmed is not seeking personal help; he is called upon to bear witness. By being interviewed, he is entering history. He is doing his share in remembering. That such interviews are conducted because of the subject's involvement with the Holocaust gives the interview the character less of a personal and more of a social and historical event." *Generations of the Holocaust*, 320.

33. "Il y avait un décalage absolu entre le savoir livresque que j'avais acquis et ce que

me racontaient ces gens. Je ne comprenais plus rien." In "Le lieu et la parole," *Cahiers du Cinéma* 374 (July/August 1985): 18.

34. This essay was originally a lecture at the International Congress on "Histoire et mémoire des crimes et génocides nazis" sponsored by the Fondation Auschwitz, Brussels, in November 1992. A French version was published in the foundation's *Bulletin trimestriel* (Actes II, 1994) and in *Le Monde Juif* (April 1994). [Ed. The essay was then revised considerably for publication in Hartman's *The Longest Shadow: In the Aftermath of the Holocaust*, first published by Indiana University Press in 1996. Hartman then revised the essay again; it is this last version that we publish here for the first time.]

10. Public Memory and Its Discontents

1. The shock factor seemed greater during the Vietnam War, the Biafra famine, and even occasionally before that. In 1941, filmed Japanese atrocities in China or, in the 1960s, pictures of southern brutality against Blacks during the Civil Rights movement caught the attention of the American public.

2. John Keats, "In drear nighted December," in *The Major Works*, ed. Elizabeth Cook (Oxford University Press, 2008), 165.

3. See Zygmunt Bauman, *Modernity and the Holocaust* (Cornell University Press, 2000), 18. The context of his discussion is Nazi bureaucracy and Hannah Arendt's thesis on the banality of evil. Concerning immediate media coverage of the Bosnian conflict, Slavenka Drakulic asks in the *New Republic*, June 21, 1993, 12, "Here they are, generations who have learned at school about concentration camps and factories of death; generations whose parents swear it could never happen again, at least not in Europe, precisely because of the living memory of the recent past. What, then, has all the documentation changed? And what is being changed now by what seems to be the conscious, precise bookkeeping of death?"

4. No wonder many in the younger generation, who are the most susceptible, are drawn to the unreality of fiction, to horror movies and other artificial plots, even more crude, gothic, and violent: One can pretend that these, at least, are mere fantasy.

5. Robert Lifton, *Death in Life: Survivors of Hiroshima* (University of North Carolina Press, 1991), xii.

6. See William Wordsworth, Preface to *Lyrical Ballads*, in *The Major Works*, ed. Stephen Gill (Oxford University Press, 2011), 599. Compare Goethe's notation circa August 8, 1797, in his *Reise in die Schweiz*: "Sehr merkwürdig ist mir aufgefallen, wie es eigentlich mit dem Publikum einer großen Stadt beschaffen ist; es lebt in einem beständigen *Taumel von Erwerben und Verzehren*" (It seems to me very peculiar and worthy of notice, the quality of public life in a great city: It is marked by a constant tumult of acquiring and consuming). Johann Wolfgang von Goethe, *Werke*, 30 vols., ed. Karl Heinemann (Bibliographisches Institut, 1901–1908), 17:87. (See also lines from Wordsworth's "The world is too much with us": "Getting and spending, we lay waste our powers." [Wordsworth, *Major Works*, 270]). He goes on to mention, in particular, theater and the inclination of the reading public toward novels and newspapers as the major distractions. These early symptoms of a consumer culture show that, from the outset, sensations are among the commodities being produced and consumed.

7. Herbert Marcuse, *One-Dimensional Man: Studies in the Ideology of Advanced Industrial Society* (Beacon, 1964), 248.

8. Robert Rosenblum, "Warhol as Art History," in *Andy Warhol: A Retrospective*, ed. Kynaston McShine (Museum of Modern Art / Bullfinch, 1989), 36. Henri Lefebvre's theory of "everydayness" diagnoses a "generalized passivity" that accompanies the increasing uniformity of everyday life (itself a functionalist result of the industrial and electronic revolutions) and is often veiled by the surface of modernity. "News stories and the turbulent affectations of art, fashion, and event veil without ever eradicating the everyday blahs. Images, the cinema and television divert the everyday by at times offering up to it its own spectacle, or sometimes the spectacle of the distinctly noneveryday; violence, death, catastrophe, the lives of kings and stars—those who we are led to believe defy everydayness." For Lefebvre, see *Yale French Studies* 73 (1987): 7–11. Or see Gianni Vattimo on what he characterizes as a "growing psychological dullness": "Technical reproduction seems to work in exactly the opposite sense to *shock*. In the age of reproduction [the reference is to Walter Benjamin's essay of 1936 on that subject], both the great art of the past and new media products reproducible from their inception, such as cinema, tend to become common objects and consequently less and less well defined against the background of intensified communication." Gianni Vattimo, *The Transparent Society*, trans. David Webb (Johns Hopkins University Press, 1992), 47–48.

9. William Shakespeare, *The Tempest*, in *The Norton Shakespeare*, ed. Stephen Greenblatt et al. (Norton, 2016), 1.2.50.

10. Ralph Waldo Emerson, "Experience," in *Essays: Second Series* (Floating Press, 2009), 67.

11. Terrence Des Pres, *Praises and Dispraises: Poetry and Politics, the 20th Century* (Penguin, 1989), xiv.

12. The result of this can also be comic: Think of the energy some expend on seeking to prove that Shakespeare was really Francis Bacon or the Earl of Essex, or consider that even children's literature is beginning to exploit this revisionism, as in "The True Story of the Three Little Pigs," by Alexander T. Wolf.

13. Des Pres, *Praises and Dispraises*, xv (my emphasis). That which "we cannot not know" is "the real," according to Henry James.

14. Such as blaming the "white devil" or the Jew for the world's suffering, or the notion of an evil empire. One of the few treatises to take up the possibility of ethics in a technological age, Hans Jonas's *Das Prinzip Verantwortung* (first published in German in 1979), argues that our sense of technological power has led to utopian expectations: that it is all too easy to conceive of action on the pattern of technological progress and that we need, therefore, a new "modesty" as the basis of moral activism. "In view of the quasi-eschatological potentials of our technical processes, ignorance about ultimate consequences becomes itself a ground for responsible hesitation—a second-best quality, would wisdom be lacking." Hans Jonas, *The Imperative of Responsibility: In Search of an Ethics for the Technological Age*, trans. Hans Jonas (University of Chicago Press, 1984), 21. In America, at the same time, televangelism spawns its own sublime simplicity: The sinful past can be overcome by turning to a savior figure. The sense of universal suffering conveyed (painfully) by the media is here relieved (painlessly) by the media.

15. Indeed, Jean-François Lyotard defines our "postmodern" condition as "incre-

dulity toward metanarratives" produced by progress in the sciences. Lyotard, *The Postmodern Condition: A Report on Knowledge* (University of Minnesota Press), xxiv. There is often a rupture, then, between the increasingly scientific history of the historians and the culture of the community, that is, collective practices structured by group memory. In Judaism this separation from communal ways of remembering becomes painfully clear after the Holocaust. The command *zakhor*, "remember!" that resounds through the Bible and Jewish tradition, used to refer to observances that stressed, in Yosef Yerushalmi's words, "not the historicity of the past, but its eternal contemporaneity." *Zakhor, Jewish History, and Jewish Memory* (University of Washington Press, 1996), 96. Today the same "remember!" documents in volume upon volume a genocide that has weakened Jewish continuity. A form of memorizing rather than remembrance, and information rather than performance oriented, it is very different from the liturgical memory, the collectively recited lamentations, petitions, and hymns, or the scripture study, by which Jews as a community healed or at least integrated the catastrophes in their past. Amos Funkenstein reintroduces the notion of "historical consciousness" to show that the split between historical and liturgical memory is not, today or in earlier times, as absolute as Yerushalmi represents it. Amos Funkenstein, "Collective Memory and Historical Consciousness," *History and Memory* 1 (1989): 5–27.

16. Two more contemporary examples. (1) East Germany's foundational cult, centered on the prewar Communist leader Thälmann. Thälmann may have been brought to Buchenwald and executed there toward the end of the war. To magnify Buchenwald as the symbol of German resistance to fascism, the East German government identified the cell where he was killed, made it a cavernous shrine, and used it to initiate young devotees of the youth movement. The Thälmann cult excluded all perspectives on the Nazi era except that of heroic Communist revolt and became a sterile and self-exculpatory "god-term" for East Germany, one that allowed its inhabitants to transfer guilt for fascism and war crimes exclusively to the citizens of the *other* (West) Germany. (2) The rebirth of Israel, as Saul Friedländer and Alan Mintz (among others) have shown, activated a "paradigm retrieval" that had long ago linked catastrophe and redemption. "The national historian," Funkenstein writes, "who in the nineteenth century enjoyed the status of a priest of culture, and whose work, even professional, was still read by a wide stratum of the educated public ... even created some of [the symbols], some almost from nothing, such as the legend of Hermann, the victorious Cheruskian hero of early Roman-Germanic encounter." Funkenstein, "Collective Memory," 21.

17. Edwin Muir, *Scott and Scotland: The Predicament of the Scottish Writer* (Routledge, 1936), 161.

18. The stories often crystallize or cluster around proper names, especially place names (Hart-Leap Well; Beth-El; Wessex; Balbec; Paris, Texas; Ole Kentucky; Chelm; Homewood). Some of these are fictional places, but such is the power of art that names outlive in our imagination referents they may never have had.

19. Alasdair MacIntyre, *After Virtue: A Study in Moral Theory*, 3rd ed. (Notre Dame University Press, 2007), 138.

20. Pierre Nora, ed., *Les lieux de mémoire, 3 tomes* (Gallimard, 1984–1992); and Marc Augé, *Non-Lieux: Introduction à une anthropologie de la surmodernité* (Seuil, 1992). The conception of *non-lieu* plays with the legal term by which courts refuse to receive a com-

plaint or nullify its basis in law. Cf. Claude Lanzmann, "Le lieu et la parole," *Les Cahiers du Cinéma* 374 (July/August 1985). He describes there how he develops a technique to overcome the "non-lieu de la mémoire" (19).

21. Michael Kammen, *The Mystic Chords of Memory: The Transformation of Tradition in American Culture* (Vintage, 1993), 696.

22. Maurice Halbwachs, *La mémoire collective*, 2nd ed. (Presses Universitaires de France, 1968), 68–69. Halbwachs's "collective memory" is a broader concept than "communal memory": No memory, according to Halbwachs (in the wake of Durkheim and Marc Bloch), is purely individual but always depends, to be a memory, on an "affective community" (which need not be religious or ritual). Edward Shils in *Tradition* (University of Chicago Press, 1981) makes the case that there is a sense of the past that is inculcated early and that is important as a general "sensibility to past things" as well as for its specific contents.

23. "Commentators on American culture note that a sense of historicity is shifting away from singular stories that are forever true—away from story-lines that are hero-oriented and confrontations. There are fewer authentic moments of 'catastrophe time.'" Don Handelman on "media events," in *Models and Mirrors: Towards an Anthropology of Public Events* (Cambridge University Press, 1990), 200ff.

24. Jacques Le Goff, in describing the work of Pierre Nora on memory-places, and a new history "which seeks to create a scientific history on the basis of collective memory," does not entirely confront this difference between public and collective memory in his rather optimistic assessment. "The whole evolution of the contemporary world, under the impact of an *immediate history* for the most part fabricated on the spot by the media, is headed toward the production of an increased number of collective memories, and history is written, much more than in earlier days, under the influence of these collective memories." *History and Memory*, trans. Steven Rendall and E. Claman (Columbia University Press, 1993), 95.

25. Cf. the description of what Jan Assmann names "das kulturelle Gedächtnis," which seeks a stability beyond the *saeculum* of oral history and the span of Halbwachs's collective memory. "Kollektives Gedächtnis und kulturelle Identität," in *Kultur und Gedächtnis*, ed. Jan Assmann and Tonio Hölscher (Surhkamp, 1988). Funkenstein, "Collective Memory," sees the difference between a purely liturgical memory and a more dynamic, heuristic collective memory emerging in the historical consciousness. The latter, according to him, appears in the *hidushim* (new insights) of rabbinic (*halakhic*) lawfinding, as well as in literature—but he does not provide us with a conceptualized understanding of the difference between "the liturgical incantations of a dynasty of tribal leaders" and "the poetry of Homer or the Book of Judges."

26. See Ellen S. Fine on post-Holocaust Jewish writers (especially the children of survivors) in "The Absent Memory: The Act of Writing in Post-Holocaust French Literature," in *Writing and the Holocaust*, ed. Berel Lang (Holmes & Meier, 1988): 41–57. Also Nadine Fresco, "Remembering the Unknown," *International Review of Pscyho-Analysis* 11 (1984): 417–27. For Henry Raczymow, see "La mémoire trouée," *Pardès* 3 (1986): 177–82.

27. See Julius Lester, *To Be a Slave* (Dial, 1998). See also John Edgar Wideman, "A Begat Chart," "Family Tree," in *Damballah* (Houston Mifflin, 1998).

28. Toni Morrison, *Beloved* (Knopf, 1987), 23.

29. Wordsworth's note to Isabella Fenwick about "Ode: Intimations of Immortality." See *Poems in Two Volumes, and Other Poems, 1800–1807*, ed. Jared Curtis (Cornell University Press, 1983), 428.

30. Raymond Federman, *To Whom It May Concern* (University of Alabama Press, 1990), 107, 104.

31. Federman, *To Whom It May Concern*, 108.

32. Haim Gouri, *Facing the Glass Booth: The Jerusalem Trial of Adolf Eichmann*, trans. Michael Swirsky (Wayne State University Press, 2004), 268.

33. Videotape adds to the dimension by allowing the recording of "stylistic" and "prosodic" features, such as gestures, visually accented pauses, etc. As in photography generally, more detail previously thought of as incidental or accidental is included. This increases oral history's movement away from *histoire événementielle*.

34. Claude Lanzmann, in "Le lieu et la parole," *Cahiers du Cinéma* 374 (July/August 1985), goes so far as to say that his film seeks an "incarnation." "Le souvenir me fait horreur: le souvenir est faible. Le film est l'abolition de toute distance entre le passé et le présent" [Recollection disgusts me: it is so weak. The film aims at the abolition of all distance between the past and the present] (21).

35. I must leave aside here the more general issue of the revival, through history or art, of memory-places. For the sensibility, for example, that joins Wordsworth to Milton in understanding memory-place, see Milton's *Paradise Lost*, IX, ll. 320–29. In terms of academic transmission the *lieu de mémoire* becomes a "topos," but the boundary between discourse, on the one hand, and poetry and even living performance, on the other, is quite porous, as was shown by E. R. Curtius's magisterial book on the way the classical tradition reaches modern European literature, *European Literature and the Latin Middle Ages* (Princeton University Press, 1973), and by the famous research of Milman Parry and Albert Lord on the formulaic compositional methods of Yugoslav bards, *The Singer of Tales*, 3rd ed. (Harvard University Press, 2019). For Halbwachs's interesting treatment of "Religious Space," see *La mémoire collective*, 145–46, 160–65. Monuments too are *lieux de mémoire*, involving, like stories, real or legendary places.

36. For Hegel it would have needed the entire history of the world, together with an intellectual odyssey of millennia, before mind is mind, free of its *subservience* to sense-perception, and able to retrieve all its memory-stages in the activity of thought. Meanwhile (i.e., in everyday rather than visionary temporality), interesting makeshift solutions are found. I have mentioned Alexander Kluge; Claude Chabrol's *L'oeil de Vichy* (1993) raises the spectator's consciousness of visual dependence by creating a film purely out of archival propaganda images, countered only by a dry historical commentary placing them in context. And Wilfried Schoeller has explained: "Every museum, every monument, every memorial site recalling the Nazi era should reserve a moment of discretion, should leave something open and perhaps even claim the status of ruin or artifact, so that the imagination can still be active toward something in it."

37. Derek Walcott, Nobel lecture, "The Antilles: Fragment of Epic Memory," *New Republic*, December 28, 1992, 27. W. B. Yeats, *Selected Poems and Two Plays of William Butler Yeats*, ed. M. L. Rosenthal (Collier, 1966), 143. However, in emphasizing the per-

formative dimension we need to distinguish between an opportunistic recomposing of the collective memory, motivated by identity politics, and the creative-heuristic use of its traditions in art. Such notions as Schiller's "aesthetic education" may provide a beginning for theorizing that difference. The formalist's deinstrumentalizing emphasis on what is distinctively literary also responds to the need for a critical perspective.

11. Shoah Literature: The Universal Aspect

1. Jorge Semprún, *Le mort qu'il faut* (Gallimard, 2000), 148, 184–85. Only the artifice of a masterly narrative, Semprún writes, will help Holocaust "reality to seem real, and truth to be believable." Charlotte Delbo, preface to *Aucun de nous ne reviendra* [*None of Us Will Return*] (Gonthier, 1965). The issue of verisimilitude in both autobiographical and novelistic narratives is carefully discussed by Karla Grierson in "Vérité littéraire et vraisemblance dans le récit de déportation," in *La Shoah: Témoignages, savoirs, oeuvres*, ed. Annette Wieviorka and Claude Mouchard (Presses Universitaires de Vincennes, 1999), 207–25. See also Yannis Thanassekos, "Positivisme historique et travail de mémoire. Les récits et les témoignages des survivants comme source historique," *Bulletin Trimestriel de la Fondation Auschwitz* 36–37 (1993): 19–37.

2. Phillip Roth, ed., *Shop Talk: A Writer and His Colleagues and Their Work* (Houghton Mifflin, 2001), 23, 28. For a cogent discussion of the realism issue, see Hayden White, "Figural Realism in Witness Literature," *parallax* 2, no. 1 (2004): 113–24, esp. 114.

3. I owe this example to Lawrence Langer, *Preempting the Holocaust* (Yale University Press, 1998), 187.

4. "For people first learning about the Holocaust, the profound cruelty and suffering described by the witnesses can seem more farfetched than claims of being abducted by aliens from outer space." Robert Kraft, *Memory Perceived: Recalling the Holocaust* (Praeger, 2002), 94–95. Marie Syrkin, an editor of the *Jewish Frontier*, has acknowledged how in August 1942 a lack of "emotional capacity" to believe detailed reports about the extermination of the Jews of Lodz characterized even many among the American Jewish leadership. Her comments are quoted by Robert Lifton and Eric Marcusen in their *The Genocidal Mentality: Nazi Holocaust and Nuclear Threat* (Basic Books, 1990), 238–39.

5. Renata Lachmann, "Danilo Kiš: Factography and Thanatography (*A Tomb for Davidovich, Psalm 44, The Hourglass*)," *Partial Answers* 4, no. 2 (2006): 219–38.

6. Jonas's statement to Ernest Simon is quoted in Michael L. Morgan, *Post-Holocaust Jewish Thought in America* (Oxford University Press, 2001), 4–5.

7. Nicolas Despréaux Boileau, *Art poétique de Boileau*, ed. Henri Bénac (1674; Hachette, 1946).

8. For a different translation of Terence's "humani nihil a me alienum puto" from *The Self-Tormentor*, see Terence, *The Comedies*, ed. and trans. Palmer Bovie (Johns Hopkins University Press, 1992), 84.

9. See Paul Celan's poem "Todesfuge" ("Death Fugue"), in *The Poems of Paul Celan*, trans. Michael Hamburger (Persea, 2002), 32–33.

10. *Diary from the Galleys*, quoted by him in "Who Owns Auschwitz," *Yale Journal of Criticism* 14 (2001): 268. Joseph Brodsky makes a similar point when he writes: "Lit-

erature is the only available tool for the cognition of phenomena whose size otherwise numbs your senses and eludes human grasp." See his introduction to Danilo Kiš, *A Tomb for Boris Davidovich* (Penguin, 1980), xvii.

11. William Samelson, *Warning and Hope: The Nazi Murder of European Jewry* (Valentine Mitchell, 2003), 123.

12. Terrence Des Pres, in an essay of that title, criticizes the oppressive rule that seeks to exclude the comic from Shoah literature. He discusses the humorous or grotesque element in Borowski and how it is complicit with the mask of "normative" behavior. See his *Writing Into the World: Essays 1973–1987* (Viking, 1991), 277–87.

13. William Shakespeare, *Hamlet*, in *The Norton Shakespeare*, 3rd ed., ed. Stephen Greenblatt et al. (Norton, 2016), 1840 (5.1.122).

14. My libertarian attitude, however, is sorely tested when I hear of Kinky Friedman, a well-known Texas musician, touting a Holocaust country music song titled "Ride 'Em, Jewboy."

15. See also Malvin Jules Buliet's "Introduction" to his anthology *Nothing Makes You Free* (Norton, 2002), 20–23. Aharon Appelfeld, himself a child survivor, reaching maturity during the Holocaust and its immediate aftermath, divides responses into the chronicler generation and that of children who accepted the kingdom of death as the reality and so exerted their play-instinct within it. Insofar as the Holocaust produced an art of its own, including Appelfeld's sophisticated version, it views itself as rooted in that childlike mode of presentation.

16. See Eva Hoffman, *After Such Knowledge: Memory, History, and the Aftermath of the Holocaust* (Public Affairs, 2004), esp. 10–16. Hoffman writes eloquently from the perspective of a second-generation witness in her first chapter, "From Event to Fable," where she distinguishes between the reception of the events by the eyewitnesses and by the second generation. Benigni, while not Jewish or a direct descendant, is contemporaneous with the first cohort of the second generation. Yet as Kertész and Appelfeld evidence, to access the domain of the literary even the survivor witnesses have to become, as it were, part of the second generation.

17. Irving Feldman, "To the Six Million," in *New and Selected Poems* (Viking, 1979), 54–55.

18. Patrick Modiano's *Dora Bruder* is a symptomatic and powerful example of that haunting quest, and like his other more fictional books, as well as his quasi-autobiography *Un pedigree*, it is full of circumstantial and sometimes picaresque detail. That fullness has a relation to the genre of "faction," motivated in this case by the sense of an emptiness caused by the Shoah's dispersion and then devastation of Jewish life. For Schindel, see esp. his "Judentum als Erinnerung und Widerstand" [Judaism as memory and resistance], in *Gott schütz uns vor den guten Menschen: Jüdisches Gedächtnis, Auskunftsbüro der Angst* (Suhrkamp, 1995).

19. Such loss also cannot be assuaged by another identitarian (or communitarian) quest, one that motivated the explosion of second-generation Jewish fiction dealing with the Holocaust. It is no slander against the zeal of that generation to say that generally it does not seek to confront directly the tragic amputation of a fully developed Yiddish culture and an assimilated German and West European intelligentsia. The Shoah and its immediate consequences are already a quasi-legendary background for

the postwar novel of this generation, so in the unsettledness, the troubled *va-et-vient* and ever-returning solitude, of Barbara Honigmann's *Eine Liebe aus Nichts* (Rowohlt, 1991), when her narrator and Jean-Marc chat together, it is mostly about their parents during the Nazi persecutions: "Ihre Emigrationsrouten und Erlebnisse in den fremden Ländern waren wie Mythen unserer Kindheit und unseres Lebens überhaupt, wie die Irrfahrten des Odysseus; Legenden, tausendmal erzählt. Jetzt wiederholten wir sie uns gegenseitig, sangen sie fast im Chor, wie verschiedene Strophen ein und desselben Liedes" [Their emigration routes and experiences in foreign countries were like our childhood myths, like the wanderings of Odysseus, legends told a thousand times. Now we repeated them to each other, singing them almost in chorus, like different verses of the same song] (55).

20. Henry James and Walter Besant, *The Art of Fiction* (Cupples and Hurd, 1884), 66.

21. To return once more to Honigmann's novella: A deceptive yet exemplary moment is created when the narrator continues in her own name the aborted, discouragingly trivial diary of her father, begun after his return to Germany after thirteen years of exile. Her citation and completion of the diary helps us recognize an emerging literary pattern reflecting the secondary witness's burden of continuity. I should also mention as paradigmatic Jorie Graham's poem "Annunciation with a Bullet in It," a goodly section of which is composed, as she signals, of sometimes slightly edited quotations from Isabella Leitner's diary, *Fragments of Isabella*. The poem also contains phrases from Jean-François Lyotard's *Le differend*. Finally, attention should be drawn to Charles Reznikoff's *Holocaust*, an "objectivist" recitative based on officially published documents. Reznikoff's long narrative, divided like old epics into twelve books, appeared just before his death in 1976 when he was over eighty years old. He notes that it was entirely based on the US government publication *Trials of the Criminals Before the Nuremberg Military Tribunal* as well as on the records of the Eichmann trial.

22. All Pagis quotations are from *Points of Departure*, trans. Stephen Mitchell (Jewish Publication Society, 1981), 25.

23. *Heshbon*, translated as "sum," is everyday Ivrit for "the bill," while *kan leolam* ("here forever") should be cross-read with its occurrence in the poem "Europe, Late," where its meaning is the opposite: "never here."

24. This shame blocks art's intrinsic desire for imitation, for achieving a resembling portrait. Aware of the dilemma, Maurice Blanchot insists that while testimony is an obligation, the life of those who survived the Holocaust may involve a "rupture with the living affirmation: the attestation of the goodness of life (life which is not narcissistic but for the other) has been so decisively impacted that nothing remains intact. From that point on, it could be that all narration, even all poetry, has lost the basis on which a different language [*un langage autre*] might be erected, because of the extinction of the happiness of speaking latent even in the most mediocre silence." Maurice Blanchot, *Après coup: Précédé par le ressassement éternel* (Éditions de Minuit, 1983), 98.

25. I am indebted to Vivian Liska, "Vom Schutteimer zum Schüttelreim: Überlegungen zu Ilse Aichingers Erzählung *Der Engel*," in *Verschwiegenes Wortspiel: Kommentare zu den Werken Ilse Aichingers*, ed. Heidy M. Müller (Aisthesis, 1999): 95–109.

26. Sidra Dekoven Ezrahi, "Representing Auschwitz," *History and Memory* 7 (1996): 152. See also her *Booking Passage* (University of California Press, 2000), on how the

"view from a distance" tries to rescue not only the voices, the culture, lost through Auschwitz, but also how the widowed or diasporic imagination builds anew in the void.

27. It may be that by now certain episodes, however gruesome, are so familiar or stylized that we feel we could or should view them again. Hollywood realities have replaced Holocaust reality by a fatality implicit in (especially video-visual) representation.

28. I know of one interesting experiment depicting the dilemma of the quester for authenticity by way of a Holocaust novel—interesting as an experiment because it seeks to abolish the distance between reader and protagonist but also, in fact, between author and protagonist. Michal Govrin comments on her *The Name* (*Ha-shem*, trans. Barbara Harshev [Riverhead, 1998]): "I chose to write *The Name* in the first person, working through the tumultuous trauma of the heroine's body and soul." She then shifts (too quickly?) to the presumed effect on the reader. "The novel invites the reader not only to read but also to perform the text, as an actor who experiences the narrator's interior monologue at first hand and prays along with her. I think of this as 'organic writing.'" Her friends among the literary critics, she adds, claimed that her book did not shelter the reader from such a radical consciousness through narrative distancing or the third person. See Michal Govrin, "In Search of the Story: A Friendship Between Critic and Writer," trans. Yael Levin, *Partial Answers* 4, no. 2 (2006): 271.

29. Igal Sarna, *The Man Who Fell Into a Puddle: Israeli Lives*, trans. Haim Watzman (Vintage, 2004), 6.

30. Sarna, *The Man Who Fell Into a Puddle*, 200.

31. Sarna, *The Man Who Fell Into a Puddle*, 202.

12. Defining a Living Genre: The Survivor Testimony

1. Boder also conducted an oral history project recording survivors of the Kansas City flood of 1951.

2. Avishai Margalit in *The Ethics of Memory* (Harvard University Press, 2002) has gone as far as anyone can in providing the analytic distinctions that describe what he calls moral witnessing in generic terms, without disparaging other kinds. The essential moral feature, according to Margalit, is that the testimony of such a witness has a special authenticity coming from suffering directly an evil or having been at risk because of it. Yet the degree of clarity we can achieve about the moral (or ethical) issues raised, not by the act of testifying itself but by the behaviors reported in the testimonies about an evil as great as the Holocaust, depends on a more complete study of the testimonies themselves and asking what risk, if any, is taken by the *intellectual* witness, by a philosopher like Margalit or a student of the testimonies like myself.

3. The excerpt is taken from my earlier discussion in this volume. See chapter 9, "Learning from Survivors: The Yale Testimony Project," note 1.

4. See the research by E. Zech and others, summarized in Sylvie Delvenne et al., *Oralités: Catégoriser l'impensable* (Université Libre de Bruxelles, 2005), 9–14. I cannot tell from that summary how extensive that research was.

5. Research into the intrapersonal aspect of testimony giving has underestimated, in my opinion, its interpersonal resonance.

6. Shoshana Felman and Dori Laub, *Testimony: Crises of Witnessing in Literature, Psychoanalysis, and History* (Routledge, 1992), 82.

7. See Aleida Assmann, "History, Memory, and the Genre of Testimony," *Poetics Today* 27, no. 2 (Summer 2006): 261–75.

8. See his essay "One Line at a Time," in *Poetics Today* 27, no. 2 (Summer 2006): 425–31.

9. Phillipe Lejeune, *Le pacte autobiographique*, 2 vols. (Seuil, 1975).

10. James Young, *The Texture of Memory: Holocaust Memorials and Meaning* (Yale University Press, 1993).

11. We too, as witnesses to the witness, cross from the question how we get to know what we know—from the epistemology of various media, such as video, or the disciplines such as history and literary studies—to ethics, which describes how we justify actions, even those choices imposed on the victims that continue to trouble them.

12. Jolly Z.'s testimony can be viewed here: https://fortunoff.aviaryplatform.com/collections/5/collection_resources/1035?u=t&keywords[]=jolly.

13. The quotation is a translation from the French text, itself translated from Srebnik's native tongue. See Claude Lanzmann, *Shoah* (Fayard, 1985), 11, 18.

14. Ernst van Alphen, "Second-Generation Testimony, Transmission of Trauma, and Postmemory," *Poetics Today* 27, no. 2 (Summer 2006): 473–88.

15. As I write this, I run across the following statement made by the Israeli writer Etgar Keret in an interview in *Tikkun* 20, no. 5 (2005): "A child of Holocaust survivors, Keret grew up with a crippling sense of insignificance. His experiences felt dwarfed by what his parents had endured. 'I would bump into a wall and I wouldn't cry, because I'd say, "You just bumped into a wall. Smile to your mum and make her happy"'" (70).

16. See Thane Rosenbaum, *The Golems of Gotham* (Harper Collins, 2002).

17. Carl Friedman, *Nightfather*, trans. Arnold and Erica Pomerans (Persea, 1995), 2, 1.

18. Quoted in Geoffrey Hartman, preface to *Le passage du témoin: Portraits et témoignages de rescapés des camps de concentration et d'extermination nazis* (La Lettre Volée, 1995), 7.

13. The Ethics of Witness: An Interview with Ian Balfour and Rebecca Comay

1. [Ed.: Interview conducted December 29, 2000.]

2. Maurice Halbwachs, *The Collective Memory*, trans. Francis J. Ditter (Harper Colophon, 1980).

3. See Geoffrey Hartman, *The Fateful Question of Culture* (Columbia University Press, 1997), chap. 3.

14. Terror and Art: A Meditation

1. See Maximilien de Robespierre, "Speech to the National Convention (February 4, 1794)," collected in *Pageant of Europe*, ed. Raymond P. Stearns (Harcourt Brace Jovanovich, 1947), 405.

2. See, for instance, Jacques Derrida, *Specters of Marx: The State of the Debt, the Work of Mourning, and the New International*, trans. Peggy Kamuf (Routledge, 1994), 65.

3. Karl Barth, *The Epistle to the Romans*, trans. Edwyn C. Hoskyns (Oxford University Press, 1977), 309.

4. See *The French Revolution: A Document Collected*, 2nd ed., ed. Laura Mason and Tracey Rizzo (Hackett, 2023), 265.

5. William Wordsworth, *The Prelude, 1799, 1805, 1850*, ed. Jonathan Wordsworth, M. H. Abrams, and Stephen Gill (Norton, 1979), 361–63 [1850, Book X, ll. 70–87].

6. Wordsworth, *The Prelude*, 363 [1850, Book X, ll. 76–77].

7. Wordsworth, *The Prelude*, 177 [1850, Book V, ll. 450–51].

8. Wordsworth, *The Prelude*, 177 [1850, Book V, ll. 448–56].

9. William Shakespeare, *Macbeth*, in *The Norton Shakespeare*, 3rd ed., ed. Stephen Greenblatt et al. (Norton, 2006), 2722, 1.1.11–12.

10. Immanuel Kant, *The Critique of the Power of Judgment*, ed. and trans. Paul Guyer (Cambridge University Press, 2001).

11. Jessie Weston, *From Ritual to Romance* (Anchor, 1957), 18.

12. Primo Levi, *Survival in Auschwitz*, trans. Stuart Woolf (Touchstone, 1996), 28.

13. See Luc Boltanski, *Distant Suffering: Morality, Media, and Politics*, trans. Graham Burchell (Cambridge University Press, 1999).

14. John Keats, "In drear nighted December," in *The Major Works*, ed. Elizabeth Cook (Oxford University Press, 2008), 165.

15. Keats, *Major Works*, 297, ll. 256–61.

16. Keats, *Major Works*, 296, ll. 199–202, 207–8.

17. Keats, *Major Works*, 299, ll. 355–57.

18. Philip Roth, *Exit Ghost* (Houghton Mifflin, 2007), 186.

19. Primo Levi, *The Drowned and the Saved*, trans. Raymond Rosenthal (Simon and Schuster, 1988), 12.

20. Alain Badiou, *Le siècle* (Éditions du Seuil, 2005), 32.

15. Future Memory: Reflections on Holocaust Testimony and Yale's Fortunoff Video Archive

1. Paul Celan, *Gesammelte Werke* (Suhrkamp, 1982), 3:183. Author's translation.

2. In genocidal episodes after the Holocaust, another delaying factor may enter: Residual political constraints (such as victim and perpetrator continuing to live in proximity) could make it hard to secure a mental and physical place safe enough to allow either public or privately offered testimony.

3. Beryl Lang's *Philosophical Witnessing: The Holocaust as Presence* (Brandeis University Press, 2009) is an intricate, important examination of what seems to be lacking (and an attempt to fill that lack): the consideration of the Holocaust by most major contemporary philosophers.

4. See Haim Gouri, *Facing the Glass Booth: The Jerusalem Trial of Adolf Eichmann*, trans. Michael Swirsky (Wayne State University Press, 2004), 268.

5. A. W. Frank, *The Wounded Storyteller: Body, Illness, and Ethics* (University of Chicago Press, 1997), 25.

6. Ellen S. Fine, *Legacy of Night: The Literary Universe of Elie Wiesel* (State University of New York Press, 1982), xiii.

7. May Sarton, "Invocation to Kali," *Poetry*, February 1971, 317.

8. Binjamin Wilkomirski, *Fragments: Memories of a Wartime Childhood*, trans. Carol Brown Janeway (Schocken, 1996).

9. D. P. Boder, *I Did Not Interview the Dead* (University of Illinois Press, 1949).

10. W. G. Sebald, *The Emigrants*, trans. Michael Hulse (New Directions, 1996), 23.

11. Primo Levi's "The Survivor" appeared as the epigraph to *Moments of Reprieve*, trans. Ruth Feldman (Summit, 1986), 13. Charlotte Delbo, *Auschwitz and After*, trans. Rosette C. Lamont (Yale University Press, 1995), 267.

12. Lawrence Langer, *Using and Abusing the Holocaust* (University of Indiana Press, 2006), xvi.

13. Paul Frosch and Amit Pinchevski, *Media Witnessing in the Age of Mass Communication* (Palgrave Macmillan, 2009), 4.

14. Frosch and Pinchevski, *Media Witnessing in the Age of Mass Communication*, 3.

15. Dori Laub, "Reestablishing the Internal 'Thou' in Testimony of Trauma," *Psychoanalysis, Culture & Society* 18, no. 2 (2013): 184. See also Dori Laub, "Testimony as Life Experience and Legacy," in *The Power of Witnessing: Reflections, Reverberations, and Traces of the Holocaust*, ed. N. R. Goodman and M. B. Meyers (Routledge, 2012): 59–79. The concept of such a space was originally developed by Donald Winnicott as a special and especially important case of Object Relations theory; it posits that the child is allowed to, as it were, "destroy" or "annihilate" what stands against its ego, an action the caretaker must suffer, so that the child, consoled by an intimation of the love object's indestructibility/immortality, can build up a first "ego organization." See D. W. Winnicott, *The Maturational Process and the Facilitating Environment: Studies in the Theory of Emotional Development* (Karnac, 1990).

16. Amit Pinchevski, "The Audiovisual Unconscious: Media and Trauma in the Video Archive for Holocaust Testimonies," *Critical Inquiry* 39 (Autumn 2012): 148.

17. Laub, "Reestablishing the Internal 'Thou' in Testimony of Trauma," 184.

18. The strongest interviews can also become a mode of bonding beyond the testimonial alliance by expanding what Maurice Halbwachs described as an "affective community" necessary for the reception, development, and maintenance of a collective memory (though not necessarily a traumatic one). This further, larger-scale bonding arose, in the Yale project, from the necessity of organizing groups in each country to make the tapings possible through fundraising, information gathering about the presence of survivors and witnesses, and interview training sessions. All this led beyond the dyad and introduced a third dimension, communitarian and intergenerational. "The apparatus of the archive doubles as the enabling context for the construction of a remembering community. It doesn't take just two to bear witness, but the promise of a whole congregation." See Pinchevski, "The Audiovisual Unconscious," 149.

19. Dan Pagis, "Testimony," in *Selected Poems*, trans. Stephen Mitchell (University of California Press, 1989), 24.

20. Dramatic instances of this are provided by journalists like Samantha Power. See her *A Problem from Hell: America and the Age of Genocide* (Basic Books, 2002), esp. the preface. She details forcefully the problematic of reception on the part of news editors

and state agencies. Consider also the chilling title of Philip Gourevitch's *We Wish to Inform You That Tomorrow We Will Be Killed with Our Families: Stories from Rwanda* (Farrar, Straus and Giroux, 1998). The radio in Rwanda was used by the perpetrators to disseminate orders and inflammatory messages.

21. Jack Hitt, "Ideas & Trends: Conspiracy Alert; Sure, It May Look Like Mars," *New York Times*, January 11, 2004.

22. Luc Boltanski, *La souffrance à distance: Morale humanitaire, médias, et politique* (Métailié, 1993).

23. Jean Améry, preface to *Unmeisterliche Wanderjahre: Aufsätze* (Klett-Cotta, 1985).

24. Robert Antelme, *Textes inédits, Sur l'espèce humaine, Essais et témoignages* (Gallimard, 1996), 68. He is thinking particularly of Maurice Blanchot's writings.

25. Here theory work becomes essential, especially that which defines the "cultural memory," given the deadly effect of Nazi ideology's *Rassenwissenschaft*, its politicized biology and phylogenetic concept of racial speciation. See Jan Assmann, "Kollektives Gedächtnis und kulturelle Identität," in *Kultur und Gedächtnis*, ed. Jan Assmann and Tonio Hölscher (Suhrkamp, 1988), 9ff.

26. Walter Benjamin, "On the Concept of History" and "Paralipomena," in *Selected Writings, vol. 4: 1938–1940*, ed. Howard Eiland and Michael W. Jennings (Harvard University Press, 2003), 390, section 2, and 401.

Index

absence, 12, 53, 96, 116–18, 126, 170. See also presence
abstract, abstraction, 9, 92, 97, 124; abstracting, 8; abstractness, 109
actuality, 16, 17, 109
Adorno, Theodor, 13, 24, 28, 44, 48, 54, 128, 188n38; "Commitment," 39; *Minima Moralia*, 25
Aeschylus, 45
aesthetic, 5, 10, 25, 29, 39, 48, 51, 74, 81–82, 139, 143, 164; distance, 29, 165, 167; education, 5, 79–80, 186n15, 213n37; idealization, 124; judgement, 42; truth, 29
affective community, 32, 128, 150, 207n30, 211n22, 219n18, *See also* community
African Americans, 98, 104, 115–16
Agamben, Giorgio, 156–58
Agnon, Shmuel Yosef, 62
Aichinger, Ilse, 128
aide-memoire, 82. *See also* memory
Akhmatova, Anna, 45
Albert Speer (Sereny), 12
Algerian crisis, 193n18
Alon, Amos, 21
Alphen, Ernst van, 137
Amanpour, Christiane, 180
Améry, Jean, 14, 26, 43, 97, 181
amnesia, 2, 60, 118
Angel, Ezra, 129–30
"The Angel" (Aichinger), 128
"Annunciation with a Bullet in It" (Graham), 215n21
Antelme, Robert, 26, 33–34, 37, 138, 181

anti-intellectualism, 26, 28
antisemitism, antisemitic, 34, 36, 37, 57, 73
Appelfeld, Aharon, 12, 120, 214n15
archive, archives, 17, 66, 98, 122, 136, 147, 150–59; Archive of Conscience, 104, 118; libraries, 152
Arendt, Hannah, 95, 208n3
Aristotle, 13, 120–21, 123, 125, 156, 165
art, 23, 163, 165, 168; aesthetic distance and, 29; memory and, 113; reality of 80; representability and 31; art-shame, 13
Assmann, Aleida, 134
Assmann, Jan, 206n24, 211n24, 220n25
atrocity, atrocities, 8, 23, 38, 54, 108, 116, 122, 146–47, 160, 164, 176, 182, 208n1; atrocity, memory of, 26, 204n2. *See also* catastrophe
audience: for art, 46, 113, 123; of modern technology, 179; for survivors, 6, 100, 103, 134, 147; for witnesses or witnessing, 18, 105, 136, 146, 177, 178, 182
audiencing, 18, 177
Auerbach, Erich, 149
Augé, Marc, 114
"Augenstimmen" (Celan), 84
Auschwitz, 34, 41, 43–44, 97, 102, 112, 149
Auschwitz Foundation, 156
Austria, 126
authenticity, 58, 100, 117, 128, 154, 158–59, 175, 216n28, 216n2
authentic reception, 176–77
autobiography, 134; collective, 136

Index

"L'azur" (Mallarmé), 84

Baal Shem-Tov, Rebbe Israel, 64
"Backlight" (Celan), 172
Bacon, Francis, 209n12
Badiou, Alain, 171
Balfour, Ian, 17, 140–59
Barth, Karl, 161
Bastiaans, Jans, 130
Baudrillard, Jean, 118
Bauman, Zygmunt, 108
Becker, Jurek, 34
Beckett, Samuel, 118
A Beggar in Jerusalem (Wiesel), 63, 65
Beloved (Morrison), 98, 115–16
Belzec, 135. *See also* camp, camps
Benigni, Roberto, 34, 123
Benjamin, Walter, 25, 29, 82, 109, 118, 196n45; "The Concept of History," 182; "Goethe's *Wahlverwandtschaften*," 44
Benn, Gottfried, 195n42
Bergmann, Martin, 207n32
Beyond Formalism (Hartman), 4
Bialik, Hayim Nahman, 60
the Bible, 61, 62, 64, 113; Book of Job, 34, 50, 70, 108; New Testament, 115. *See also* Hebrew Bible; Genesis; Psalms; Song of Solomon
Bitburg in Moral and Political Perspective (Hartman), 2
Blanchot, Maurice, 7, 12–16, 36–44, 86, 128, 193n18, 195n42, 215n24; *L'écriture du désastre*, 158; *Friendship*, 27; *The Instant of My Death*, 170; literary space and, 51; *Thomas l'obscur*, 40; *The Writing of the Disaster*, 27, 42, 48, 49, 52, 53, 158, 170
Blonski, Jan, 22
Blum, Léon, 37
Boder, David, 100, 131, 133, 174, 175
Boileau, Nicolas Despréaux, 31, 122
Boltanski, Luc, 167, 180

Bonnefoy, Yves, 27
The Book of Laughter and Forgetting (Kundera), 109
Borowski, Tadeusz, 29, 124
Bosnia, 3, 57, 104, 108, 119, 180
Brandeis, Louis, 30
Buber, Martin, 43, 60
Buchenwald, 23, 24, 26, 33, 74, 114, 181, 210n16. *See also* camp, camps
Buddhism, 159
Buñuel, Luis, 169
Burke, Edmund, 168
bystander, bystanders, 8, 22, 25–28, 47, 95, 97, 108, 119, 128, 155, 158, 180

Cambodia, 3
camp, camps, 23, 34–35, 73, 96, 99, 100, 101, 123–25, 127, 130, 132, 135, 139, 148, 166, 174–76, 188n37, 203–4n7. *See also* concentration camps
Candide (Voltaire), 39
Captive Mind (Milosz), 41
catastrophe, 12, 28–29, 38, 45, 108, 129, 142, 152, 159, 203n46, 209n8, 210n116; creation, 53; poetry and, 39
Celan, Paul, 14, 30–33, 36, 45, 79–81, 89–93, 128, 135; "Augenstimmen," 84; "Backlight," 172; "Death Fugue" ("Todesfuge"), 47, 122, 189n45; "Engführung," 83–84, 91, 92, 203n47, 203n48; Holzstern," 90–93, 202n37
Chabrol, Claude, 212n36
Charles R. Revson Foundation, 207n29
Chatterton, Thomas, 113
Chaucer, Geoffrey, 113
"Child of Europe" (Milosz), 57
Les Chimeres (Nerval), 85
Christianity, 26, 34, 84, 182
"Christopher Smart's *Magnificat*" (Hartman), 4
Churchill, Winston, 74

cinema, 24, 129
Clout, Colin, 165
Cohen, Arthur A., 33
collective, 25, 30, 41, 58, 95, 98, 125, 128, 136, 180
collective memory, 7, 67, 113–14, 117–19, 136, 150–52, 211n22
Comay, Rebecca, 17, 140–59
comedy, 123–25
"Commitment" (Adorno), 39
communication, 5, 86, 102, 128, 133, 138, 154, 178
community, 66, 70, 84, 105, 112–13, 116–17, 128, 147, 151; affective, 32, 128, 150, 219n18; promise of, 50
concentration camps, 12, 71, 73, 101, 108, 123; Auschwitz, 34, 41, 43–44, 97, 102, 112, 149; Belzec, 135; Buchenwald, 23, 24, 26, 33, 74, 114, 181, 210n16; Dachau, 26, 138, 181
"The Concept of History" (Benjamin), 182
consciousness, 4, 7–8, 10, 26, 44, 47, 52–53, 77, 157, 173, 177, 180, 212n36; historical, 211n25; self-, 84, 86; word-, 36–37
conversation, 31–32, 36–38, 91
Un cri sans voix (*Writing the Book of Esther*) (Raczymow), 126
Criticism in the Wilderness (Hartman), 4
A Critic's Journey (Hartman), 5
culture, cultural, 5, 30–31, 44, 112, 113, 121, 128; activities, 68; difference, 132, 151; heritage, 35; ideal, 75, 113; inheritance, 112; literary, 83; memory, 113, 181, 207n26, 220n25; of remembrance, 20; revolution, 112

Dachau (concentration camp), 26, 138, 181
Damballah (Wideman), 115
Dante, 43
Darfur, 3

Davis, Natalie, 152
Dawn (Wiesel), 61
"Death Fugue" ("Todesfuge") (Celan), 47, 122, 189n45
decorum, 29, 52, 123–24, 148, 167
dehumanization, dehumanizing, 6, 96, 106, 179
Delbo, Charlotte, 24, 33, 47, 100, 120, 127, 176
Demjanjuk Trial, 96
denial, 2, 72, 76, 78, 108, 112; of the holocaust, 75, 77, 121, 173. *See also* revisionism derealiization, 179–80
Derrida, Jacques, 4, 27, 42, 82, 156–57, 161, 194n30; and archive fever, 156
Desbois, Patrick, 171
desire, 25, 49–50, 52, 88, 91, 133; for immediacy, 3; for justice, 161; visual, 166
Des Pres, Terrence, 21, 38, 110, 111, 123, 214n12
derealization, 179–80. *See also* unreal, unreality
Deuteronomy 32:1, 6:4, 140
Diderot, Denis, 116
The Differend (Lyotard), 188n37
displaced persons, 100, 174–75, 178
displacement, 80, 83, 95, 114, 129, 131
distancing, 25, 32, 109, 123, 128, 216n28. *See also* distant suffering
distant suffering, 167
documentary, documentaries, 16, 24, 25, 74, 100, 117. *See also* historical documentation
documentation, 11, 95, 125; historical, 11, 12, 16; oral, 96, 100, 131, 138, 148, 149, 152, 154, 206n17, 208n3
Donne, John, 85
Dora Bruder (Modiano), 214n18
Drakulic, Slavenka, 208n3
dreams, 14, 40, 59, 61, 102
The Drowned and the Saved (Levi), 28, 102, 158, 175, 205n7
Dubnov, Simon, 125

Duino Elegies (Rilke), 87

Easy Pieces (Hartman), 4
eclogue, 43, 165
écriture, 82, 157
L'écriture du désastre (Blanchot). See *The Writing of the Disaster*
Eichmann trial, 22, 34, 103, 117, 151, 159, 174
The Eighteenth Brumaire (Marx), 112
Elective Affinities (Goethe), 196n45
Eliot, T. S., 52
embodiment, 104, 143, 148, 154
Emerson, Ralph Waldo, 110
emotion, 8, 70, 74, 98–102, 121, 126, 130, 134, 138, 164, 167, 182; and catharsis, 24; and impact, 15, 131
empathy, 26, 99
Empson, William, 8
"Engführung" (Celan), 83–84, 91, 92, 203n47, 203n48
the Enlightenment, 22, 80, 82, 83, 168
Epistle to the Romans (Barth), 161
L'espéce humaine (Antelme), 37, 181
The Ethics of Memory (Margalit), 216n2
Euripides, 45
Exit Ghost (Roth), 169
experience, 11, 20–23, 28, 53, 94, 100, 101, 104, 107, 128, 133, 138, 152, 156, 158, 159, 160, 172, 179; everyday, 99; historial, 118, 137; limit, 122; modern, 25, 31, 114; personal, 98; recorded, 132; traumatic, 134
Eyes on the Prize (documentary), 117

The Fall of Hyperion: A Dream (Keats), 168
The Fantastic (Todorov), 166
fascism, 26, 210n16
The Fateful Question of Culture (Hartman), 5
The Fate of Reading and Other Essays (Hartman), 4

Faurisson, Robert, 186n21
Federman, Raymond, 116–17
Feldman, Irving, 125, 126, 127
Fergusson, Francis, 165–66
fiction, 11–14, 24, 55, 56, 58, 59–65, 77, 99, 120, 126, 128; nonfiction, 121, 123; postmodernist, 118; realism in, 107; silence and, 62; unreality of, 208n4
Fiction in the Archives (Davis), 152
The Fifth Son (Wiesel), 61
film, 100, 110
Final Solution, 3, 7, 68, 73, 122, 166, 171
"The 'Final Solution': On the Unease in Historical Interpretation" (Friedländer), 77
Fine, Ellen, 115
Fink, Ida, 25, 29, 33, 136
Finkielkraut, Alain, 126
First Temple, 34
First World War, 21, 87
Flucht und Verwandlung (*Flight and Metamorphosis*) (Sachs), 87
The Forgotten (Wiesel), 60
Fortunoff Video Archive for Holocaust Testimonies, Yale, 1, 5, 15, 94–95, 104–5, 117, 131, 140, 152–53, 173, 181
frame, 138–39; conditions, 15, 131–32, 189n41; narrative, 13, 164. See also narrative
France, 21, 37, 117, 122, 151
Frank, Anne, 170
Frank, Arthur, 174–75
Frazer, James, 165
free associations, 47
free speech, 110
French Revolution, 25, 112, 160, 162
French tragedy, 124
Freud, Sigmund, 26, 60, 156
Friedländer, Saul, 77, 206n17, 210n16
Friedman, Carl, 124, 139
Friedman, Thomas, 96
Friendship (Blanchot), 27

Frosh, Paul, 18, 177
Fussell, Paul, 204n5

Gadamer, Hans-Georg, 31, 81
Gance, Abel, 118
Gaza, 3
Geertz, Clifford, 96
Geis, Raphael, 74
generation: first-generation witness, 21–22, 128; intergenerational, 30, 137, 181, 185n4; postgeneration, 2, 17; second-generation witness, 7, 21, 33, 214n16
Genesis, 30, 69, 83
genocide, 5, 15, 19, 33, 37, 45, 47, 57, 105, 121, 125, 131, 133, 134, 135, 136, 152, 172, 177, 180, 218n
genre, 6, 42, 63, 106, 124, 174
Germany, 34, 54, 71; East, 210n16; Nazi, 6, 35
globalization, 180–81
Goethe, Johann Wolfgang von, 44, 45, 196n45
"Goethe's *Wahlverwandtschaften*" (Benjamin), 44
Goldhagen, Daniel, 27, 72
Gouri, Haim, 117, 174
Govrin, Michal, 216n28
Graham, Jorie, 215n21
Gray, Thomas, 169
gray zone (Levi), 28, 175
Great Depression, 132
The Great War and Modern Memory (Fussell), 204n5
Greece, ancient, 121
Greeks, 29, 113
Greek tragedy, 45
grief, 33, 38, 112; and globalization, 180–81
Gross, Jan T., 54–58, 135
Grossman, David, 124, 139
guilt, 28, 37, 62, 73, 74, 77, 108, 210n16

Habermas, Jürgen, 21, 25, 29, 31

Halbwachs, Maurice, 7, 32, 114–15, 128, 150–51, 211n22, 219n18
Halivni, David Weiss, 34
Hamlet (Shakespeare), 124, 159, 165, 166
Handelman, Susan, 141
Harrison, Jane, 165
"Hart-Leap Well" (Wordsworth), 113
Hartman, Geoffrey, 1–5, 8–10, 187n33, 188n39
hate speech, 62–63
Hebrew Bible, 152, 200n14
Hebrew language, 65
Hegel, G. W. F., 3, 38–41, 49, 85–86, 141, 212n36
Heidegger, Martin, 36, 194n30
Helen K. (witness), 105
Hell (Dante), 43
hermeneutics, 15, 30, 79, 81–82, 112, 148
heroic, unheroic, 41, 103, 112–13, 116, 192n7
Hilberg, Raul, 57
Himmler, Heinrich, 72–73, 75–77
Hirsch, Marianne, 2, 7, 24, 185n4
historical documentation. *See* documentation
historiography, 16, 56, 142, 166
history, 16; African American, 104, 115–16; eventful (*événementielle*), 105, 207n31, 212n33; official, 109, 111–12; oral, 95, 104–5, 118, 132, 152–53, 167, 174, 206n26, 211n25, 212n33; positivistic, 81, 102, 153; written, 95, 97, 114
Hitler, Adolf, 12, 22, 27, 71, 72, 75
Hitler's Willing Executioners (Goldhagen), 27, 72
Hitler Youth, 75
Hölderlin, Friedrich, 80
Holocaust (TV serial), 34, 103
Holocaust annihilation, 29–30
Holocaust industry, 158
"Holocaust laughter," 123

Holocaust Memorial. *See* Yad Vashem
Holocaust Remembrance (Hartman), 2
Holocaust Remembrance Day, 19
Holocaust Survivors Film Project, 104.
    See also Fortunoff Video Archive
Holocaust Testimonies (Langer), 150
"Holzstern" (Celan), 90–93, 202n37
Homer, 149
Homo Ludens (Huizinga), 160
hope, 2–3, 8, 13, 19, 25, 31, 33–46, 52, 53, 67, 89, 91, 92, 123, 129, 130, 133, 134, 139, 153, 165, 167, 172, 181, 186n15; deceptive, 68; false, 66; messianic, 49, 193n19; qualified, 80
"An Horatian Ode Upon Cromwell's Return from Ireland" (Marvell), 161
Howe, Irving, 27
Huizinga, Johan, 160
human rights, 107, 172, 173, 180, 181
humor, 35, 41, 66, 124, 175
hyperbole, 82, 91, 149
Hyperion: A Fragment (Keats), 168

The Idea of a Theater (Fergusson), 165
identification, 25–26, 101, 102–3, 126, 185n4
I Did Not Interview the Dead (Boder), 175
imagination, 25, 84, 107, 109, 114–15, 120, 126, 139, 162–64, 176, 204n2, 210n18, 212n86, 215n26; exegetical, 5; sympathetic, 8–9, 23, 99
imaginative condensation or modification, 13, 17, 132, 164
imaginative literature, 3, 11, 24, 85, 120, 123
impartial spectator, 22
indifference, 2, 8–9, 14, 16, 48, 58, 95, 108, 134, 188n33
Industrial Revolution, 109
information sickness, 107
Instagram, 18
The Instant of My Death (Blanchot), 170

intellectual, 22, 26
intellectualism, 26
intelligibility, 32
interpretability, 148
interruption, 145, 196n45
intergenerational. *See* generation
Iphigenia in Tauris (Goethe), 44–46
Islamic Sharia law, 161
Israel, 19, 125, 144, 155, 210n16
Italy, 151

Jacob the Liar (film), 34–35
James, Henry, 49, 126
Jedwabne, Poland, 54–57
La jeune parque (Valéry), 85
Jewishness, 126, 129
Jewish studies, 5
Job, Book of, 34, 50, 70, 108
John the Baptist, 152
Jonas, Hans, 122
Journal des Débats, 37
journalism, 55, 111
Judaism, 42, 84, 140
Judeocide, 75

Kafka, Franz, 42, 161
Kammen, Michael, 114
Kant, Immanuel, 30, 42, 82, 164, 168
Katznelson, Yitzhak, 33
Keats, John, 8, 108, 113, 168–69
Kee, Robert, 204n5
Kennedy, John F., 111
Keret, Etgar, 217n15
Kertész, Imre, 33, 43, 123
Kierkegaard, Søren, 50–51
King Lear (Shakespeare), 58
Kiš, Danilo, 122
Klein, Dana, 146
Klemperer, Victor, 35, 133
Kluge, Alexander, 212n36
Kofman, Sarah, 39
Kohl, Helmut, 21
Kraft, Robert, 132

Kraus, Karl, 63
Kundera, Milan, 109

labor, 23, 71–72, 166, 175; of the negative (Hegel), 42. *See also* camp, camps
LaCapra, Dominick, 23, 26
Lachmann, Renata, 122
Langer, Lawrence, 21, 38, 101, 121, 136, 150, 176–77
Langgässer, Elisabeth, 35
"Language and Culture After the Holocaust" (Hartman), 157
Language of the Third Reich (LTI), 35
Lanzmann, Claude, 26, 56, 106, 135, 137, 143, 163; *Shoah*, 22, 105, 117, 174
Last Year at Marienbad (film), 117
latency period, 22, 103, 138
Laub, Dori, 6, 104, 133, 135, 144, 149, 177–78, 186n21
law: Islamic Sharia, 161; Jewish, 57, 59, 84, 88–89; natural, 162–63
Lebensraum ("living space,"), 178
Lebenslüge (Speer), 76–78
Lefebvre, Henri, 209n8
legacy, 7, 19, 31, 38, 80, 97, 104, 117, 187n22, 191n5, 192n7, 207n26
Le Goff, Jacques, 211n24
Lejeune, Phillipe, 136
Lekh Lekho (Shayevitch), 69–70
Lenin, Vladimir, 171
Lester, Julius, 115
Levi, Primo, 14, 32–33, 43, 67, 70, 100–103, 136, 170; *The Drowned and the Saved*, 28, 29, 102, 158, 175, 205n7; "The Survivor," 176
Levinas, Emmanuel, 36, 39–41, 65, 141, 194n30
Lewis, Wyndham, 21
Libeskind, Daniel, 41
lieu de mémoire (memory-milieu, memory place), 106, 114, 116–17, 132, 150–51, 210–11n20, 212n35; non-*lieu*, 114, 116, 210–11n20, 211n24, 212n25
Life Is Beautiful (film), 34–35, 123, 192n9
Lifton, Robert J., 109
Lind, Jakov, 121
Lipkin, Aharon, 6
literary language, 6, 14, 36–37, 42, 43, 83, 91, 92
literary space, 32, 49, 51, 85–86, 89, 91, 123, 170
literature: and audiovisual testimony, 6, 14–15, 17, 99–101, 148–49; and cure, 6; and the Holocaust, 120–30; and memory, 115–19; and nationalism, 35, 168, 170; and witnessing, 33, 99–101, 174–75; as knowledge, 5–6, 14, 79–85; Blanchot on, 36–44, 48, 86; imaginative, 3, 11, 120–23; non-remedial, 6, 24, 28, 34–38. *See also* literary language; literary space
Literature or Life (Semprún), 23, 25
Litzmannstadt death, 69
"living deposit" (Halbwachs), 7, 114–15
Lodz Ghetto, 11, 19, 66–70
The Longest Shadow (Hartman), 1, 2, 9, 11
Lyotard, Jean-François, 186n21, 188n37, 209–10n15

Macbeth (Shakespeare), 164, 169
MacIntyre, Alasdair, 113
Maimonides, 84
Makom shel Osher (Sarna), 129–30
Mallarmé, Stéphane, 38, 42, 52, 80, 82–84, 194n27
Malraux, Andre, 25
Mann, Heinrich, 35
Mao Zedong, 171
Marcuse, Herbert, 109
Margalit, Avishai, 216n2
Marquardt, Wilhelm, 34
Marvell, Andrew, 161
Marx, Karl, 112
Maurras, Charles, 36

228 Index

Maus (Spiegelman), 167
meanings, 38–39, 83, 103, 137
media, 8–11, 15, 16, 18, 25, 28, 47, 107–11, 114, 158, 160, 162, 166–67, 170, 176–61, 185n8, 189n40, 108n3, 209n14, 211n24. *See also* news, 4, 15, 185n8, 189n40; Hegelian, 39, 86
Media Witnessing in the Age of Mass Communication (Frosh and Pinchevski), 18, 177
medicine, narrative, 133
memoirs, 48, 115, 128, 130, 151, 159, 174, 191n22, 204n5; oral, 94–103
memorial(s), 11, 56, 67, 111–12, 130, 157, 180, 187n23, 212n36. *See also* United States Holocaust Memorial Museum; Yad Vashem
memory, 11, 19–20, 22–26, 29–32, 58, 61, 63–64, 86, 89, 95–98, 101–2, 105–6, 107–19, 126–27, 119, 130, 132–33, 136–39, 141–42, 145, 150–52, 158–59, 182, 192n7, 193n14, 204n2, 204n4, 205n12, 206–7n26, 208n3, 212n34, 213n37; absent, 115–18; African American, 115–16; "collected," 117, 136, 151; collective, 7, 17, 56, 67, 113–19, 120–26, 135–36, 151–52, 156, 158; and integrity, 119; official, 7, 110; personal, 7, 107, 151; postmemory (Marianne Hirsch), 7, 24, 126, 138; public, 2, 7–8, 17–18, 20–21, 107–19; rememory (Toni Morrison), 116, 205n12, 210n16, 211n22, 211n24, 219n18, 220n25. *See also lieu de memoire;* remembrance
memory-envy, 118–19, 159, 176
memory-places. *See lieu de memoire*
Mengele, Josef, 102
Metaphor, 6, 13, 17, 23, 52, 83, 87, 127, 132, 149, 189n5
Middle Passage, 98
migration, 170; emigration, 192n12, 215n19; immigrants, 104

Milosz, Czeslaw, 41, 57, 58
"Milton's Counterplot" (Hartman), 4
mimesis, 23–24, 92, 99, 203n46
minimalist poetry, 109
Minima Moralia (Adorno), 25
Minor Prophecies (Hartman), 4
Mintz, Alan, 210n16
Mitscherlich, Alexander and Margarete, 75
Mnemosyne, 113
modernism, 36, 50–51, 94, 128, 157, 193n15
modernity, 83, 112, 209n8
modesty, 59, 80, 209n14
Modiano, Patrick, 214n18
Morality, 14, 41, 58, 63, 69, 77, 108, 110–11
Morrison, Toni, 98, 115–16
mourning, 14, 47, 49, 91, 96, 138, 176, 180
"Mourning and Melancholia" (Freud), 26, 47
Muir, Edward, 113
Murray, Gilbert, 165
Muselmänner, 68, 158
museum(s), 15, 155–56, 164, 181, 212n36
Mystic Chords of Memory (Kammen), 114

narrative, 11, 13, 17, 26, 28, 34, 42–43, 55, 57–58, 86, 99–106, 109–10, 112–13, 117, 119, 131–34, 143, 147, 149–50, 163–64, 168, 175–76, 178, 182, 188n35, 200n14, 203n46, 204n2, 206n18, 213n1, 215n21, 216n28
Native Americans, 104
NATO, 111
natural law, 163
Nazi racialism, 99
Nazism, 31, 40, 57, 122, 179, 188n35
Neighbors (Gross), 54–55
Nerval, Gérard de, 85
Netanyahu, Benjamin, 19
"never forget," 11–12, 19, 31, 67

New-Man Nation, 171
"The New Midrash" (Simon), 43
New Testament, 115
The New Yorker, 54, 56
The New York Times, 96, 180
news (the), 6, 8, 9, 11, 14, 15, 18, 41, 108, 112, 167, 174, 179, 180, 208n6, 209n8, 219n20
Nietzsche, Friedrich, 48, 54, 82, 153
Night and Fog (Resnais), 24
Nightfather (Friedman, C.), 124, 139
nonescapist thoughtfulness, 3, 10, 13, 123
nonfiction, 121, 123. *See also* fiction
nostalgia, 113, 119
Nouvelle Révue Française, 37
novel(s), 13, 24, 40, 59–65, 98–99, 116–17, 123, 159, 165, 167, 169, 170, 176, 205n12, 208n6, 213n1, 215n19, 216n28
numbing (psychic), 8, 109; numbness, 18, 132
Nunca Más, 139
Nuremberg Tribunal, 71

objective, objectivity, 16, 52, 134
Object Relations theory, 219n15
obscenity, 26, 56
Oedipus, 77, 110
official history, 109, 111–12
official memory, 7–8, 11
The Official Story (film), 110
One Generation After (Wiesel), 62
Oneg Shabbat, 66
Operation Barbarossa, 56
oral documentation, 96, 100, 131, 138, 154
oral history, 95, 97, 104–5, 132, 152–53, 167, 174–75, 181, 206n26, 211n25, 212n33, 216n1. *See also* oral testimony
oral memoirs, 96, 101
oral testimony, 9, 14, 94, 102, 117–18, 133, 136, 174, 204n4. *See also* oral history

oral tradition, 20, 45, 97, 119, 150
Orwell, George, 36
overidentification, 25, 102–3

Pagis, Dan, 32–33, 125–28; "The Roll Call," 126; "Testimony," 179
Palestine, 19, 61
parody, 69, 86, 165, 206n17
Parsifal, story of, 166
Paz, Octavio, 36
Pensées (Pascal), 42
Perec, Georges, 22
perpetrators, 21–22, 26, 55, 57, 60, 75–78, 95–96, 125, 136–37, 166, 174, 206n17, 220n20
The Phenomenology of Spirit (Hegel), 40, 86
Phillips, Adam, 5
The Pianist (film), 129
Pinchevski, Amit, 18, 177, 178
Plato, 118, 156, 157
pleasure, 92; from suffering, 23–24, 122
"Poem and Ideology" (Hartman), 4
poetics, 121–22; symbolist, 89–90; modernist impersonality, 127–28; and testimony, 132–34
Poetics (Aristotle), 120, 121, 156, 165
poetry, 43, 80–82, 91, 125; catastrophe and, 39; minimalist, 109; poetics, 132; Romantic, 83
Poland, 21, 54–57, 58, 66, 95
Polanski, Roman, 129
police, 21, 55, 67
"Politics and the English Language" (Orwell), 36
The Politics of Friendship (Derrida), 27
Pollak, Michael, 32
Pollin-Galay, Hannah, 16–17, 189n41
"A Poor Christian Looks at the Ghetto" (Milosz), 57
positivistic history, 81; and testimony, 102, 153, 207
postgeneration, 2, 17

postmemory, 7, 24, 126, 185n4. *See also* memory
postmodern, 116, 157–58, 209–10n15; postmodernism, 26, 118, 17
Pound, Ezra, 195n42
The Prelude (Wordsworth), 162, 164
presence, 6, 39, 59, 114, 134–35, 17. *See also* absence
probability, 13, 35, 56, 165; Aristotelian, 120, 122–23
"Prose" (Mallarmé), 82
Proust, Marcel, 118
Psalms, 19, 23, 60, 83–85, 89–90, 127–28
public (the), 5, 7, 9, 20–21, 110, 152, 173
public memory, 2, 7–8, 17–18, 20–21, 107–19
Puenzo, Luis, 110

Quixotism, 109

race, 44, 77, 99, 121–22, 192n12, Nazi pseudoscience of (*Rassenwissenschaft*), 99, 117, 220n25
Raczymow, Henri, 115, 126
Radnoti, Miklos, 43
Rashomon effect, 102
reading, 11, 45, 80–81, 145, 147, 149, 162–63, 170; close reading, 83, 178; reading-fatigue, 38
Reagan, Ronald, 111
realism, 10–11, 107, 116, 167
reality, 2, 9–14, 18, 19, 21, 23–25, 40, 52, 61, 80, 82–83, 86, 90–92, 108–9, 121, 123, 124, 129, 134, 137, 139, 164, 166–67, 179–80, 187n31, 189n43, 203n46, 213n1, 216n27. *See also* "the real"; unreal, unreality
Realpolitik, 31, 171
reception, 10–11, 20, 22, 118, 121, 123, 151, 176–77, 187–88n33, 215n16, 219n18, 219n20
reembodiment, 178–79
Reframing the Holocaust (Shenker), 15

remembrance, 20, 22, 29, 34, 117, 126, 142, 158, 210n15; culture of, 20
Remembrance Book, 66
Remembrance Day, 19
rememory, 116, 205n12, 210n16, 211n22, 211n24, 219n18, 220n25
Remnants of Auschwitz (Agamben), 158
representation, 3, 10–11, 14, 18, 21, 25, 30, 92, 98, 105–6, 107, 163, 166–67, 175, 206n17, 216n27
representability, 31, 47; unrepresentability, 120
Resnais, Alain, 24
resocialization, 133, 145, 176
revisionism, 73, 153. *See also* denial
Richards, I. A., 4
Riefenstahl, Leni, 143
Rieff, David, 107
Rilke, Rainer Maria, 79, 86–88
Rimbaud, Arthur, 118
Robespierre, Maximilien de, 160
"The Roll Call" (Pagis), 126
Roman Empire, 112
Romantic, 4, 42, 83, 113; Romanticism, 3, 113
"Romantic Poetry and the Genius Loci" (Hartman), 4
Rosenbaum, Thane, 138
Rosenberg, William, 104
Rosenblum, Robert, 109
Rosenfeld, Oskar, 70
Roth, Philip, 169–70
Rudof, Joanne, 1, 146, 147, 153
Rumkowski, Chaim, 67–68, 70
"Rumpelstiltskin" (fairy tale), 88
Russia, 54, 119
Rwanda, 3, 220n20

Sachs, Nelly, 25, 86–92
Saint-Just, Louis Antoine de, 160
Sarna, Igal, 129–30
Sarton, May, 175
Saving the Text (Hartman), 4

Index   231

Scars of the Spirit (Hartman), 5
Schindel, Robert, 126
Schindler's List (film), 9, 109, 129, 143, 152, 163
Schoeller, Wilfried, 212n36
Scholem, Gershom, 200n5
Scholl, Sophie, 128
Scott, Walter, 113
Sebald, W. G., 176
secondary trauma, 9–10, 15, 17, 19, 23, 101. *See also* trauma
secondary witness, 18, 21, 32, 125–26, 129, 137–39, 173, 187n33, 215n21. *See also* witness
second-generation, 20, 22, 214n16; fiction of, 124, 214n19; second-generation witness, 7, 21, 33, 214n16
Second Temple, 34
Second World War, 11, 54, 131
See Under: Love (Grossman), 124, 139
self-abnegation, 50
self-consciousness, 84, 85, 86, 168
Semprún, Jorge, 23–25, 33, 120
September Massacres, 161
Sereny, Gitta, 12, 71–78
Shakespeare, William, 45, 63, 70, 209n12; *Hamlet*, 124, 159, 165, 166; *King Lear*, 58; *Macbeth*, 164, 169
Shalamov, Varlam, 43
shame, 11, 31, 67, 70, 122, 128, 138, 179, 192n12, 215n24; art-shame, 13, 47
Shayevitch, Simkha-Bunim, 69–70
Shenker, Noah, 15
Shoah (Lanzmann), 22, 38, 105, 117, 135, 137, 143, 163, 174
"Shoah and Intellectual Witness" (Hartman), 2–3, 19, 20–32, 187n33
"Shoah Literature: The Universal Aspect" (Hartman), 10–13, 18–19, 120–30
Shoah Foundation, USC, 15, 16, 155, 181
The Sickness Unto Death (Kierkegaard), 50–51

silence: about the Holocaust, 30–31, 34, 38, 138, 148; and Blanchot, 13, 49, 215n24; of survivors, 186n21, 188n37; in survivor testimony, 16, 98, 102, 106, 133–35, 145–46, 148; Wiesel's fiction, 64–65
Simon, Ernst, 43
Singer, Oskar, 69
Smart, Christopher, 6, 186n17
Smith, Adam, 22
social criticism, 96
social identity, 32
social memory, 114, 150–52. *See also* memory
"social sharing," 17, 133, 207n32. *See also* Dori Laub
Solidarity, 25–27, 29
Sonderkommando, 139
Song of Songs, 116, 126, 128
Sophocles, 77
"Soul of Wood" (Lind), 121
South Africa, 73
Spandau Prison, 71
Spanish Civil War, 25
speech, 7, 32, 35–37, 40, 42, 44, 50, 58, 62–63, 83–86, 90–92, 128, 140, 149, 165, 186n17, 193n18, 203n46; free, 110; hate, 62–63; in testimony, 16, 32, 131, 141, 145, 149, 154, 173
Speer, Albert, 12, 71–78
Spenser, Edmund, 165
Spiegelman, Art, 167
Spielberg, Steven, 15, 109, 129, 143, 152, 154–55, 163
spirituality, 42, 59, 194n27
spiritual: element in Judaism, 59, 64; element of testimony, 96, 141; language, 42; resistance, 68
Spitzer, Leo, 35, 45
"Spring Morning" (Fink), 136
Srebnik, Simon, 137
Stalin, Joseph, 22, 27, 171
Stalinism, 26

star: of David, 202n33, 202n43; yellow (worn by Jews), 202n33
stars, 2, 52, 79, 83–93
Sterling Memorial Library, 207n29
Stevens, Wallace, 50, 107
style, 14, 27, 42, 43, 62, 87, 92, 124, 165, 181, 204n5
Styron, William, 136
subjectivity: testimony and, 134–35, 181, 204n4; Wordsworthian, 169. *See also* consciousness
suffering at a distance (*souffrance à distance*), 167
survival, 16, 31, 64, 67, 97, 102–3, 128, 131, 152, 160, 173, 192n9. *See also* survivors
"The Survivor" (Levi), 176
survivors, 2, 6–7, 10, 15–17, 20–23, 31–32, 33–34, 47, 59, 61, 63, 94–130, 166, 186n21, 206n18, 207n28; and testimony, 131–39, 142–43, 145, 147–50, 152–59, 172–79, 182, 219n18
Sutzkever, Abraham, 43
Symbolist movement, 89–90
symbols, symbolism, 83, 85–86, 89–90, 91, 112, 118, 158, 178, 210n16
sympathy, 66, 72, 79, 86, 101, 135, 145; sympathetic imagination, 8, 23, 99; sympathy paradox, 8
Szondi, Peter, 79–83, 91–92, 186n15, 199n2, 200n12

Tallien, Jean-Lambert, 161
Talmud, 34, 59, 63–64
technology, 9–10, 14, 16, 18, 28, 111, 117–18, 142, 154, 172; and expansion of the senses, 9–10, 111; ethics of, 209n14, 206n19; and information, 180, 200n3; telecommunications, 8, 107, 180; in testimony, 18, 153–55, 172, 177–78. *See also* media; news
telecommunications, 8, 107, 180
telesuffering, 8, 18

"the real," 10, 171, 180, 209n13
The Terror, 161–62
terror, 14, 30, 34, 38, 45, 87, 105, 160–64, 167–68, 170–71; pity and (Aristotle), 70, 120
terrorism, terrorist, 61, 160, 163, 169–70
testimonial alliance, 3, 134, 144, 173, 177, 219n18
testimonial pact, 136
testimony, 2, 5, 6, 7, 37–38, 70, 96, 98, 101, 119, 128, 147, 150, 151, 158, 172–82; eyewitness, 21, 125; oral, 9, 14, 94, 102, 117, 174; performative aspect of, 16, 17, 18, 134; personal experience in, 98; public, 105; subjectivity and, 181; survivor, 11, 14–17, 62, 102, 131–39; trauma and, 133–34; video, 3, 11, 15–16, 33, 100, 104, 134, 136–37, 142, 143, 144, 149, 154, 173. *See also* testimonial alliance
"Testimony" (Pagis), 127, 179
Thälmann Cult, 210n16
Thanasseikos, Yannis, 156
That Obscure Object of Desire (film), 169
Theory of Moral Sentiments (Smith), 22
therapy, therapeutic, 26, 144, 165, 186n17, 207n32; therapeutic alliance, 144
theology, 34, 42, 48, 60, 82, 84, 140, 158, 160, 167; counter-theological, 170
Theresienstadt, 112
The Third Pillar (Hartman), 1
This Way for the Gas, Ladies and Gentlemen (Borowski), 29, 124
Thomas l'obscur (Blanchot), 40
TikTok, 18
To Be a Slave (Lester), 115
Todorov, Tzvetan, 166
Tolstoy, Leo, 111
Torah, 84
torture, 26, 122, 125, 170
totalitarianism, 6, 27, 36, 119

"To the Six Million" (Feldman), 125, 126
To Whom It May Concern (Federman), 116
tragedy, 46, 55, 70, 123, 139; French, 124; Greek, 45; Shakespearean, 45
trauma, 2, 5–6, 7, 23–24, 26, 28, 29–31, 38, 53, 60, 67, 77, 91, 94, 107, 115, 125, 130, 133–34, 141, 148–49, 158–59, 160, 172, 175, 176, 179, 180–82, 186n17, 205n14; collective or communal, 125, 207n30; secondary, 9–10, 15, 17, 19, 23, 101; testimony and, 94, 101–5, 133–34, 137–38, 177–78, 179, 182, 206n18
truth, 3, 8–9, 43, 56, 92, 108, 110, 118, 122; aesthetic or artistic, 29, 109; factual, 17, 95, 150; half-, 55, 80; in fiction, 13, 120, 124; historical, 17, 96, 150; vs. realism, 167; in testimony, 16, 23 136, 175; untruth, 110. *See also* probability; realism; reality; truthfulness
Truth and Reconciliation Commissions, 139, 173
truthfulness, 13, 123
truthiness, 120
Twilight (Wiesel), 59, 60, 63
Twitter (X), 18

"Über philologische Erkenntnis" (Szondi), 80
Ukraine, 171
United States Holocaust Memorial Museum, 15, 155
The Unmediated Vision (Hartman), 3
Unmeisterliche Wanderjahre (Améry), 181
unreal, 49, 80, 109, 119, 123, 171, 179; unreality, 10, 18, 111, 187n31, 208n4. *See also* derealization
The Unremarkable Wordsworth (Hartman), 4

Valéry, Paul, 85, 156
veracity, 16, 17, 133, 189n45. *See also* truth
verisimilitude, 120, 213n1
video testimony, 3, 5, 11, 14, 15–16, 33, 100, 104–5, 117, 134, 136–37, 142–44, 149, 152–56, 154, 167, 173–76, 179, 181
videotape, 9, 117–18, 131, 137, 154, 178, 207n32, 212n33
violence, 5–6, 8–9, 15, 17, 19, 28, 39, 40, 107–9, 114, 195n23; divine, 160. *See also* genocide
Virgil, 100
visions, 59, 61–62
visuality, 142
Vlock, Laurel, 104
Voegelin, Erich, 119
voice, 11, 15–16, 30, 42–43, 62, 64, 67, 70, 85, 84, 94, 96, 103–4, 117, 126, 134–35, 142, 157, 164–65, 182
Voltaire, 39

Waffen SS, 111
Walcott, Derek, 119
Walzer, Michael, 96
war crime, war criminals, 74, 210n26
Warhol, Andy, 109
Warsaw Ghetto, 58, 66, 95
weak anamnestic power, 29
weak messianic power, 29
Weigel, Sigrid, 176
Weinreich, Max, 27, 121
Weston, Jessie, 166
"white devil" (as name for Jews), 209n14
"White Rose" resistance, 128
Wideman, John Edgar, 115
Wiesel, Elie, 14, 33–34, 43, 59–65; *A Beggar in Jerusalem*, 63, 65; *Dawn*, 61; *The Fifth Son*, 61; *One Generation After*, 62; *Twilight*, 59, 60, 63
Wieviorka, Annette, 151

Wilkomirski, Binjamin, 175, 176
Winnicott, Donald, 219n15
Wirklichkeit, 16, 80, 91–92, 189n43
witness, 15, 22, 44, 50, 70, 99, 102, 126, 135, 141, 146, 150, 173, 174, 179; accounts, 16, 34, 94, 95, 100, 104, 105, 120, 132, 133, 134, 137, 143, 144, 148, 177; against false witness, 58; bearing witness, 2, 7, 9, 37, 140, 177, 178; eyewitnesses, 20; first-generation, 21–22, 128; for the witness, 18, 151; future, 10; intellectual, 20–21, 27, 30–32; oral, 117; primary, 17; public, 146, 147; secondary, 18, 21, 32, 125–26, 129, 137–39, 173, 187n33, 215n21; second-generation, 7, 21, 33, 214n16; survivor of, 174; transgenerational, 64
witnessing, 2, 7, 10, 17, 31–32, 140–41, 157, 188n33, 188n37; concept of, 172–73; development of, 172–73, intellectual, 27, 158; intelligibility and, 32; media, 177–81; moral, 216n2; voluntary, 23
word-consciousness, 37
"Words and Wounds" (Hartman), 6
Wordsworth, William, 4, 109, 113, 162–64, 169

Wordsworth's Poetry, 1797–1814 (Hartman), 4, 188n39
World War I, 21, 87
World War II, 11, 54, 131, 152, 171
The Wounded Storyteller (Frank, Arthur), 174–75
wound(s), 5–6, 42, 57–58, 67
The Writing of the Disaster (Blanchot), 6, 42, 48–49, 52–53, 170
Writing The Book of Esther (*Un cri sans voix*) (Raczymow), 126
written history, 95–97, 114. *See also* historiography
Wyschogrod, Edith, 41

X (Twitter), 18

Yad Vashem (Holocaust Memorial, Jerusalem), 19, 155
Yale University, 173
Yeats, W. B., 119
Yerushalmi, Yosef, 33, 56, 114
Yiddish, 65
Young, James E., 117, 136

Zakhor (Yerushalmi), 56
Zuckerman, Nathan, 170

Geoffrey Hartman was Sterling Professor of English and Comparative Literature at Yale University and Project Director of its Fortunoff Video Archive for Holocaust Testimonies. His many books include *The Third Pillar: Essays in Judaic Studies* (2011), *A Scholar's Tale: Intellectual Journey of a Displaced Child of Europe* (2007), *The Geoffrey Hartman Reader* (2004, winner, Truman Capote Prize for Literary Criticism), *Scars of the Spirit: The Struggle Against Inauthenticity* (2004), *The Fateful Question of Culture* (1997), *The Longest Shadow: In the Aftermath of the Holocaust* (1996), *The Unremarkable Wordsworth* (1987), *Criticism in the Wilderness: The Study of Literature Today* (1980, 2nd ed., 2007), *The Fate of Reading and Other Essays* (1975), *Beyond Formalism: Literary Essays, 1958–1970* (1970), and *Wordsworth's Poetry, 1787–1814* (1964, winner, Christian Gauss Award).

Kevis Goodman is Professor and John F. Hotchkis Chair in English at the University of California, Berkeley. She is the author of *Pathologies of Motion: Historical Thinking in Medicine, Aesthetics, and Poetics* (2023) and *Georgic Modernity and British Romanticism: Poetry and the Mediation of History* (2004).

Brian McGrath is Professor of English at Clemson University. He is the author of *Look Round for Poetry: Untimely Romanticisms* (2022) and *The Poetics of Unremembered Acts: Reading, Lyric, Pedagogy* (2013).

Sara Guyer and Brian McGrath, series editors

Sara Guyer, *Reading with John Clare: Biopoetics, Sovereignty, Romanticism.*

Philippe Lacoue-Labarthe, *Ending and Unending Agony: On Maurice Blanchot.* Translated by Hannes Opelz.

Emily Rohrbach, *Modernity's Mist: British Romanticism and the Poetics of Anticipation.*

Marc Redfield, *Theory at Yale: The Strange Case of Deconstruction in America.*

Jacques Khalip and Forest Pyle (eds.), *Constellations of a Contemporary Romanticism.*

Geoffrey Bennington, *Kant on the Frontier: Philosophy, Politics, and the Ends of the Earth.*

Frédéric Neyrat, *Atopias: Manifesto for a Radical Existentialism.* Translated by Walt Hunter and Lindsay Turner, Foreword by Steven Shaviro.

Jacques Khalip, *Last Things: Disastrous Form from Kant to Hujar.*

Jacques Lezra, *On the Nature of Marx's Things: Translation as Necrophilology.* Foreword by Vittorio Morfino.

Jean-Luc Nancy, *Portrait.* Translated by Sarah Clift and Simon Sparks, Foreword by Jeffrey S. Librett.

Karen Swann, *Lives of the Dead Poets: Keats, Shelley, Coleridge.*

Erin Graff Zivin, *Anarchaeologies: Reading as Misreading.*

Ramsey McGlazer, *Old Schools: Modernism, Education, and the Critique of Progress.*

Zachary Sng, *Middling Romanticism: Reading in the Gaps, from Kant to Ashbery.*

Marc Redfield, *Shibboleth: Judges, Derrida, Celan.*

Emily Sun, *On the Horizon of World Literature: Forms of Modernity in Romantic England and Republican China.*

Robert Mitchell, *Infectious Liberty: Biopolotics between Romanticism and Liberalism.*

Orrin N. C. Wang, *Techno-Magism: Media, Mediation, and the Cut of Romanticism.*

Brian McGrath, *Look Round for Poetry: Untimely Romanticisms.*

Christopher Rovee, *New Critical Nostalgia: Romantic Lyric and the Crisis of Academic Life.*

Adela Pinch, *The Location of Experience: Victorian Women Writers, the Novel, and the Feeling of Living.*

www.ingramcontent.com/pod-product-compliance
Lightning Source LLC
Chambersburg PA
CBHW020404080526
44584CB00014B/1166